OUR FAMILY AFFAIRS
1867–1896

BY

E. F. BENSON

AUTHOR OF "DODO," "DAVID BLAIZE,"
"MICHAEL," "QUEEN LUCIA," ETC.

WITH PORTRAITS

NEW YORK

GEORGE H. DORAN COMPANY

OUR FAMILY AFFAIRS

E. F. BENSON

MY FATHER, ÆT. 50

13254

CONTENTS

vii

CONTENTS

PORTRAITS

OUR FAMILY AFFAIRS

OUR FAMILY AFFAIRS

CHAPTER I

WELLINGTON AND THE BEGINNING

MY father was headmaster of Wellington College,
where and when I was born, but of him there, in
spite of his extraordinarily forcible personality, I have
no clear memory, though the first precise and definite
recollection that I retain at all, heaving out of nothing-
ness, was connected with him, for it certainly was he,
who, standing by the table in the window of the dining-
room with an open newspaper in his hand, told me never
to forget this day on which the Franco-German war
came to an end. Otherwise as regards him, somebody
swept by in an academic cap and gown, a figure not at
all awe-inspiring as he became to me very soon after, but
simply a rather distinguished natural phenomenon to be
regarded in the same light as rain or wall-paper or sunshine. Cudgel my memory as I may, I can evoke no
other figure of him at Wellington, except as something
shining and swift; an external object whirling along on
an orbit as inconjecturable as those of the stars, and
wholly uninteresting. He had a study on the left of the
front door into the Master's Lodge, where there was a
big desk with a shiny circular cover. I know that I was
taken in there to say good night to him, but the most

13

remarkable thing there was the big desk with large handles, and perhaps a boy standing by it, mountainous in height and looking extremely polite and gentle. There was the same ceremony every evening: my father kissed me, put his hand on my head and said, "God bless you and make you a good boy always." The most significant detail of that ritual was that my father's face was rough, not smooth like the face of my mother and of Beth, and that there lingered round him or the room a smell of books and a smell of soap.

A little later on than that there came a period when for half an hour before bedtime my two sisters and I (for the present the youngest) used to visit him in that same study while he drew entrancing pictures for us, each in turn. One of these I found only the other day: it represents a hill crowned with a castle and a church, in front of which is a small knight waving his sword in the direction of a terrifying dragon, horned and tailed, who is flying across the sky. Below in minute capitals runs a rhyming legend. Or I went to the College chapel, though not often, and by way of a treat, and there was the same figure in a surplice, in a stall on the right hand of the door of entrance. I believe I was there on the last Sunday of his Headmastership and that they sang a hymn which he wrote.

Emotionally, I have no picture-book illustrated with memories of my first five years, but externally I have impressions that possess a haunting vividness comparable only to the texture of dreams, when dreams are tumultuously alive. All these (and I think the experience is universal) were external happenings, trivial in themselves, but far more lasting than emotional affairs in later life. Never shall I forget, though I have forgotten so much of far vaster import since then, the discovery of an adder on the croquet lawn outside the nursery windows. The gardener attacked it with the shears that he had been using for clipping the edges of the grass: he made fine chopping gestures, and presently disappeared into the belt of wood with the adder slung on the blades. There is the vignette: something terribly vivid but girt about with mist. I have no other knowledge of the gardener but that he killed an adder with his shears and went into the belt of wood with the corpse dangling thereon.

There was an evening when, having had my bath in the nursery I escaped from the hands of my nurse, slippery with soapy water, and looked out of the nursery window. Then a miracle burst upon my astounded eyes, for, though it was bedtime my mother was in the act of putting her foot on her own croquet ball, and with a smart stroke sending the adversary into the limbo of a flower-bed. That was allowed by the rule of 1870 or thereabouts, and it gave me the impression of consummate skill and energy. My mother, you must understand, stood quite still with her own ball in chancery below her foot. The concussion of her violent mallet sent the adversary into a flower-bed, and the calceolarias nodded. . . . Then Beth, my nurse, caught me, and rubbed me dry, and I went to bed with the delicious sense of my mother's magnificence, and the marvel of people still playing croquet in daylight when I had to go to bed. I think that this occasion was the first on which I recognised my mother as having a personality of her own. The next confused me again, for on some birthday of one of us, or at Christmas, Beth told me that Abracadabra was coming, and that I mustn't be frightened. I was then taken to see my mother, who was lying down in her bedroom, and said that she was very sleepy, and I returned to the nursery. Shortly afterwards there was a general hubbub in the house, and on being taken downstairs from the nursery into the hall, I saw a huge bedizened fairy standing in front of the fireplace. She blew a piercing trumpet at intervals, and made dance-steps to the right and left. She had a wonderful hat covered with lilies, and a dress covered with jewels, and in front of her was a thing that might have been mistaken for the clothes-basket out of which Beth took clean shirts and socks, but it could not possibly have been that, because it gleamed with pure gold. A sheet lay on the top of it, and Abracadabra blew her trumpet, and Beth, holding me close, said, "Eh, dear, don't be frightened; it's all right!"

Obviously it was all right; for to put an end to all tearful tendencies, Abracadabra, with a magnificent gesture, withdrew the sheet, and hastily presented me with a clockwork train, just what I had always wanted. She turned a key in the engine, and the engine then capsized with loud buzzings, but when Abracadabra put it on its wheels again, it proceeded to draw three tin carriages after it. And it was mine, the very thing I had wanted, and Abracadabra smiled as she gave it me, and I thought that her face was rather like Mamma's. But the likeness must have been purely accidental, because Mamma was in her bedroom feeling sleepy. And when Abracadabra went through the door into the kitchen passage blowing loudly on her trumpet, and when, after a few excursions of the clockwork train, I was allowed to go up to her room again, and found her still sleepy, it might be indeed considered proved that she was not Abracadabra. Besides, when I told her about Abracadabra's visit, she was very much vexed that she had missed her, and asked whether Abracadabra had not left any present for her, which she had not. That is the first clear and definite memory I have of Abracadabra, and also, in a way, it is the last, for when next that amiable fairy visited us, I knew, alas, that she was no fairy at all, but my mother, dressed in the amazing garb of fairyland. But though that particular brand of fairyland was finished for me, those subsequent occasions were girt with grandeur, for I, concealing my own superior knowledge, must pretend that this was genuine Abracadabra, thus indulging and buttressing the belief of my youngest brother Hugh, who still, innocent thing, had no grown-up doubts on the subject. . . . I found those selfsame garments only lately in a trunk stowed away in an attic at the last home my mother lived in; a skirt covered with sprays of artificial flowers, a bodice and stomacher set with gems of pure glass, a hat of white satin embowered in flowers, a pair of wings, gauze and gold, and a pair of high-heeled shoes covered with gilt paper. They were moth-eaten and mouldy, and it was scarcely possible for the most sentimental pilgrim to preserve them. Besides I had the memory of the day when the authentic fairy appeared in them, and that memory was sweeter than the condition, forty-five years later, of the robes themselves. My mother had kept them, I make no doubt, when her own days of Abracadabra were over by reason of our emergence from childhood, in the hope that one day a daughter or daughter-in-law would assume them again for the joy and mystification of grandchildren, but that day never came. So the robes of fairyland stowed away in their trunk were forgotten, until that day at Tremans when I found them, as I turned out the treasures and the rubbish of the vanished years before the house passed into other hands. It was a dark autumn day, and the rain beat softly on the roof, but verily, when I opened the trunk and found them there, the sunlight of the dawn of life shot level and delicious rays from the far horizon, and cast a rainbow over the weeping sky.

People in those very early days, with the exception of Beth, were more part of the general landscape of life than human beings, similar in kind to myself, with an individuality of their own. They were not loved or feared: they were but a part of the general environment, like the walls of the nursery, or trees or dinner or beds. But, as by some superior swiftness of evolution, Beth ceased to be landscape, and became a human being, wholly to be adored and generally to be obeyed, sooner than any of the family. She was well over fifty when first I remember her, and had by now almost completed the nursing of a second generation, for she had been nursery-maid with Mrs. Sidgwick, my mother's mother, when her family came into the world, and had gone to my mother when at the mature age of nineteen the first of her six children was born. Thereafter Beth remained with my mother until the end of her long and utterly beautiful life of love and service. Very soon after she came to my grandmother, at the age of fifteen, she gave notice because she wanted to go back from Rugby to her native Yorkshire, and did not settle into more southerly ways. But my grandmother encouraged her to think that she soon would do so, and so Beth, instead of leaving, stopped on till the age of ninety-three, in an unbroken devotion to us of seventy-eight years. That devotion was returned: we were all her children, and the darlingest of all to Beth's big heart was Hugh.

Beth then, to my sense, emerged first of all into the

MY MOTHER, ÆT. 20

[*Page* 19

ranks of human beings, servant and friend and to a very considerable extent mistress. But she gave us no weak and sentimental devotion, and though she never inspired the smallest degree of fear, her rare displeasure caused an awful feeling of loneliness and desolation. If we had done wrong, she demanded sorrow before her forgiveness was granted, and if to her wise mind the sorrow was not sufficiently sincere, she was quite capable of saying, when we said we were sorry in too superficial a manner, "I don't want your sorrer," and the day grew black, until she accepted it and beamed forgiveness. That granted, there was never any nagging, and next minute she would be running races with us again until panting and bright-eyed she would stop and say, "Eh, dear, I can't run any more: I've got a bone in my leg."

She mingles in almost every memory that I have of those days, a loved and protecting presence. She it was who lifted me up to look out of the nursery window when a sham fight was going on, perhaps at Aldershot. There were reports of guns to be heard and, so I fancy, flashes and wreaths of smoke, and like George III I got it firmly embedded in my mind that this was the battle of Water-loo that I had witnessed. The connection I think lay through the fact of this place being Wellington. She it was who led me through a delicious sandy piece of waste ground near the house called the Wilderness, and allowed me to pick and eat a blackberry from a bramble that grew by a rubbish heap on which was a broken plate. Never have I seen such a blackberry. I can still hardly believe it was not of the size of an apricot, for I know it entirely filled my mouth and the juice spurted therefrom as out of a wine-vat. She too consoled me for the loss of two front teeth which came out into a piece of butter-scotch that she had given me. She removed the teeth and I proceeded with the toffee. She too allowed me to take out of the Noah's ark with which we played on Sundays a brown dog remotely resembling a setter, two of whose legs had been broken. Her brilliant surgery had repaired this loss by inserting in the stumps a couple of pins so that it stood up as well as ever. This I was permitted to carry about with me, partly in my pocket, but mostly in a warm damp hand, which caused the setter to exude a pleasant smell of paint and varnish. A moment of tragedy, the first that I had known, was the sequel, and I do not believe that ever in my life I have been more utterly miserable. What happened was this.

It was Christmas Eve, and the five of us, Martin, Arthur, Nellie, Maggie, and myself—Hugh, so I guess, being then little more than a month old—were returning from our walk, and the setter should have been in my hand or in my pocket. We were going through a wood of fir trees, the ground was brown and slippery with pine-needles, and the sun low and red shone through the tall trunks making, with the fact that it was Christmas Eve, an enchanted moment. I had just found out that my breath steamed, as it came out of my mouth, and Beth and I were playing steamers. Then suddenly I became aware that the setter was neither in my hand nor my pocket, and the abomination of desolation descended on me. For a little while we looked for it, and then Beth decreed that we must go on. But Martin—this is the first thing that I can recollect about him—being eleven years old and able to walk alone after dark, got leave to stop behind and look for it, while the rest of the bereaved procession went homewards. At that point my memory fails, and I have no idea whether he found it or not. But here were the two first crystallized emotions of my life; the black misery of the loss of the setter, and the sense of Martin's amazing kindness and bravery in stopping behind by himself in the terrible wood. There was a moon in the sky when we came out into the open and frosty stars, but no heart within me to care for playing steamers any more that day.

Next morning, after nursery-breakfast, I went down to the dining-room, and was given a cup of milk to drink by my father. This was an unusual proceeding, and as I progressed towards the bottom of the cup he told me to drink slowly. Something inside the cup clinked as I finished it, and there was a shilling which was mine.

On Sunday morning, towards the end of the Wellington days, I went down to breakfast in the dining-room. There were short prayers first, about which I remember nothing except the sight of servants' backs, kneeling at chairs. But on one such morning, in the summer I suppose, because all the windows were wide open, a very delightful thing happened. There was a tame squirrel that used to scamper about the house, and run up and down stairs, and on this occasion he suddenly descended from a curtain rod, crossed the floor and scampered up the cook's back. Probably she pushed him off, for he chattered with rage and went and sat on the sideboard and began nibbling ham.

After prayers were over, while breakfast was being brought up, it was my task to go round the walls of the dining-room, where hung engravings of eminent personages, and name them. There was the Prince Consort in striped trousers with a bowler hat in his hand, the Duke of Wellington in knee-breeches, the head and shoulders of Dr. Walford, a full length of Dean Stanley, and Dr.

Martin Routh in a wig reading a book. Round the edge of this which I think must have been a mezzotint were various small sketches of the said Dr. Martin Routh in other attitudes. Then came the smell of sausages and the advent of two or three sixth form boys who in turn breakfasted with my father. These were very glorious persons and I marvelled at their condescension in coming. Once the head of the school came, and following my father's example I addressed him by his surname (whatever it was) without the prefix of "Mister," for which omission I was corrected. But out of his magnificence he did not seem to mind.

Slowly, as the mists of infancy dispersed through which like sundered mountain-tops were seen these scattered incidents, a more panoramic vision of life as a coherent whole made its appearance. There had been vignettes, now of the Wilderness, now of my father's study, now of the nursery, with nothing except the continuous association with Beth to bind them together. But now these scattered localities became parts of one connected picture, and I could form some sort of complete idea of the place. Most important was the house, the Master's Lodge, a red brick building standing in its own grounds. You entered through a gabled porch into a broad passage, on one side of which lay my father's study. Glass doors separated this from the huge immensity of the hall, with my mother's sitting-room, the drawing-room and the dining-room opening out of it. The stairs started in the centre of it and after one flight separated into two, each of which led up into a gallery that skirted three sides of the hall. Bedrooms opened out of this, also the day nursery and night nursery, and pitch-pine banisters (a wood much admired at that time) ran round it, and it

was through these banisters that one morning my sister
Maggie, in a fit of wonderful audacity inserted her foot,
and exclaimed, "That's my foot, Alleluia." In the
nursery, the room with which I was chiefly concerned, was
a rocking-horse with wide red nostrils and movable pummels. These pummels penetrated right through his dap-
pled skin, and by removing them it was possible to drop
small objects like pebbles into his inside, where they rattled agreeably as he rocked. Once some one of us, tempt-
ing Fate, held a penny at this remarkable aperture, and
the penny dropped inside, so that Beth had to turn the
rocking-horse upside down and shake him until it was
restored to currency again. There was a low deal table,
quantities of lead soldiers, and a swing hung from the
ceiling, so that altogether it presented most agreeable
features. There was also a large cupboard where play-
things must be put away when they were done with, and
I remember with excitement a Homeric struggle that took
place there between Martin and Arthur for the possession of a stick which was painted blue and red. But the
most remarkable feature of the nursery was its walls,
which, by the time we left Wellington, were entirely
covered with pictures. These pictures we children used
to cut out on wet days from old illustrated papers under
my father's supervision, and he, clad in a dressing-gown
to defend his clothes from splashes of paste, fixed them
up on the walls, till the entire surface was covered. He
had a step-ladder on which he attacked the higher altitudes, and a roller with which he pressed down the affixed
pictures to the wall. There were battles there and historical scenes, notable buildings, and numerous cartoons
from *Punch*. But one ought never to have been put there,
for I dreaded seeing it, and, like a child, kept my dread to

myself. It was the outcome, I imagine, of some enquiry
into sweated trades, and represented a dressmaker talking
to a client and saying, "I wouldn't disappoint your lady-
ship for anything," or words to that effect. At the back
was a glimpse into her workroom, and there falling backwards with closed eyes was a girl, fainting I suppose in
the artist's intention, but I knew better and was aware
that she was dead. Nightmares pictured her as falling
across my bed in the sleeping-nursery next door, and Beth,
in her frilled nightcap came close and said, "Now, dear,
go to sleep again. I'm taking care of you." Doors in
the hall led I suppose to kitchens and servants' bedrooms,
but of these I remember nothing except the fact of a
flagged passage and the smell of a store-cupboard to
which I once went with my mother. That part of the
house did not matter.

Outside, the lawn was spread round two sides of the
house; if you crossed it, you found a wicket-gate in a
fence that bordered the belt of trees where the gardener
cast the dead adder, and through this you passed to the
kitchen garden. On the right of the lawn below the
trees stood a summer-house where the croquet mallets
were kept, and through these trees was a path that led
out into the school playing fields. A gravel sweep faced
the front door; there were laburnums and rhododendrons
by the gate, to the right lay the Wilderness and straight
in front the College buildings with the spired chapel at
the far end. Somewhere in these buildings was the school
library, only notable because it contained a glass case in
which was a white ant. Below the playing fields lay two
immeasurable lakes, in the lower of which was the school
bathing-place: the upper, though also immeasurable, was
smaller, and a waterfall of gigantic height severed the

two. By degrees the same world extended even further than that, for by walking laboriously you could reach either of two hills called Edgebarrow and Ambarrow, and then it was time to come home again.

Simultaneously with this growing reality of the world, its inhabitants (still with the exception of my father) assumed an individuality of their own. Far the most individual of them was my mother, who seemed to live entirely for pleasure except when she taught us our lessons. She played croquet with consummate skill, she drove herself in a pony carriage, she put on a low shining dress every evening with turquoise brooches and bracelets, and had as much eau-de-Cologne as she wished on her handkerchief. When she was dressing for dinner we used to go into her room, examine that Golconda of a jewel-case, and bring her clean handkerchiefs of our own still folded up, for her to "make moons" on them, as the phrase was, with eau-de-Cologne. She took the stopper out of the bottle, and reversed it on to these folded handkerchiefs, making three or four applications. Then we unfolded these odorous handkerchiefs, held them up to the light, and lo, they were penetrated with full wet moons of eau-de-Cologne. She was, too, enormously wealthy, for every Saturday we went to see her in her sitting-room, and she opened the front of her inlaid Italian cabinet, and drew from one of the pigeon-holes within, a little wicker-basket, and out of it paid our weekly allowances. For elders there was as much as sixpence, but sixpences came out of a japanned cash-box, for juniors there was twopence or a penny according to age, and all these pennies, infinite apparently in number came out of the wicker-basket. She had a rosewood work-box, lined with red silk, which contained what was known as her "treasures." These were two white china elephants with gilded feet, a small silk parasol, the ferrule of which was a pencil, an amber necklace, a cornelian heart, and boxes that made loud pops when you opened them. If any of us had a cold, or some ailment that kept us indoors, we were allowed to play with her treasures, to while away the solitude. But for some reason I did not think much of the treasures, and after being consoled with them during an afternoon indoors gave vent to the appalling criticism, "What Mamma calls tessors, I call 'Ubbish." But that, as far as I know, was the only disloyalty of which I was ever guilty with regard to her. I just did not care about that particular sort of treasures.

What a life was hers! She ordered lunch and dinner precisely as she chose; she had a silver card-case with cards in it, stating who she was and where she was, and we all belonged to her, and so in some dim way did my father, and even the biggest boys of the great sixth form itself touched their caps to her as she passed. And slowly, slowly I became aware that she was worthy of all these pleasures and this homage.

There were certainly lessons in those days, I suppose for about an hour a day. There was a book called *Reading without Tears*, which said that a-b was "ab," and d-o-g was "dog." There must have been certain crises over this learning for I was kept in instead of going out one day, and, with the fatal habit of inversion which has clung to me all my life, said, so my mother told me, "I call it tears without reading!" I record this anecdote in pure self-condemnation: I don't suppose I knew that this *obiter dictum* made sense; it was only the beginning of a habit to play about with words, and see to what fashion of affairs they could be suited. Every morning also, when we came downstairs we went into my mother's sitting-room, and learned a new verse of a Psalm, repeating the verses previously learned. The Twenty-Third Psalm was one of these, and the Ninety-First I think must have been another, since I cannot remember the time when I did not know it by heart. I do not think that these religious repetitions meant anything to me; they were part of the inevitable day, which was full of glee.

That my mother had any other life of her own, full as I know it to have been of worries and anxieties and of marvellous happinesses, never, as was natural, occurred to any of us. She was, as far as concerns my memory of her at Wellington, a glorious sunlit figure, living a life that appeared to be the apotheosis of hedonism, the mistress of a shouting houseful of children, all wilful, all set on having their own way, and she calmly ruled us all, without even letting us know that we were being ruled. All the time she was a very young woman married to a man twelve years her senior who was as violently individual as anyone could be. But for us she floated there like the moons of eau-de-Cologne which embellished our handkerchiefs, carrying something of the fairyhood of Abracadabra, and all the wizardry of her own inimitable wisdom. After Beth it was she who first emerged out of the landscape which once embraced trees and people alike, and to us soared upwards like a rising constellation. She could not take Beth's place, for Beth filled that, but she enlarged a child's heart, and dwelt there. She never ceased from her own enlargements: in my mother's house there were many mansions. There were mansions for everybody, and none of the tenants usurped the place of another. As we grew up, all of us, without exception, felt that we were especially hers, and were in

a unique relation to her. We were all quite right about
that, and so were a myriad friends of hers. There was
"the best room" for each of them. How she did it, how
she conveyed that adorable truth I know now, because
I know that love is of infinite dimensions, and has the
same perfect room for all. But the childish instinct was
right: she cared supremely, and gave her whole heart to
each of us.

My sisters, presently to be kindled for me with a great
illumination, were for the period of the Wellington days
quite dim, so too were Martin and Arthur now at a
private school at East Sheen, where, some years later, I
followed them, and the rest of the world at that time
consisted of vague visitors, among whom were my
mother's three brothers, William, Henry, and Arthur
Sidgwick (remarkable only for their beards and their
use of tobacco), and her mother, who is a much clearer
figure. She encouraged small visitors when she was
dressing for dinner, was generous in making moons, and
had a ritual with regard to the dressing of her hair which
filled me with wonder. It was parted in the middle and
she drew down two strands of it over the top of her
ears, and holding each of these in place applied to it a
stick of brown cosmetic which I now know to have been
bandoline. The effect of this was that the hair stuck
together in the manner of a thin board, absolutely smooth
and in one piece. Sometimes a crack or fissure appeared
it it, and more bandoline was employed. It formed in
fact a little stiff roof, and on the top she put a lace cap.
She had long chains round her neck, and carried a silver
vinaigrette containing a small piece of sponge soaked in
aromatic vinegar. It was chiefly used in chapel when she
was standing up during the Psalms. On the other side

of the family there were three aunts who corresponded with the three uncles, sisters of my father, two of whom were very handsome and of a high colour; the third, Aunt Ada, seemed to me to be like a horse. They all floated in a sort of remote ether, like clouds coming up and passing again.

CHAPTER II

IN 1873 my father was appointed Chancellor of Lincoln, and the move there was made in the summer of that year, during July and August. We four younger children, Nellie, Maggie, myself and Hugh went with Beth to stay with my grandmother at Rugby while it was in progress. That visit was memorable for several reasons: in the first place I celebrated a birthday there, and great-Aunt Henrietta had no idea that I was long past fairies, for on the morning of that day she met me in the hall, and said she would go out to see if there were any fairies about, for she fancied she had heard them singing. Accordingly she went out of the front door, closing it after her, and leaving me in the hall. Sure enough from the other side of the door there instantly came a crooning kind of noise, which I knew was Aunt Henrietta singing, and there was a rattle in the letter-box in the door of something dropped into it. Aunt Henrietta then returned in considerable excitement, and asked me if I hadn't heard the fairies singing, and of course I said I had. One had come right on to the doorstep, she continued, while she stood there, and had dropped something for me into the letter-box. And there was a velvet purse with a brass clasp, and inside five shillings. This was an opulence hitherto undreamed of. Aunt Henrietta was remarkable in other ways besides generosity:

she wore a curious cap with pink blobs on it, and when asked how they were made instantly replied that they were made by coral insects underneath the sea. It was also said of her that she went to church one Sunday with a friend, and found they had only one prayer book, and that with small print, between them. They were both short-sighted and they each pulled so lustily on the prayer book in order to see better, that it came in half about the middle of the Psalms.

One day there came a moment which still ranks in my mind as an experience of transcendent happiness. It had been a delicious day already, for not only had my mother arrived, but the ceiling of the dining-room was being white-washed, and we had our meals in my grandmother's sitting-room, which gave something of the thrill of a picnic. That evening we were playing in the garden when Beth came out to tell us it was time to go to bed. She took me along the path, and there close to an open window my mother and grandmother were having dinner. We stopped a moment, and I asked if I might not have ten minutes more in the garden. That was granted, and, as if that was not enough, my grandmother gave me three grapes from a bunch on the table. As I ate them a breeze brought across me the warm scent of a lilac bush, and the combination of these things made me touch a new apex of happiness. Something, the joy of the level sunlight, of the three grapes, of the lilac scent, of having ten minutes more to play in, rushed simultaneously over me, and at that moment some new consciousness of the world and its exquisiteness was unsealed in me. And I doubt if I have ever been so happy since, or if anything, owing to that moment, will ever smell so sweet to me as lilac.

Whatever that unsealing was, the wax was broken for

ever, and from then a more vivid perception was mine. According to Wordsworth I ought, just about then, to have ceased trailing my clouds of glory, instead of which they trailed in far more radiant profusion. The arrival at Lincoln still wonderfully etched in my memory was an adventure of the finest kind, and the exploration of the new land teemed with unique discoveries. The fact that the house dated from the fourteenth century naturally mattered not at all: its joy lay in its present suitability to the diversions of children. There was a winding stone staircase, opening from a nail-studded door in the hall with pentagrams carved on the steps to keep off evil spirits: there was a day nursery made of two bedrooms thrown into one; there was a suite of amazing attics, steeped in twilight, with rafters close above the head, and loose boards underfoot. Here in dark corners lay water-cisterns which gurgled unexpectedly in the dusk with mirthless goblin chuckles; cobwebs hung in corners and mice scuttled. Here too was a bare tremendous apartment also under the roof, spread with pears and apples. Up one side of it went a buttress, which certainly contained the chimney from the kitchen, for it was warm to the touch and altogether mysterious.

Instantly, so it seems to me now, we began playing the most blood-curdling games in that floor of attics; people hid there and groaned and jumped out on you with maniacal screams. A short steep flight of steps led down from it to the nursery floor, and how often, giddy with pleasing terror, have I tumbled down those steps, because somebody (who ought to have been a sister, but might easily have become a goblin) was yelling behind me. One's mind, the sensible part of it much in abeyance, knew quite well that it was Nellie or Maggie, but

supposing one's sensible mind was wrong for once? It
was wiser to run, just in case. . . . From which vivid
memory I perceive that though I knew about Abracadabra
I was not so firmly rationalistic about the rooms with
gurgling cisterns in them. In the dark, strange metamor-
phoses might have occurred, and when one day I found in
the darkest corner of one of these attics, a figure apparently human, and certainly resembling Nellie, lying flat
down and not moving (though it was for the hider to
catch the seeker) the light of my sensible mind was
snuffed out like a candlewick, and I shrieked out, "Oh,
Nellie, don't!" Observe the confusion of an infant
mind! I knew the corpse to be Nellie, for I addressed
it as Nellie, and told it not to; on the other hand, by an
involuntary exercise of the imagination I conceived that
this still twilight object might be something quite different.

My sisters were now of an age to sleep together in a
large apartment somewhere at the top of the stone stairs,
while I still slept in the night nursery, in a bed near
the window. Beth occupied another bed, and in a corner
was Hugh's crib with high sides, where he—being now
about two years old—was stowed away before the day
was over for me. Next door to the nursery was a room
smaller than any room I have ever seen, and this was of-
ficially known as "My Room." It had a tiny window,
was quite uninhabitable, for it was always shrouded
in a deadly gloom and piled up with boxes, but the fact
that it was my room, though I lived in the day nursery
by day, and slept in the night nursery by night, gave me
a sense of pomp and dignity, and I resented the fact
that presently my father had the wing of the house which
lay above the stone staircase connected with the night

nursery by a wooden passage across the roof. This turned my room into part of the passage, and though he called this ten yards of passage "the Rialto," I felt that I had been robbed of some ancestral domain. After all it was My Room. . . .

The rest of the house was not particularly interesting; it consisted of sitting-rooms and dining-room, and school-room and lobbies, the sort of thing that you naturally supposed would be there. But one day my father presented my sisters and me with a room at the top of the stone stairs, with which we were allowed to deal precisely as we wished. We instantly called it "The Museum," and put in it any unusual objects that we obtained. One day Maggie found a piece of sheep's wool stuck in a hedge, so that of course was brought home, washed white and carefully combed and put in a cardboard box with a glass lid. Then (to anticipate as regards the Museum) we spent a summer holiday at Torquay, and collected various attractive pebbles, and madrepores, and shells. These were dedicated to the Museum, and a large earthenware bread-bowl was lined with them, and filled up with water to the top, so that they gleamed deliciously through the liquid. Then there came a memorable day when my mother killed a hornet on her window; she gave us the squalid corpse, and after consultation we put it in the water of the bowl, lined with spa and madrepore, in order to preserve it. It floated about there and was supposed to be in process of preservation. An addled swan's egg joined the collection, which, very prudently, we decided not to blow. But it began to smell so terribly even through the shell that with great reluctance we scrapped it. My father gave us a case of butterfles, collected by his father, in which, without doubt were two "large cop-

pers." "As rare things will" that case vanished, and I
wonder what fortunate dealer eventually got the "large
coppers." . . . Then on a bookshelf was the great stamp-
collection, and I wish I knew what had happened to that.
There was all South Australia complete, and complete
too was Tasmania, and complete the Cape of Good Hope,
the stamps of which for the sake of variety were triangu-
lar. Heligoland was there and the Ionian Islands and
New Caledonia (black and only one of it). But the
stamp-collection was considered rather dull: the hornet
disintegrating in the bread-bowl, and the piece of sheep's
wool were far more interesting. They had the timbre of
personal acquisition, and rang with first-hand emotion.
Personal and precious too were the bits of oxydised glass
smouldering into rainbows which we dug up in the garden
and displayed here; there too we found bowls and broken
stems of tobacco-pipes which I think were Cromwellian.
But Cromwell was no good to us, so we said that they
were Roman tobacco-pipes. Then there was a collection
of fossils, which, with the aid of geological hammers that
my father gave us, we rapped out of stones in lime quar-
ries, or from the heaps that lay by the roadside for mend-
ings. Amateur stone-breakers indeed we were, and often
bruised fingers were of the party, but they added preciousness to the trophies that we brought back to the Museum.
On the door of the Museum was a paper label, on which
was emblazoned in large letters tinted with water-colour,
"Museum. Private." The privacy was part of the joy
of it. Occasionally we asked my mother to have tea with
us there, and she came in her hat formally. This very
proper behaviour was duly appreciated.

Indeed that was a good house for children with its
attics and its winding-stairs, and its multitude of pas-

sages.   Judging the virtue of a house by the standards of hide-and-seek, than which there is no more authentic rule, I never saw so laudable a habitation.   Endless were the dark places for the concealment of hiders, endless also the various routes by which the seekers might get back uncaught to the sanctuary where Beth sat with her sewing over the fire and said, "Eh now, you'll be falling down and hurting yourselves."   There was the route up the kitchen stairs, the route through my father's dressing-room and study, only practicable (as on the days when the Khyber Pass is open to caravans) when he was away: there were the stairs up from the hall into the lobby; there were the winding-stairs communicating through the Rialto with the nursery passage, at the other end of which were the nursery stairs.   How rare again was the cul-de-sac, that infernal invention of degraded architects and the ruin of all good hide-and-seek, which makes capture inevitable, when once you are in the trap.   For magnificence of design, judging by these standards, I unhesitatingly allot the palm to the Chancery house in the Close at Lincoln.

Gardens, in like manner, must be judged by their serviceableness in the pursuit of games, and here again we were fortunate.   Adjacent to the house itself was a big lawn, levelled and sown afresh, which was the arena of cricket and rounders.   Behind that was an asphalted yard with a stable, a coach-house and a wood-shed, erected no doubt in order that we might play fives against them: a covered passage led to the kitchen garden. There was sufficient space here for a lawn-tennis court, the lines of which were laid down with tape secured by hairpins.   Occasionally the foot caught in the tape; "zp, zp, zp," went most of the hairpins and the shape of the

court changed for the moment from an oblong to a trape-
zium with no right-angles. By one side of this was a
steep grassy bank with elder bushes growing on the top.
Here you laid yourself stiffly out on the ground, and like
that rolled bodily down the bank, sitting up again at the
bottom to find the world reeling and spinning round you.
When you felt a little less sick, you refreshed yourself
with elderberries, and rolled down again. Beyond this
was a pear tree large enough to climb, and high enough
not to fall out of, and an asparagus bed. The edible
properties of that vegetable were of no interest, but when
it went to seed and grew up in tall fern-like stems with
orange berries it was valuable as a hiding-place. Narrow grass paths led this way and that between the garden
beds, and they had been well constructed, for they were
of such a width that it was possible, though difficult, to
bowl a hoop down them without invading the cabbages.
A fool would have made them either wider or narrower,
and then they would have been useless. In a corner of
the garden were our own particular plots, and against
the red brick wall grew a fig tree, which I thought had
some connection with the biblical tree that withered away,
because it never yielded its fruit. All round the garden
ran a high wall, now brick, now ancient limestone, and
at the bottom was a mediæval tower partly in ruins, where
we habitually played the most dangerous game that has
ever been invented since the world began. Why no one
was killed I cannot understand to this day. The game was
called "Sieges," and the manner of it was as follows:

A flight of some twenty high stone steps led up to a
chamber in the tower, which was roofless and ivy-clad.
They lay against the wall with a turn half-way up, and
up to that point had no protection whatever on one side,

so that nothing could have been simpler than to have fallen off them to the ground. From the chamber a further short flight led up on to an open turret defended at the top by a low iron railing of doubtful solidity. One child was constituted King of the Castle, the others were the besiegers. The besiegers stormed the castle and the besieger and besieged tried to hurl each other downstairs. The besieged had the advantage of superior height, for he stood usually at the top of the stairs by the chamber; the besiegers the advantage of weight and numbers. You were allowed to resort to any form of violence in order to win your object, except kicking; blows and pushings and wrestlings and trippings-up formed legitimate warfare. Even the rule about kicking must have been rather slack, for I remember once seeking my mother with a bleeding nose, and saying that Nellie had kicked me in the face at "Sieges." Her defence, a singularly weak one as it still appears to me, was that she hadn't kicked me in the face at all: she had only put her foot against my face and then pushed. Whereon the judge went into such fits of laughter that the trial was adjourned.

At first my mother taught us entirely, and the sight of the schoolroom when lessons were going on would certainly have conveyed a very false impression to a stranger, for close to my mother's hand lay a silver-mounted riding-whip of plaited horsehair. But it was not for purposes of correction: its use was that if as we were writing our exercises and copies she saw we were not sitting upright, her hand would stealthily take up the whip and bring it down with a sounding thwack on to the table, startling us into erect attitudes again. To these instructions there was soon added Latin, and I remember the charm of new words just because they were new. It was also interesting

to grasp the fact that there really had been people once
who, when they wanted to say "table" preferred to say
"mensa," and found that their friends understood them
perfectly.   I suppose that soon my mother became too
busy to continue the instruction of my sisters and me, for
a day-governess appeared, a quiet melancholy German
lady with brown eyes, and a manner that commanded respect.   She was not with us very long, and on her departure we three went to a day-school kept by a widow.
She had a Roman nose, and though rather terrible was
kind.   She lived in a house just outside the close which
smelt of mackintosh: the schoolroom was a larger wooden
apartment built out over the garden.

In between these curricula we had a temporary governess who seemed to us all the most admirable and en-
viable person who ever lived.   This was Miss Bramston,
a great personal friend of my mother's, whose brother,
beloved subsequently by generation after generation of
Wykehamists, had been a master at Wellington under
my father.   Never was there so delightful an instructress;
by dint of her being so pleasant when we disobeyed her,
we soon got to obey her not out of discipline, of which
she had not the faintest notion, but out of affection, of
which she had a great deal.   She wrote us a play in
rhymed verse, all out of her own head, which we acted
one Christmas, rather like *Hamlet*, with rhymes thrown
in, and ending much more comfortably than that tragedy.
There was a king on a throne, only he wasn't the right
king and when alone he soliloquized, saying:

> I'm a usurper, though I seem a swell;
> The true King lies within a dungeon cell,

and I wish I could remember more of it.   She painted

not in water-colour only but in oils, and could make any
canvas of hers recognizable. For instance, you knew at
once that this was the Cathedral. But not only to us
was she not a usurper but a swell; she was a Public
Authoress, and wrote stories, printed and published,
which she gave us to read. The S.P.C.K. published them,
and the whole world could buy them, and she got paid for
writing them. One of her early works was *Elly's Choice;*
there was a poor good girl called Elly, and a rather nasty
rich cousin called Cordelia, a boy called Alick, and everybody who mattered was about nine years old. A piece of
stained glass was broken in the "Octagon Room," and
Cordelia let Elly be punished for it though Cordelia had
broken it, and then Elly received apologies from Grand-
mamma Farmer, and Cordelia learned a lesson, and all
got wonderfully happy again. The extreme vividness
with which I remember it, surely shows that the book
fulfilled its purpose, that is, of interesting children. Later
Miss Bramston spread larger pinions, and I do not think
she did so well. To our intense joy she came back to us
at Truro a year or two later, and was as lovable as ever.

It was in those few years at Lincoln that my father
began to be individual, instead of being part of the landscape, and as I got to know him, I, like the rest of us,
also got to fear him. For many years we were none of
us at our ease with him, as we always were with my
mother, and it is tragic that it was so, for I know that he
regarded us all with the tenderest love. Often and often
his glorious vitality, keener and more splendid than any
I have ever come across, enchanted us, and the sunlight
of him was of a midsummer radiance. But he had no idea
how blighting his displeasure was to small children, and
for fear of incurring it we went delicately like Agag, at-

tending so strictly to our behaviour that all spontaneity withered. Nothing would have pleased him more, had we taken him into our confidence, but we feared his disapproval more than we were drawn to intimacy with him. It was always uncertain whether he would not pull us up with stinging rebukes for offences that were certainly venial, and in his watchfulness over our mental and moral education, he came down upon faults of laziness and carelessness as if to explode such tendencies out of our nature. Earnest and eager all through, and gloriously and tumultuously alive, he brought too heavy guns to bear on positions so lightly fortified as children's hearts, and from fear of the bombardment we did not dare to make a sortie and go to him. Too much noise, an ordinary childish carelessness might, so we believed, bring down on us a schoolmaster's reproof instead of such remonstrances as we got from my mother, which were completely successful, and with him we were careful to be decorous to the verge of woodenness. We had washed hands and neat hair and low voices, because thus we minimized the risks of his society. We were never frank with him, we did not talk about the things that interested us, but those which interested him and which we thought he would wish us to be interested in. We sat on the edge of our chairs, and were glad to be gone. If we had been natural with him, I know that his appreciation of that would somehow have made cement between us, but how are you to be natural when, rightly or wrongly, you are being careful? Tearing spirits moderated themselves on his approach, we became as mild as children on chocolate boxes. If he was pleased with us, we breathed sighs of relief: if he was displeased we waited for the clouds to pass. With him I, at least, was a prig and a hypocrite, assuming a demure demeanour, and pretending to be interested in the journal of Bishop Heber of Bombay, which I still maintain is a dreary work, and not suited to young gentlemen of between six and nine years old. But the journal of Bishop Heber was given me as a book to read on Sunday and helped to add to the wearisomeness of that rather appalling day.

Below our lovely Museum, and opening out of the winding stone stairs, there was a room fitted up as a chapel. There was stained glass in the windows, Arundel prints on the walls, and a quite unique harmonium that cost five pounds. The keyboard was only of three octaves, extending from

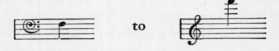

which, as it was used if not designed to be as an instrument to accompany hymns, seems to me to be a truly remarkable compass, since in order to accompany hymns on it at all, you had to leave out the bass, or transfer the whole tune to the higher octave. When fully extended for purposes of melody, it stood about two and a half feet high, but on its black japanned front were two steel catches which, if pressed, caused it to subside into itself, the foot-bellows becoming flat, and the harmonium itself so small that a man could put it under his arm. Sometimes when playing it (as I was presently to do) a too vigorous knee, in the movement of blowing, would touch these catches, and it collapsed in the middle of the hymn on to the feet of the organist, dealing them a severe blow, and necessitating its readjustment before the hymn proceeded. It had two stops, one of which allowed the air to get to its pipes, the other was a tremolo which caused its voice to be transformed into a series of swift little bleats with pauses in between like a soprano lamb much out of breath. Perhaps it was designed to take the solo part of a flute in one of those curious bastard orchestras on which Mr. Oscar Browning, with the help of three undergraduates, used to render quartettes in his rooms at King's College, Cambridge, but here it was as an accompanying instrument at prayers in the chapel of the Chancery, and took its part in the religious exercises of the morning.

Sunday, in fact, began in the chapel for us children after the early service for our elders in the Cathedral. There was a hymn, my father read certain Sunday prayers, and then came breakfast. The collection of hymns which we used in chapel was Bishop Wordsworth's "Holy Year." There are many admirable hymns in it, others not so good. For instance, the one for the feast of St. Philip and St. James began:

> Let us emulate the names
> Of St. Philip and St. James.

We children, therefore, could hardly help making up another hymn for the feast of St. Simon and St. Jude beginning (and then stopping):

> Let us try to be as good
> As St. Simon and St. Jude.

Matins at the Cathedral was at half-past ten, so we often bore a crude sausage there, as Juvenal would have said. The service was fully choral, and the *pièce de résistance*, as far as I was concerned, was the Litany, chanted by two lay-clerks at a desk in the middle of the gangway between the seats. Together I think (or perhaps separately, while the other was in reserve) they chanted the first sentences as follows:

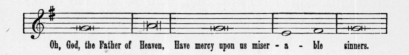

Oh, God, the Father of Heaven, Have mercy upon us miser - a - ble sinners.

The choir then repeated it in harmony, and the same simple musical material furnished the whole of the subsequent responses.

Sung thus very slowly the Litany took a full quarter of an hour, but when that was over, I was at liberty to find my hat and steal out. I used to put my hat, a round soft felt hat with elastic under the chin, in an aperture at the corner of our seat below the stalls, which had in it an opening for ventilation. Sometimes my hat slipped down this, and after an excited groping for it, it came up covered with the dust of ages. The service had already lasted an hour or more, and I made my jaded way back to the Chancery, while my mother and sisters, and in the holidays, my two elder brothers, remained for the rest of the service. Martin and Arthur occupied stalls near my father and were still dim figures to me, at home only for a comparatively few weeks in the year, and having a sitting-room of their own. I used to be rather glad when they went to school, because my mother invented for me the title of "The Eldest Son at Home," which could only be used in their absence.

In the afternoon there was a family walk, and then Cathedral service again. Then came a reading of Sunday books, or a reading of the Bible with my father, and we went utterly fatigued to bed. It was not so much the plethora of religious exercises that caused this lassitude, but the entire absence of any recreation. Spare time (and there was not much of it) was supposed to be taken up with Bishop Heber's Journal, *Agathos* and *The Rocky Island*. Once a certain brightness came into these Sunday readings, because we were allowed a book called *Sunday Echoes in Week-day Hours.* There was a widowed mother in it, and her boy called Cecil, and their conversation about collects was so excruciatingly pious that it became merely humorous, and we invented fresh Cecil-talk among ourselves. We once indulged in this before my mother, who with a controlled countenance withdrew the delightful volume. I remember waking up after falling asleep one Sunday night, and hearing Compline going on in the chapel with another hymn, and thinking with amazement that they were still at it. In the way of a child, I think I was, from certain evidence that will appear, religious, but to put it quite frankly, I was sick of the whole affair by Sunday evening.

I cannot chronologize the events in our life at Lincoln, which only lasted for three and a half years, and I do not quite know when the Cathedral services began to wear a perfectly new complexion for me. The reason of this was that I was violently attracted by a choir-boy, or rather a chorister, one of four, who instead of wearing a surplice like the common choir-boy, wore a long dark blue coat down to the knees faced with white. A similar experience, I fancy, is almost universal: the first romantic affection a girl is conscious of is nearly always towards a girl, and in the same way, a small boy, when first his physical nature begins to grope, still quite blindly and innocently, in the misty country of emotion, is pretty certain to take as his idol for secret romantic worship, one of his own sex. It was so at any rate with me, and instead of the Cathedral services being of incomparable tedium, they became exciting and exalting. He, the nameless he, came in procession at the end of the choir-boys just before the lay-clerks, and besides having this soul-stirring effect on me, he woke in me, by means of his singing, my first love of music. He sat at the end of the choir nearest our seat, and luckily on the other side, so that I could see him without the intervention of dull people's heads. I could hear his voice, sexless and un-emotional, above the rest of the trebles, but with what emotion did that voice inspire me! He used to sing solos as well, and I am sure that the sneaking love that I have still for Mendelssohn, was due to the fact that (unaccompanied) he sang "The night is departing, de-pa-a-art (A in alt) ing." I would have welcomed the interminable Litany becoming literally interminable, so long as he continued singing, "We beseech thee to hear us, Good Lord," with his chin a little stuck out, and his eyes roving about the pews. Sometimes I thought he saw me and noticed me, and then my imagination took wings to itself, and I saw myself meeting him somewhere alone, him in his chorister's cope. What we should have to say to each other, I had not the smallest idea, but we should be together, and there lay completion. It was due to his unconscious influence that I began to sing loudly in the chapel at the Chancery, and never shall I forget my father once saying to me, "Perhaps some day you will sing an anthem in the Cathedral." That supplied a fresh imaginative chapter to my secret book; I should be a chorister too, and sit next the idol, and we would sing together. I was not egoistic in this vision: I had no thought of ravishing the world by the beauty of my

voice: it merely became a sunlit possibility (after all my
father had said as much) that I should sing in the Cathedral. But I knew, though he did not, that I should be
singing with the chorister. Thanks to my idol, Sunday
became, as long as this passion lasted, a day in which joy
watered the arid sands of Bishop Heber's Journal, and
made it, literally, "break forth into singing." That emotion, the fulfilment of which was brought into the realms
of possibility by my father's remark, touched such religion as I had with ecstasy, and I added to my prayers
the following petition, which I said night and morning.

"O God, let me enter into Lincoln Cathedral choir,
and abide there in happiness evermore with Thee!"

Who "Thee" was I cannot determine: I believe it to
have been a mixture of God and the chorister, and, I
think, chiefly the chorister.

This quickening of emotion gave rise to a sort of waking vision in which I used then consciously to indulge,
promising myself as I undressed for bed a night of Holy
Convocation. Two minutes of Holy Convocation were
about the duration of it, and then I went to sleep. There
was a hymn in the "Holy Year" in which there were
lines

> To Holy Convocations
> The silver trumpets call,

and with that and the chorister as yeast, there used to
bubble out, when I had gone to bed, this curious waking
vision. I would not be asleep at all, but with open eyes
I distinctly saw against the blackness of the night nursery
a line of golden rails, very ornamental, before which I
knelt. There was the sound of silver trumpets in my
ears, there was the sound of the chorister, anthems in the

Cathedral, and the presence of God. But all these things were secret and apart, never told of to this day, and they did not in the least interfere with wrestlings in the tower, and violent games of rounders and the pleasing terrors of hide-and-seek. The shrine usually stood shut, but when it opened it disclosed blinding splendours.

The Cathedral had, apart from the chorister and the services, certain pains and pleasures of its own. Occasionally assizes were held in Lincoln, and then on Sunday the judges would attend in robes of majesty with full wigs falling on to their shoulders. They walked in procession up the choir, and, reaching their seats, turned round awful pink clean-shaven faces of eternal calm, awful mouths that pronounced death-sentences. Once to my knowledge there was a murder-trial at Lincoln and a man condemned to death and the judge on that occasion became more terrible than death itself, and I slunk out after the Litany with apprehension that I should be called back, and hear some appalling sentence pronounced on me. Again, one day, a canon of the Cathedral stepped backwards through a skylight and was killed and Great Tom, the big bell in the central tower, tolled for the funeral. But the whole circumstances of that were so interesting that, though terror was mingled with them, they were more exciting than terrible. Wholly delightful on the other hand was a scientific demonstration that took place in the nave. A long cord was hung from one of the arches, to the end of which depended a heavy lead weight. On the pavement beneath it there was marked out a circle in white chalk, and this pendulum was then set swinging. As the hours passed, it swung in a different direction from that in which it was started, and instead of oscillating up and down the nave it moved along the transepts, thus demonstrating the motion of the earth. Why that delightful piece of science was shown in the Cathedral I have no idea; certain it is, however, that my mother took me to see the pendulum after breakfast one morning and again before tea when it was swinging in quite another direction. I never had any doubts about the rotary movement of the earth after that, nor, as far as I can remember, before.

CHAPTER III

THOSE three and a half years at Lincoln appear to have lasted for decades, so eventful was the unfolding of the world, and all the years which have passed since then, with their travels to many foreign lands, and climbings of perilous peaks, seem to have contained no exploration so thrilling as the revelation of Riseholme, where lived Bishop Wordsworth of Lincoln, who wrote the "Holy Year," and his wife, and his family and Janet the housekeeper. (The latter, like Mrs. Wordsworth, had ringlets down the sides of her face, and dispensed Marie biscuits and cowslip wine in unstinted profusion.) The family, too, were interesting, for one daughter when she laughed said, "Sss-sss," and another, "Kick-kick-kick," and the Bishop himself had a face like a lion, and a hollow ecclesiastical voice. My sisters considered him very formidable, but I was not afraid of him, chiefly because at an early stage of our acquaintance he gave me an ink-bottle of pottery, with a gilded lion (like himself) on top of it, and a receptacle to hold sand for the blotting of your letter, if you had managed to write it. This argued an amiable disposition, and when I came in contact with him, I was conscious of no embarrassment.

> In Xanadu did Kubla Khan
> A stately pleasure-dome decree,

but Xanadu was nothing to Riseholme for domes and

stateliness. There were two lakes peopled with dace and water-lilies and pike and swans, and an island where the swans nested, and a sluice, around which the water was of fabulous depth, where we fished for dace. There was a boat-house, on the roof of which in the autumn a great chestnut tree used to shed its fruit, bursting the husks, and disclosing the shiny brown kernels; and at Riseholme, as far as I remember, we were allowed to do precisely as we pleased. We used to go out alone in the boat, with paste for bait, and splash the water at each other, and come home with a couple of dace, dirty and wet and hopelessly happy. Swans used to scold and hiss at us, the boat did everything but capsize, and æons of bliss were our portion. There were water-snails to be collected, if the fish would not bite (they seldom did), and wreaths of stinking water-weed, and broken fragments of swan eggs lined inside with a tough kind of parchment, which we called "swan-paper." Then dace (when there were any) were cooked for tea, and provided a bony mouthful for one; the swan-paper was taken home for the Museum, together, on one glorious occasion, with the addled swan's egg; and the wreaths of stinking water-weed were laid out on sheets of cartridge-paper and pressed. This pressing resulted in an awful fricassee of weed and paper, and then something else occupied us. On the banks of the lake, at intervals, appeared a sympathetic Bishop with daughters, to whom we shouted the results of our explorations, and one of the daughters said, "Kick-kick-kick," and another, "Sss-sss-sss." For larger people, such as Arthur, there was more grown-up fishing, and once with a spoon-bait he caught a pike that weighed three pounds. But not even the sympathetic and combined appetites of the juniors could finish that toothsome dish.

Then there were expeditions into the vast forest that lay below the sluice, where marsh-marigolds grew, and the willow shoots flew back and slapped the faces of those who followed the leader in these excursions. Maggie and I formed a small club or society (I suppose Nellie was too old then, being about eleven) to get lost in this pathless place, but we never quite succeeded in doing so. Just as we thought there was no hope of our ever being discovered, in which case we proposed to live on leaves and drink the water that came from the sluice in a small stream, Beth's voice would sound quite near at hand, or, by mistake, we came back into the meadow beyond the lake, or into the path that bordered it. So instead, we collected chestnuts, if there was not a marine or lacustrine expedition, and ground up the kernels into a nutritive powder, or mixed it with lake-water to form a paste. About this time Maggie and I formed a special alliance, which continued till the end of her life, and the light of it was never quite obscured by those dusky years of darkened mind through which her way led, for she was always willing to talk of the days at Lincoln, and the collections and the amazing stories which we invented to beguile our walks. They were compounded of strange adventures, with the finding of gold and immense diamonds, of desert islands and bandits, and the central figures were she and I and the collie, Watch. All was coloured with the vividness of dreams, and the seriousness of childhood.

Riseholme was about two and a half miles from Lincoln, and the most exciting experience I ever had in its connection was that of being sent over there by my father with a note for the Bishop. I took Watch with me, and "Kick-kick-kick" and "Sss-sss-sss" were so entertaining and the Bishop so long in writing his answer that it was nearly dark before, with sinkings of the heart, I started on my return. "Sss-sss-sss" I think offered to accompany me till I got out of the loneliness of the road and in touch with the lights of Lincoln, but I was too cowardly to say I was afraid of the darkness and the emptiness, and started off alone. Wanting to get it over as quickly as possible, I ran, and was frightened at the noise of my running. Then, one after the other, my stockings came down, and I thought that the strip of whiteness would encourage highwaymen to attack me, and so had to stop every third step to pull them up. Then I talked to Watch in order to hearten myself, saying, in so many words, "Watch, aren't we benighted?" (new word) and then was frightened at the sound of my voice in the frosty stillness. But there was pleasure in this sense of adventure, and I was given an egg for tea.

There were expeditions to Nocton, where in a wood of vast extent the whole ground was white with lilies of the valley growing wild, and the still languid air beneath the trees swooned with the scent of them, which, I am told (though never since that day have I been able to believe it), is extremely pleasant. For the last of these expeditions to Nocton had a tragic sequel so far as I was concerned. We had lunch there after picking lilies all the morning, and I suppose I ate too much, and it began to rain as we drove homewards so that the carriage, full of hot children and lilies of the valley, had to be closed. The effect was that I was exceedingly unwell and never since that day have been able to dissociate the smell of lilies of the valley from being sick. To balance that bilious day was a glorious expedition to Skegness, where I saw the sea for the first time, and fell in love with it with a devotion that has never wavered. I took with me a small black handbag in which to stow the treasures of the shore, among which I rather mistakenly selected a dead decaying skate. An odour as unpleasant to others as was that of lilies of the valley to me filled the railway carriage on the return, which was eventually traced to my bag, and the dead skate which would have looked, anyhow, interesting in the Museum, was thrown out of the window. That first impression of the sea was confirmed by summer holidays spent at Torquay, and it was there, I think, that I must have learned to swim, and then have forgotten that I knew how. For when some years later I went to Marlborough and began to learn in the school bathing-place, I instantly did swim, and the old instructor who sat with small boys in a strap at the end of a fishing-rod, said with disgust, "Why you swims already!" Torquay was responsible for a whole host of further activities, for it was there, I believe, that we began those scribblings which subsequently developed into the *Saturday Magazine* (an industry so important that it must presently have a paragraph to itself) and it was certainly there that there were hot twisty rolls for breakfast which were only to be obtained by reciting some sort of rhyme, of which one of my mother's seemed to me to touch the high-water mark of inspired wit and poetry. This ran:

> Bread is the staff of life, the proverbs say,
> So give me of its twisted staff to-day.

Surely that was far better than a miserable effusion by Bishop Temple, of Exeter, who merely said:

An egg,
I beg,

and was sycophantically applauded by the grown-up people present. You could have eggs without making rhymes . . . but perhaps he didn't understand, and anyhow it was no use wasting time over him. There, among the diversions of Torquay we all violently embraced the career of artists, and drew miles of cottages and churches and painted leagues of the English Channel. The shell collection was started then, so also collections of wild flowers, and there was bathing and Devonshire cream, and a steep garden with gladioli and aloes in its beds. I think my birthday must have been celebrated there, for certainly I received a present of a terra-cotta teapot with lines of blue enamel on it, after receiving which it was difficult to imagine circumstances that could have the power to hurt one ever again.

Never can I sufficiently admire or be sufficiently thankful for the encouragement my father and mother both gave to these multitudinous hobbies, for hobbies, as they well knew, whether literary, artistic, or scientific, are a priceless panacea for the preservation of youth, and the stimulation of the world-wonder of beauty. At this time we were all of us draughtsmen, ornithologists, conchologists, geologists, poets, and literary folk: we all drew and wrote and collected shells and birds' eggs, and smashed stones in order to discover fossils. I claim no measure of eminence or even promise in any of us, but that is not the point. The point is that under parental encouragement we did all these things with extreme zest and interest. In sports and games my father gave us less support, for he looked on them only as a recreation which would enable the mind to get to work again, and as having no intrinsic value beyond what a brisk walk could have brought. But we had enough keenness among ourselves for these, and a ball and something to hit it with filled the rest of the vacant hours with ardour. For music, among the arts, he had likewise no sympathy at all: he liked the singing of Psalms and Handel and hymns entirely because of the words, and when he joined in the hymns in chapel, he produced a buzzing noise that bore no relation to any known melody. By this time my own love of music, sown in me by the adored chorister, had taken firm hold, and with help from my mother to start me, and an elementary book of instruction, music became to me a thing apart. I wanted no companionship or sympathizer in it, and though as far as execution on the piano went I was leagues behind my sisters, I felt certain in my own mind that I had opened a door for myself into a kingdom to which they did not really penetrate though they could execute (both counting very loud) Diabelli's Celebrated Duet in D which I considered below contempt, though it was very clever of them to move their fingers so fast. At that time my mother, who had always an Athenian disposition with regard to the joy of a new thing, went in for a course of instruction somehow connected with Dr. Farmer of Harrow. There was founded at Lincoln a Farmer Society of some kind, and the ladies met once a week or thereabouts and played easy Bach to each other, and one of the most rapturous Lincoln days was a certain wet afternoon, when the Society met at the Chancery. My sisters and I were allowed to sit in the window-seat, provided we remained quiet, and we all had acid drops to suck, and books to read when we got tired of listening. They were soon deep in *Little*

Women and *Good Wives*, but for me, in spite of a toothache, I listened in an entranced bliss to a series of Gavottes and Sarabands and Allemandes, while the rain beat on the windows, and the melodious dusk gathered. The time of the year must have been near Christmas, for I feel as if I went straight from there to the nursery, on the floor of which was laid out a large sheet piled with holly and laurel and ivy, out of which we made wreaths for the doors. The remaining leaves, when all was done, were put in the fire and roared and crackled up the chimney, filling the room with an aromatic smell of burning, that ranks next in preciousness of recollection to the smell of lilac.

It was in this last year at Lincoln that I had a fit of demoniacal possession, for I committed three heinous crimes one after the other. On a shelf in the drawing-room with Dresden figures and vases there was an Easter egg which had been sent to my father. It was decorated with a cross and a crown and a halo and some flowers, and was without doubt a goose's egg. This trophy was singularly sacred, and my father had told us that we were never to touch it. Because of that prohibition I wetted my finger and rubbed off a piece of the crown and the halo. I followed this up by stealing a quantity of sugar from the tea-table in a yellow box which I think had contained sweetmeats, and kept it on my knees under the table-cloth. I suppose I then forgot about it and, getting up, I caused it to fall to the ground, and spill its contents all over the floor.

The third piece of devil work was far more daring and inexplicable. I had a cold one day and was not allowed to go out, but was left instead by the fire in the sitting-room belonging to my two elder brothers. There

was a white sheepskin rug in front of it, and as soon as
my father with the four eldest children had left the
house, I ladled the whole of the burning coals out of the
grate and put them on the hearthrug. An appalling
stench arose as the wool caught fire; the place was filled
with smoke, and I left the room, quite impenitent and
merely interested to know what on earth would happen
next. The smoke must by now have penetrated to the
rest of the house, for I met my mother running downstairs, and she asked me if I knew what that smell was.
I told her that I didn't, and went up to the nursery.
Presently, having extinguished the fire, she followed me,
and again asked me if I was sure I didn't know anything
about it. Upon which I told her that it was I who had
emptied the fire on to the rug. A fine spanking followed,
which I did not in the least resent, and I was told to go
to bed till I was sorry. I never was sorry—for it was
demoniacal possession—but I suppose that some time I
must have got up again.

Friendships had sprung up between us and other children at Mrs. Giles's day-school, and among these was
May Copeland, who was Nellie's particular friend, and
told us that she was descended from Oliver Cromwell.
This was very distinguished, and I fully meant to marry
her. There was also a girl whose name I forget, and she
was responsible for one of the greatest surprises of my
young life, for one day while she and I were looking
for a tennis ball in the bushes, she took my hands and
drew them upwards against her bosom. I found to my
astonishment that instead of being flat, she had two
swellings there, and I asked her if they were bruises. She
seemed rather offended and said that they certainly were
not. Then there was Willie Burton to whom I told, in

the spirit of bravado, what I had done to the sheep-skin hearthrug, and he thought it very magnificent. He used to get phosphorus matches from his father's table, which was grand, for we only used Bryant and May's safety matches, and our great game was to retire into the blackness of the tool-house, wet the palms of our hands, and rub on the phosphorus which glowed with a mysterious light. He had an awful story which I entirely believed of an aunt of his on whom a practical joker played a dreadful trick, for he wrote up in phosphorus above his aunt's bed the text, "This night shall thy soul be required of thee." On which his poor aunt went raving mad, and I got a general distrust of phosphorus. . . . Willie Burton was dressed in sailor clothes, and I in a short jacket and knickerbockers, and one day with a sense of almost excessive adventure, we undressed in the tool-house and each put on the other's clothes. We then opened the door in order to let daylight behold this transformation, and swiftly changed back again. That was a wonderful thing to have done, and when we met next day at the gymnasium we looked at each other's clothes with glances of secret knowledge.

My final remembrance at Lincoln is perhaps the most vivid of all, for the sense of it was not that of a momentary impression, but of a growing reality. Every evening now we came down to my mother's room and for half an hour before bedtime she read Dickens aloud to us, sitting in front of the fire. She liked to have her hair stroked, so I used to stand behind her chair, passing my fingers over the smooth brown hair above her forehead, and listening to the story of the Kenwigses. Her voice and the contact of my fingers on her hair wakened in me the knowledge of how I loved her.

CHAPTER IV

THE NEW HOME AT TRURO

ONE morning a most exciting bomb-shell exploded in the Chancery and blew Lincoln into fragments. It came in the shape of two letters, one from the Prime Minister, Lord Beaconsfield, offering my father the Bishopric of the newly created see of Truro in Cornwall, the other from Queen Victoria, saying that she personally hoped that he would accept it. These letters must have arrived a few days before we knew of them, for that day my father told us that he had thought it over and had settled to go. I felt nothing whatever except wild delight and excitement, unmingled as far as I am aware, with any regret for leaving Lincoln, and all the time that we were out for our walk that morning Maggie and I, instead of telling each other stories, whispered with secret smiles, "The Lord Bishop of Truro! The Lord Bishop of Truro!" We were vastly proud of my father, and thought it most sensible of Lord Beaconsfield and the Queen to have selected him.*

The fresh move came in the spring of 1877, and in that loveliest of all seasons the train slid one evening across the tall wooden viaducts with the lights of Truro pricking the dusk, where the town lay below, and the enchantment of Cornwall instantly began to weave its

---

* Lord Beaconsfield seems to have been as pleased as we were at my father's accepting the bishopric, for he wrote exultantly to a friend, saying, "Well, we *have* got a Bishop."

spell. The new home was the Vicarage of Kenwyn, a small village high on the western hills and perhaps a mile from the centre of the town. As a house it was not comparable for amenities and mysteries with the Chancery of Lincoln, but what was the garden at Lincoln, for all its towers and rolling banks, in comparison to the garden here and the fields and water-haunted valleys which encompassed it? The garden at Lincoln, confined within its brick walls and planted down in the middle of a town, was like some caged animal that here roamed wild and untamed.

Oh, unforgettable morning when for the first time I awoke in the new house, and saw on the ceiling the light of the early sun that shone in through the copse outside, making a green and yellow dapple on the whitewash! The house was still silent; opposite me was Hugh's bed with his head half-hidden in the sheet, and I dressed stealthily and went downstairs and out. From the lawn I could see the viaduct over which we had come, and below it the misty roofs of the town, with one steeple piercing the vapour into sunlight. Then the mist faded like a frosty breath and beyond the town there stretched broad and shining the estuary of the Fal. Instead of the sorry serge of ivy, the house was clad with tree-fuchsias, and magnolia, and climbing roses and japonica: never was there such a bower of a habitation. On that April morning no doubt the fuchsia and the roses were not in flower, but looking back now, that moment seems to have sucked into itself the decorations of all the months, making in my mind a composite picture, from which I cannot now disentangle the true component parts. But surely there was a gorse bush at the corner of the house, on the edge of the copse through which the sun had shone, and surely it was on that morning that I found a mossy feathery little football of a tit's nest, woven inextricably among the spines of the gorse, and a virago of an infinitesimal bird peeped out of the circular door, when I drew too near, and scolded me well for my intrusion. I passed up the winding path that led through the shrubbery, and found a circular pleasance with a summer-house. I went cautiously past a row of beehives; I came through a door into a lane below the churchyard, where ferns (the sort of things not known before to exist in other localities than greenhouses and tables laid for dinner-parties) grew quite carelessly in the crevices, and so back, now breathlessly scampering and surfeited with impressions past woodshed and haystack and stable, and upstairs again with heart and shoes alike drenched with the spring-dew.

All that ensuing summer, lessons I fancy were considerably relaxed, and the lovely months passed like some fugue built on the subjects of that early walk, coloured, amplified and decorated. My father gave us a prize for botany (all specimens to be personally gathered, personally pressed, and mounted on sheets of cartridge paper with the English, and, if possible, the Latin name written below), and we scoured the hedges and liquid water-sides and the edges of the growing hay meadows, with a definite object in view. Study was necessitated by the addition of those names (Latin if possible), but this, like some homœopathic dose conveyed in honey, was drowned in the delight of rambling explorations. The appetite of the collector was whetted; there was a certain craving created for exact knowledge, but far above that was the interest in the loveliness that we should not otherwise have noticed, and the admiration which the interest engendered. Definitely also I think I trace a love of words in themselves which this studied collecting gave us, for what child could write "centaury" or "meadow-sweet," "bee-orchis," "comfrey," "loosestrife," or in more exalted spheres, "Osmunda regalis" on the virgin sheet of cartridge paper without tasting something of the flavour of these blossom-like syllables? Or what child could fail to whoop with gladness when one of us brought an unknown bloom to a certain botanist friend of my father's, and was apologetically told that its name was "Stinking Archangel"? For in the lives of all of us, words and due discrimination in their use came to play a considerable part, and somewhere we hoarded these rich additions to our vocabulary. My sister Nellie won the prize, and I remember that she afterwards confessed to me that she had stolen some of my pressed specimens and added them to her own. I never was more astonished, and class this lapse of hers with instances already given of my own demoniacal possession in the matter of the Easter egg and the sheepskin hearthrug. We both agreed that she could not possibly resign the prize, for that would lead to investigation, and she gave me a shilling by way of compensation.

Birds' eggs as a collection had hitherto been represented in the Museum by one addled swan's egg, but now they took rank among the objects of existence. Here my father dictated the conditions under which they might be acquired, namely, that no egg was to be taken from any nest unless that nest contained four, and under no circumstances was more than one to be taken. There was of course no questioning his decision, but it seemed a pity to leave the great tit in the gorse bush to bring up a family of fifteen after our levy had been made, and never to be able to get a wood-pigeon's egg at all, since those prudent birds refused to lay more than two. But here Charles the groom shone forth gilded with the glory of celestial charity, for he came to me one morning with his entire collection of eggs and "would I accept of them?" Was there ever such a groom? And among these was a pair of wood-pigeon's eggs, so those parsimonious parents were thwarted.

For a while games were quite in abeyance, romantic natural history held the field. For consider: my sister Maggie and I had heard that otters were found in Cornwall, and on that simple fact we built up the following fairy-like adventure. There was a round copse, rather lonely, on the edge of our fields; from it the ground declined in a steep down to the bottom of a valley, through which ran a stream so small that by wetting only one foot you could get across it at its widest part. But it ran below bushes and under steep banks, and it seemed highly probable that some of these Cornish otters lived there. Well, otters went about on land as well as in the water, and the lure of imagination pictured them taking a nice walk up this down and coming to the lonely copse. This grew very thick in brushwood, through which the otters (now indigenous in the copse) would certainly walk. So we hung nooses of string here and there a foot or so from the ground so that the otter might, in his walks, insert his head in the noose which would then be pulled tight, and we should come and capture him. This gave rise to further considerations; he might struggle, and get hurt if not strangled in the noose, so we must clearly be on the spot to loosen the noose, and substitute for it a chain and collar of one of the dogs. But if the otter saw us, he would probably gallop back over the down to his stream, so we built a hut woven of withies between two trees in which we could lie *perdus*, and watch for the otter. Then we should lead him chained to the stables, and gradually tame him till he could come out walking with us in company with Watch and the nanny-goat which already formed part of the family procession. (A second goat, called Capricorn, was presently added, but he had an odious habit of standing upright on his hind legs and hurling himself like a battering-ram against the hinder-parts of the unobservant, and when harnessed to a small truck which was used for gardening purposes, galloped with it at such speed that sparks flew from its wheels as they spurned the gravel.)

A much larger bowl was now granted us for the aquarium, and the spa and madrepores carefully brought from Lincoln (though the preserved hornet seemed to have been forgotten) did not more than cover the bottom of the new and sumptuous receptacle. Caddis-worms were culled from the streams that flowed Fal-wards, and whelk-like water-snails were comforted for their expatriation by having the chance of eating bread crumbs if so they wished. But the aquarium was still but a crawling democracy, and needed some denizen of livelier locomotive power to fill the post of king in this water-world. And then one day, as I have told before, in a book now mercifully forgotten, we caught the unique and famous stickleback, by accident you may say (if you believe in accidents), for certainly at the moment of his capture we had not even seen him, though it is true that we were dredging in the stream in which the otter still failed to make his appearance.

My sister Maggie and I then were just emptying out the dredging (butterfly) net thinking we had found no great treasure on that cast, when something stirred in the residuary mud, after we had extracted no more than a caddis worm or two, and it was he. With tremulous rapture we popped him in a jar for transport to the aquarium, and overcome with the greatness of the moment (like Paolo and Francesco) we fished no more that day. For perhaps a week he swam gorgeously about this new kingdom, never getting over his delusion that if he swam swiftly enough against the side of it, he would find himself at liberty again, and then the tragedy happened.

It was our custom every morning to empty out the contents of the aquarium, down the drain in the stable yard, and replace them with fresh water. During this operation one of us held a piece of gauze over the lip of the aquarium so that none of its inhabitants should be poured away. And on one of these occasions, when the water was nearly drained out, and the stickleback swimming in short indignant circles in the residue, Maggie's hand which was holding the gauze slipped suddenly and in a flood the remaining pint or two rushed out, the stickleback in the midst of it. With one flick of his tail, he disappeared down the drain in the stable yard, leaving us looking at each other in incredulous dismay. . . .

It was certainly during this summer that another idol came to fill that shrine of worship in my heart once occupied by the chorister, and once again music was the hot coal that fired my incense, and the music in question was the mellow thunder of the organ in Kenwyn Church. I still believe that it was very skilfully and sympathetically played by the unconscious object of my adoration. I must have fallen in love not really with what she was, but with what she did, for my passion was all ablaze before ever I had seen her face, or had the slightest idea

ELIZABETH COOPER; "BETH." ÆT. 78

what she was like. All I knew of her was that she produced these enchanting noises, since from our pew I could see nothing of her except her back, and a hand which reached out to shut a stop or open another bleating fount of melody. She played the pedals, those great wooden keys, and swayed slightly from side to side as her feet reached out for them. Once or twice, entering or leaving the church I had a glimpse of her in less than profile, and that served my adoration well enough. Her name was Mrs. Carter, and I daresay she was thirty years old or thereabouts, for she had a son of about my own age who used sometimes to turn over leaves for her, sitting by her on the organ bench, and though I don't think I would quite have exchanged mothers with him, I would have given most other things to take his place there.

This seemed likely to be a barren affair, for Sunday after Sunday passed and I never saw more than the swaying back of Mrs. Carter. But by way of killing one bird and possibly two with one stone, I got leave somehow (with the gardener's boy to blow the bellows for an occasional quarter of an hour) to find my way about the organ. That exploration was a good bird in itself, but a better lurked in my mind, for I thought that Mrs. Carter might so easily come up to Kenwyn Church during the week to arrange her music or what not, and she would find Me sitting in her place and making tentative experiments with the stops, and straining after the nearer pedals with my short legs. Surely some day I should look up and see her standing by, and she would say, "Who taught you to play so nicely?" (I perceive that vanity was mingled with passion) and I, in a happy tumult of emotion, would reply, "Oh, Mrs. Carter!"

But this trap for Mrs. Carter never brought the hunter

his quarry, and quite independent circumstances led me closer. It was decreed that my sisters should have music lessons and who but Mrs. Carter was engaged to be the teacher? Twice a week she would come to the house, so now no human agency, it would appear, could prevent us from meeting. But for some time a human agency did do so, that human agency being myself, for on observing Mrs. Carter's approach up the drive, an agony of shyness seized me, and I sat distracted in the day nursery until she had gone upstairs, and the noise of the piano from the schoolroom showed that she was engaged. Once, summoning up all my courage, I went in while the lesson was in progress, but she did not take her eyes off the copy of Schubert's Impromptu in A flat, which Maggie was fumbling at, and I went out and listened in the garden for the cessation of the piano, on which, I determined, I would walk quite calmly towards the front door and thus meet Mrs. Carter there or thereabouts. But, alas for this faint-hearted lover, as soon as the piano ceased I walked in precisely the other direction, and it was not likely that Mrs. Carter instead of going down the drive would force her way through the laurel shrubbery in order to find me.

I blush to record the next step of my wooing. An invincible shyness (though I was not otherwise shy) forbade my walking down the drive as Mrs. Carter was coming up, or taking any direct initiative, so I laid a lure for her. Observing her approach to the house, I regret to say that it was my custom to lean out of the schoolroom window, singing loudly. This would certainly attract her attention (indeed I think that once it did, and I rushed, panic-stricken, away) and she would say to one of my sisters, "Was that your brother who was singing?

What a charming voice!" And one of my sisters would
say, "Oh yes, he is very fond of music." Then surely,
surely Mrs. Carter would say, "I don't think we have
met," or perhaps even, "I should like to see him," and
then my sister would come and find me (for after these
bursts of melody out of the window I always fled like a
frightened dove to the nursery) and say that Mrs. Carter
would like to see me. I had looked on her face by now,
and I pictured to myself how her kind mouth would smile
as she shook hands, and she would say, "We must be
friends, mustn't we, for we are both so fond of music."

This bleating piece of Platonism came to an end somehow, and I grew to be able to contemplate Mrs. Carter's
back swaying to her pedal-playing without emotion. But
I think that this warm soft Cornish climate must have
brought out a sort of measles of sentimentality in me,
for without pause I transferred my sloppy heart to the
curate at Kenwyn, the Rev. J. A. Reeve, who subsequently was appointed Rector of Lambeth by my father,
and was an intimate friend of all of us. He was a man
who was habitually surrounded by an atmosphere of
ecstasy, an adorer of children, and next door to a fanatic
in matters of religion, beloved and blissful, living in a
light that never was on sea or land. To the outward
view he presented a long lean figure, walking at a tremendous pace, and perspiring profusely, with his umbrella
tucked under his arm, and his hands clasped in perpetual
admiration of this inimitable world, and the saints that
he constantly discovered in it under the most deceptive
of disguises. There were no "miserable sinners" in his
sight; the most impenitent were but rather wilful children of the Father. He had a mane of yellow hair which
he tossed back as he laughed peals of uproarious appreci-

ation of any joke at all. But whereas with the chorister
and Mrs. Carter there certainly was some personal, physical attraction (though no doubt the main source of the
inspiration was music), with Mr. Reeve there was no
personal attraction of any kind, and the experience was
of the stained-glass window order, in which I was cast for
the stained-glass window, and Mr. Reeve for the worshipper. At the bottom of it all perhaps there was some
grain of genuine religious sentiment, but this was so
largely diluted by mawkishness and vanity, that examination fails to find more than that minute presence described
in the analysis of medicinal waters as "some traces." He
used to breakfast with us after a short service in Kenwyn
Church at a quarter to eight every morning, to which we
children were encouraged though not obliged to go, and
he was a kind of unofficial chaplain to my father, writing
his letters for him half the morning with a puckered brow,
but ready to burst into peals of laughter on the smallest
opportunity for mirth. Every Sunday also, he came to
tea before service, and afterwards to supper, and every
Sunday evening after tea I went with him into a spare
bedroom where, with his arm round my neck, he read me
the sermon he was about to preach. I suppose my comments were very edifying and satisfactory, for he certainly told my mother that "that boy was not far from
the kingdom of God." She must very wisely have begged
him not to tell me that, for I had no idea of it at the
time. Once, indeed, he sadly failed me, for meeting me
as I was being taken to the dentist by Beth, there to have
two teeth out under gas, he said that to have gas was
the same as getting drunk, and I went on my weary way
feeling not only terrified but wicked as well. It is true,
though scarcely credible, that the gas was administered by

Mrs. Tuck the dentist's wife, and that there was no anæsthetist or doctor present. But I daresay Mrs. Tuck performed her office very well, for I had a delightful dream about being in a balloon in the middle of a rainbow.

That autumn lessons began again, and until I went to a private school next Easter I suffered under the awful rule of a German governess, not our kind Miss Braun of Lincoln, but a dark-eyed and formidable woman who, I was firmly convinced, must truly have been the terrible Madame de la Rougierre in the tale of Uncle Silas which I was reading then in small instalments, being too frightened to read much at a time. She cannot have been with us long, for before I went to school the beloved Miss Bramston came back, not originally as governess but for another and a tragic reason.

The Christmas holidays of 1877 were the last when the whole of the family of six, with my father and mother and Beth, who was absolutely of the family also, were together. My eldest brother Martin was then seventeen, and so great a gulf is fixed between that age and ten, that never, till the day I saw him last, did I form any clear idea of him. Here, then, I must abandon the standpoint I have hitherto maintained, namely, that of speaking of the events of these early years through my own personal recollection of what impression they made on me as the jolly days slipped by, and mingle recollection with subsequent knowledge.

At the age of fourteen Martin had won the first open scholarship at Winchester, and had now mentally developed into an extraordinary maturity and wisdom. He took an amazing interest in the political affairs of the day, in classics he was considered to be perhaps the most remarkable scholar that Winchester ever had, and as witness to his innate love of learning there was a library which he had himself acquired, and which must have been unique for a boy of his age. Already at Lincoln he had "spotted" an Albert Dürer woodcut pasted on to the fly-leaf of some trumpery book at a penny bookstall, and had breathlessly conveyed the treasure home, and he and my father used to exchange original Latin versions of hymns. But this precocity of scholarship did not in the least check his boyishness, which verged on the fantastic, for once he appeared in school with four little Japanese dolls attached to the four strings of his shoe-laces, and gravely proceeded with his construing. There are notebooks full of his exquisite ridiculous drawings with appropriate text in his minute handwriting: there are poems as ridiculous, and behind it all was this serious limpid spirit. . . .

He went back that January to Winchester, and Arthur to Eton, and one day, early in February he had a sudden attack of giddiness, and then followed an attack of meningitis. My father and mother were sent for; he was then unconscious. Arthur went there from Eton, but my mother decided that we younger children should not go and instead Miss Bramston came down to us in Cornwall. The rest I will tell by means of two letters which my mother wrote to Beth. I found them, after my mother's death, forty years after, in a little packet of papers which had belonged to Beth, and consisted of letters from all of us which she had always kept.

"WINCHESTER,
Friday (Feb. 8, 1878).

DEAREST BETH,

I must write you a few lines to-day. Our dear one is no better at all. Nothing can be done for him but to watch him and to give nourishment and to pray and trust in God. Everything possible is done for him; he has two nurses, day and night. We go in and out of his room from time to time. He lies quite peacefully, mostly sleeping, and evidently quite unconscious of any pain. There is no sign of pain about his face. He knows us now and then, we think, but he does not speak. He takes a little nourishment from time to time, but with difficulty. Sir William Jenner has been sent for, though there does not seem anything he can do.

Dearest Beth, it is such a comfort to think that you are with those dear ones at home. I don't know what they would do without you, or how we could bear to think of leaving them unless they had you. We are both quite sure that it is better they should not come. They could not be with him, and it is no use their hearing details. We ought to and must keep before their young minds just the Love of God, whether He shews it in giving our darling back to our prayers, or in taking to Himself so beautiful and holy a life.

But we must not, and do not give up hope. Though as far as man knows or sees there is nothing to be done, and the doctors dare not give us hope of recovery, yet just where man is most powerless, God *does* work, often, and we continue to pray to Him in hope for our darling's restoration. While there is life, we will not despair.

Dearest Beth, God keep you all: the thought of you is such a comfort to us. Pray yourself continually,—encourage them all to pray. One of the Psalms to-day begins, 'I waited patiently for the Lord, and He inclined unto me, and heard my calling.'

All our heart's love is with you all always.

Your most loving

MARY BENSON."

This is the second letter:

"DEAREST FRIEND AND MOTHER BETH,

Be comforted for Martin. He is in perfect peace, in wonderful joy, far happier than we could ever have made him. And what did we desire in our hearts but to make him happy? And now he will help us out of his perfect happiness. He died without a struggle—his pure and gentle spirit passed straight to God his Father, and now he is ours and with us more than ever. Ours now, in a way that nothing can take away.

Dearest Beth, we are all going to be more loving than ever, living in love we shall live in God, and we shall live close to our dear one.

One is so sure now, that sin is the only separation, and that sting is taken out of death by Jesus Christ. My heart aches for the dear ones at home, but I know you are a mother to them, and will support and comfort their hearts, and keep before them that God is love, and that He is loving us in this thing also. And I want them to think of Martin, our darling, in perfect peace for ever, free from fear, free from pain, from anxiety for evermore, and to think how he will rejoice to see us walking more and more in Love for his dear sake.

We cannot grudge him his happiness.

Dearest Beth, our boy is with God: he knows everything now, and will help us. The peace of God Almighty be with you.

Your own child, your fellow-mother,

M. B."

There is nothing that could tell so simply and completely, not only what my mother was, but what Beth was, as this letter which my mother wrote on the morning after the death of her eldest son. It gives the soul of them both, of my mother that she could write it, and of Beth the "fellow-mother," to whom it was written.

When I was old enough to understand my mother told me about the day on which that second letter was written. She had, so she said to me, a couple of hours of the most wonderful happiness she had ever experienced on that day, when she realized that though God had taken, yet she could give. Her inmost being knew that, and when she came back to us a few days later, there was no shadow on her, for all that she said to Beth was the simple untouched copy of the writing on her heart. But even now I can remember my father's face, as he stepped from the carriage into the lamplight, for it was the face of a most loving man stricken with the death of the boy he loved best, who had been nearest his heart, and was knit into his very soul. Often has my mother told me that though he accepted Martin's death as God's will, he could not, out of the very strength of his human love, adapt himself to it. His faith was unshaken, but the deep waters had gone over him, and years afterwards, when he saw the martins skimming about the eaves of the house at Addington, he wrote about them and his own Martin a little poem infinitely touching; and never, so I believe, did some part of him cease to wonder why his Martin had been taken from him.

CHAPTER V

AFTER Easter, 1878, I was sent to a private school presided over by Mr. Ottiwell Waterfield, at Temple Grove, East Sheen, and remained there three years. The house and grounds vanished entirely somewhere about 1908, under the trail of the suburban builder, and now hideous rows of small residences occupy their spaciousness. For the purposes of a school numbering some hundred and thirty boys, the original George I and Queen Anne house had been largely supplemented with dormitories and schoolrooms, and a modern wing as large as the house ran at right angles by the edge of the cricket field. But the part where Mr. Waterfield and his family lived had not been touched: there was a fine library, drawing-room, and his study (how awful was that place!) *en suite*, a paved hall, with a full-sized billiard table and a piano where a frail widow lady called Mrs. Russell gave music-lessons, and the French master, whose name really was M. Voltaire, conducted a dancing-class as well as teaching French and being, I think, slightly immoral. A passage out of the hall gave on to the private garden of Mr. Waterfield, where there were fine cedar trees, and a broad oak-staircase led up from it to the bedrooms of the family.

Already, darkly in the glass of fiction and under the title of David Blaize, I have hinted at some of the habits

of the young gentlemen who led a life, alternately uproarious and terror-stricken, in the other part of the house,
but now more personal details can be indulged in. By
far the most salient feature in the school, even as the
sun is the most salient feature in the day, making it
precisely what it is, was Mr. Waterfield himself. He
seems now to me to have been nine feet high, and he
certainly walked with a curious rocking motion, which
was convenient, because if you were where you should
not be, you could detect his coming long before he could
detect anybody. He had a square grey beard which smelt
of cigars, a fact known from his practice, when he had
frightened the life out of you by terrible harangues, of
saying, "Well, that's all over, my boy," and kissing you.
I believe him to have been about the best private school-
master who ever lived, for he ruled by love and fear combined in a manner that while it inspired small boys with
hellish terror, yet rewarded them with the sweet fruits
of hero-worship. He exacted blind obedience, under
peril of really infamous torture with a thick ruler with
which he savagely caned offending hands, but he managed at the same time to make us appreciate his approba-
tion. The ruler was kept in a convenient drawer of the
knee-hole table in his study, and was a perfectly brutal
instrument, but the approach of the ruler, like a depression over the Atlantic, was always heralded by storm-
cones. The first of these was the taking of the keys
from his trousers-pocket, and then you had time to pull
yourself together to retract an equivocation, to confess
a fault, or try to remember something you had been re-
peatedly told. The second storm-cone was the insertion
of the key into the drawer where the ruler was kept. You
had to be of very strong nerve when that second storm-

cone was hoisted, and divert your mind from the possible future to the supine which you could not recollect, for when the key was once inserted there might any moment be a sudden startling explosion of wrath, and out flew the ruler. Then came a short agonizing scene, and the blubbering victim after six smart blows had the handle of the door turned for him by somebody else, because his hands were useless through pain. The ruler was quite rare, and probably well deserved; anyhow it was the counter-balance to the hero-worship born of Mr. Waterfield's approval. For more heinous offences there was birching, but that had certain compensations, for afterwards you took down your breeches and showed the injured parts to admiring companions. But there was nothing to show, as Mrs. Pullet said about the boluses, when you were caned. Besides you could play cricket quite easily, shortly after a whipping, but no human hand could hold a bat shortly after the application of the ruler.

The top form (called the first form, not the sixth form) had certain specified lessons every week taken by Waterfield, and he did not teach regularly in other forms. But he was liable to make meteoric appearances soon after the beginning of a lesson in the big schoolroom where the next three forms were at work, and take any lesson himself. A hush fell as he strode in, and we all cowered like partridges below a kite, while he glared round, selecting the covey on to which he pounced. This was a subtle plan, for you could never be sure that it would not be he who would hear any particular lesson, and the chance of that made it most unwise to neglect any preparation altogether.

The school got its fair share of public-school scholarships, so I suppose the teaching of the other masters was sound, but I cannot believe that a stranger set of instructors were ever got together. Rawlings, who taught the first form, used habitually to read the *Sporting Times* in school with his feet up on the desk until the time came for him to hear us construe. Daubeny, the master of the second form, had no thought but for the encouragement of a small moustache; Davy of the third form used mostly to be asleep; Geoghehan of the fourth form (called "Geege") had lost his right arm, and used always to have some favourite in his class, who sat on his knee in school time and was an important personage, for he could, if you were friends with him, always persuade Geege not to report misconduct to Waterfield. One such boy, now a steady hereditary legislator, I well remember: he pulled Geege's beard, and altered the marks in his register, and ruled him with a rod of iron. Geege was otherwise an effective disciplinarian, and had an unpleasant habit, if he thought you were not attending, of spearing the back of your hand with the nib of his pen, dipped in purple ink. Then there was a handwriting specialist called Prior who gave out stationery on Saturdays. His appearance was always hailed by a sort of Gregorian chant to which the words were, "All boys wanting ink, go to Mr. Prior." Then came Mr. Voltaire, the gay young Frenchman, and these with one or two more of whom I cherish no recollection all lived together at a house in East Sheen called Clarence House, and were, I think, a shade more frightened of Waterfield than we.

The ways of boys are past finding out, and what could have induced us to believe that the food supplied was disgusting to the verge of being poisonous I have no idea. But tradition, at the time of which I am speaking, ordained that this was so, and how often when I was long-

ing to eat a plateful of pudding have I shovelled it into
an envelope to bury in the playground, since the currants
in it were held to be squashed flies and the suet to be
made with scourings from dirty plates. Then somebody
once saw potatoes, no doubt intended for school consump-
tion, lying on the floor in a shed in the garden, which
was considered a terrible way in which to keep potatoes.
I remembering telling my father this, and with the utmost
gravity he answered that every potato ought to be
wrapped up singly in silver paper. He also asked if it was
true that Mr. Waterfield had been seen, with his trousers
turned up diluting the beer for dinner out of a garden
watering-can. Most poisonous of all were supposed to
be the sausages which we had for breakfast now and
then: it was a point of honour not to eat a single mouthful
of this garbage. Then suddenly for no reason the fashion
changed, and the food was supposed to be, and indeed
it probably was, excellent. We gobbled up our sausages,
asked for more and got it, and ate the potatoes that had
once lain on the dirty ground, and had even degraded
themselves by growing in it. . . .

I plunged headlong into this riot of school life and for
the first year enjoyed it enormously. I had been placed
too low in the school and without the slightest effort I
found myself term after term at the top of the class, and
loaded with prizes, for no merit of my own but for the
fact that I had the kind of superficial memory that re-
tained what it had scarcely attended to at all. In consequence for a whole year I had no fear of Waterfield as
regards lessons, and devoted myself to games, stag-beetles,
and friendship, and I find it hard to decide whether the
rapture of making twenty at cricket against overhand
bowling (not lobs from sisters) was greater or less than

finding a stag-beetle on the palings, or in the early dawn
of summer mornings going on tiptoe into the next dormitory, and, after waking up my special friend, sitting on
his bed, propped up with pillows and talking in whispers
till there came the sound of the dressing-bell, which por-
tended the entrance of the matron. Then it was necessary to steal round the corner of his cubicle, and slide
back into my own bed, there apparently to fall into a
refreshing slumber, for to be caught out of bed before
it was time to dress meant to be reported to Waterfield,
who took a serious, and to me then an unintelligible view
of such an offence. But an hour's whispered conversation
with a friend was worth that risk, indeed probably the
risk added a certain savour to it, and perhaps our present
Minister at the Vatican has recollections similar to mine.
Or else it would be I who was awakened by the soft-step-
ping night-shirted figure, and moved aside in bed to give
room for him to sit there, and there would be plans to
be made, and then combining friendship with stag-beetles
into one incomparable compound we would take the stag-
beetles (for there were two of them, male and female
called "The Monarch of the Glen" and "Queen") out
of my washing basin, where they passed the night in
optimistic attempts to climb its slippery sides, and refresh
them with a breakfast of elm leaves and perhaps the half
of a strawberry. They had to be put back into two match-
boxes which were their travelling carriages before Jane
the matron came round, for she had said that if ever she
found stag-beetles in basins again she would throw them
out of the window.

An "Exeat" now and then diversified the course of the
term, and these I spent with my Aunt Eleanor who had
married Mr. Thomas Hare, famous for his book on the

Representation of Minorities. He was a great friend of John Stuart Mill, whom Aunt Eleanor, for some reason of her own, always called "Mr. Mills." They lived in a house near Surbiton which had a tower in it, on the top floor of which was Uncle Hare's laboratory, chemistry being a hobby of his, and he made oxygen in glass retorts, and put snippets of potassium to scurry, flaring and self-lit, on the surface of a basin of water. . . . On the 5th of November every year I was asked to a children's party, given by Princess Mary, Duchess of Teck, at the White Lodge, Richmond Park, and there was an immense tea followed by fireworks in the garden. There we were given squibs and told to be sure to throw them away as soon as they burned low, before the explosion came at the end, and on one of these occasions the Duke of Teck wanting a light for his cigar told me to give him my squib, for he had no matches. I told him that it was already burning low, but he said "Wass?" rather alarmingly, and so I handed it to him. He had just applied the burning end of it to his cigar when the explosion came, and his face and hair were covered with sparks, and he danced about, and said sonorous things in German, and I gathered that he was vexed. . . .

The minds of children as they grow have those diseases incident to childhood much as their bodies have. I had had my measles of sentimentality, and having got over that I developed during this year a kind of whooping-cough of lying. I used to invent and repeat extraordinary experiences, which had their root in fact, but were embellished by my imagination to scenes of unparalleled magnificence. For instance, the family spent that summer holidays at Etretat, crossing from Southampton to

Havre, and I came back with Arthur who was going to Eton, a day late for the assembling of Temple Grove. The crossing was an extremely rough one; all night the water broke over the decks heavy and solid, and certainly some unfortunate passenger came into the cabin drenched through. All next day as I travelled to Temple Grove my imagination worked on these promising materials, and I told my admiring schoolfellows that we had barely escaped shipwreck. The waves, which certainly did deluge the decks, I represented as having poured in torrents down the funnels, extinguishing the furnaces, so that we had to stop till the fires were relit, while out of the passenger who came down drenched into the cabin I constructed a Frenchman who was supposed to have said to me in broken English, "Ze water is not coming over in bucketfuls it is coming over in shipfuls." So vividly did I imagine this, that before long I really half believed it. Again the next winter holidays were marked by a heavy snowfall in Cornwall succeeded by a partial thaw and a hard frost. In consequence the horses had to be roughed, and it is certainly a fact that the carriage which was bringing my father home one evening slewed so violently that, according to his quite authentic description, he looked out of the window, and saw instead of the hedgerows the steep glazed road in front of him. I seized hungrily on that incident, and on returning to school said that we had enjoyed delightful sledging in the holidays, over roads and lakes, adding the further embellishment that I personally drove the horses. . . . There were more of these fictions which I cannot now remember, all of which had some exiguous foundation of fact, and great was my horror when an implacable enemy handed me one morning a scrap of paper, in the manner of an ultimatum headed:

"BENSON'S LIES"

and there below, neatly summarized were all these stories which I thought had been listened to with such respectful envy. The implacable enemy added darkly that "they" (whoever "they" might be) were considering what they were going to do about it all. I suppose consternation was graven on me, for he stonily added, "Yes, you may well turn pale," and I pictured (my imagination again rioting off) this damning text being handed to Waterfield, who would send it to my father. What was the public upshot, I cannot remember, but by aid of that terrifying medicine I made a marvellously brisk recovery from that particular disease.

Some time during that first year at school, there occurred a scene which I still look back on as among the most awful I have ever witnessed. Two boys, one high in the school, a merry handsome creature, the other quite a small boy, suddenly disappeared. They were in their places at breakfast, but during breakfast were sent for by Waterfield and at school that morning their places were empty. They did not appear at dinner, they did not appear at tea, and that night in the next dormitory their beds were vacant. Jane said they were not ill, and forbade any further questions, and curious whisperings went about, of which I could not grasp the import. Next morning there came a sudden order that all the school should be assembled, and we crowded into the big schoolroom. Presently Waterfield entered with his cap and gown on, followed by the two missing boys. He took his place at his desk, and motioned them to stand out in the middle of the room. There was a long silence.

Then Waterfield began to speak in a low voice that grew gradually louder. He told us all to look at them, which we did. He then told us that they had brought utter ruin and disgrace on themselves, that no public school would receive them, and that they had broken their parents' hearts. They were not going to stop an hour longer amongst us, for their presence was filthy and contaminating. They were publicly expelled and would now go back to the homes on which they had brought disgrace.

He then told us all to go out, and was left with those two, and I wondered, limp with terror, whether he was going to kill them, and what on earth it was that they had done. And if I was limp then, you may judge what was my condition, when presently the school sergeant who brought summonses from Waterfield told me that he wished to see me. . . . Indeed that imaginative habit which had made up so many glorious adventures for myself on slender grounds was a poor friend at that moment, for as I went to the study, it vividly suggested to me that I too, for some unintelligible reason, would be despatched to Cornwall, a ruined and disgraced boy.

I tapped at the door, tapped again without receiving any answer and entered. Waterfield was sitting at his table and he was crying. He indicated to me that I was to sit down, which I did. Then he blew his nose with an awful explosion of sound, and came with his rocking walk across to the chimney-piece.

"I want to ask you a question," he said. "Do you understand why those two boys were sent away?"

"No, sir," said I.

His voice choked for a moment.

"I am very glad to hear it," he said. "I thank God for that. You may go."

Here was a mysterious affair! I went out wondering about a million things, why Waterfield was crying, why he had sent for me, and above all why those two boys were publicly disgraced. I began to grub in my memory for any clue, and recalled trivial incidents. The elder of the two had been rather kind to a junior like myself: he had nodded good night to me one evening on the stairs, and I think the next night had given me a lump of Turkish delight. Finally, only a few days before, he had by virtue of his first-form privileges taken me for a stroll round the wooded grounds, where the first-form might go at pleasure, and I felt highly honoured at his notice. He had become rather odd: he began questions like, "I say, do you ever——," and stopped. As I did not know what he was talking about, and only grew puzzled, he remarked rather contemptuously, "I didn't know you were such a kid. Why, when I was your age . . ."

Then our privacy came to an abrupt conclusion, for we suddenly met Waterfield, with a large cigar, strolling along a path. He took us both into a greenhouse, and gave us some grapes, and walked back with us, one on each side of him.

There was nothing there at the time which had roused any strong curiosity in me. I had wondered vaguely why these sentences were left unfinished, and why he had only then discovered that I was such a kid. But now, in an intensity of wonder as to why Waterfield had been so glad to know that the reason for this expulsion was incomprehensible to me, and as to what that reason was, I began, with the groping instincts of a young thing, that has either to guess its way, or to be told it, to fit meaning-less little pieces of the puzzle together, trying first one pair of fragments and then another, intensely curious and instinctively certain that there was something here which other boys understood, and which Waterfield certainly understood, but which I did not. I supposed that the completed puzzle contained something in which right and wrong were involved, since a transgression such as the two expelled boys had been guilty of was an affair that could not be atoned for by a caning or a birching.

For days after that, hints, fragments, surmises floated as thickly about the school as motes of dust in a sunbeam. We were forbidden to talk about the subject at all, which gave an additional zest to discussion. Some knew a great deal, some knew a little, some knew nothing. Those who knew nothing learned a little, those who knew a little learned more, and we seethed with things that were un-savoury, because the secrecy and the prohibition made the unsavouriness of them. . . . But in heaven's name, why could we not all have been given clean lessons in natural history? Is it better that young boys should guess and experiment and be left to find things out for themselves, with the gusto that arises from the notion of forbidden mysteries, than that they should be taught cleanness by their elders, instead of being left to experimentalize in dirtiness? Until there is extracted from boyhood its proper legitimate inquisitiveness which is the reason of its growth, nothing can prevent boys from seeking to learn about those things which its elders cover up in a silence so indiscreet as to be criminal. It is a libellous silence, for it surrounds, in an atmosphere of suspicion, knowledge which is perfectly wholesome and necessary.

Between terms came holidays full of things just as

wonderful as the swamping of the furnaces of the Havre boat and "Benson's lies" generally, and these must be lumped together, to form a general summary as to how we amused ourselves for the next three years or so, when holidays brought us together.   About now a joint literary effort of all us children, called (for no known reason) the *Saturday Magazine*, made its punctual appearance. Already we were such savage wielders of the pen that one issue every holidays no longer contented us, but two or three times between term and term my father and mother were regaled of an evening with a flood of prose and poetry.   Arthur would say one morning, "Let's have a Saturday Magazine next Tuesday," and straightway we called for a supply of that useful paper known as "sermon paper," which contains exactly twenty-three lines to a small quarto page, faintly ruled in blue. Dialogues, satirical sketches, tales of adventure, essays, and poems, were poured out in rank profusion, the rule being that each member of the family should contribute "at least" four pages of prose, or one page of verse.   There was, after we had all got blooded with the lust of production, little cause for this minimum regulation, and perhaps it would have been better, in view of subsequent fruitfulness, to have substituted for the minimum restriction of " at least" a maximum restriction of "at most." Yet this habit of swift composition gave us all a certain ease in expressing ourselves if only because we expressed ourselves so freely.   The contents of the *Saturday Magazine* were, since all choice of subject was left to the author, of the most varied description.   Arthur would produce (at least) an essay in the style of *The Spectator* (Addison's) describing how he threw a cake of yellow soap at a serenading cat, Nellie would refresh us with an

imaginary interview with our Scotch coachman on the
subject of sore backs, Maggie, whose chief avocation now
was to rear an enormous number of guinea-pigs and find
names for them, gave a dialogue between Atahualpa and
Ixlitchochitl (only she knew how to spell them); poor
Fred treated them to a poem on the Devil, which he felt
sure solved the very difficult question about the origin
of evil, and Hugh, who by reason of his youth was let
off with two pages of prose, produced adventures so
bloody, that out of sheer reaction his audience rocked with
unquenchable laughter. There was a Saturnalian liberty
allowed, and my mother's experiences with a runaway
pony, or her fondness for cheese, were treated with sharp-
edged mockery, and even my father made a ludicrous appearance in some dialogue, where he was supposed to be
worsted by the superior wit of his children. . . .

In lighter mood (save the mark) we played a poetry
game called "American nouns," in which you had to
answer, metrically and with rhyme, a question written
down at the top of a half-sheet of paper, and bring in
a particular word like "unconstitutional" or some stumper
of that kind. This particular word was given to my Uncle
Henry Sidgwick together with the question, "What do
you know of astronomy?" to which in the winking of an
eye he produced the following gem:

> Phœbus, the glorious king of the sky,
>   In his unconstitutional way,
> Dispenses at will his bounties on high
>   And royally orders the day.
> No starry assembly controls his bright flow,
> No critical comet presumes to say "No."

Or again, my mother having to answer the question,

"Does the moon draw the sea?" and to bring in the word "artist," made a glorious last stanza:

> Ask me no more, but let me be;
> My temper's of the tartest:
> For if the moon doth draw the sea,
> Why, then she is an artist.

Somehow she got the reputation of being an indifferent poet, but that was considered remarkably good "for her," and worthy of being immortalized on the printing press which belonged to this epoch. This was a small wooden box, at the bottom of which you set the type backwards if you were capable of a sustained effort, and if not, anyhow. The "forme" was then smudged over with a black roller anointed with printer's ink, and letters of the set type used to stick to it (like teeth in toffee) and must be replaced if possible. Then a piece of paper was gingerly laid on the top, a lid was fitted on, and a lever was turned which pressed the lid (and of course the paper) against the inked type. The lever got out of order and I think broke, so instead several smart hammer-blows were given to the lid in order to produce the same result. The printed paper was then taken out, and the marks of punctuation inserted by hand, because there weren't any commas and colons and so forth in our fount, or because it was easier to put them in afterwards. "E's" had often to be left out too, and inserted afterwards, because "e" being a common letter was not sufficiently represented if you wanted to print a long piece like Uncle Henry's. . . . Chemistry, also, among the Arts and Sciences claimed our attention, especially Maggie's (when she was not too busy about guinea-pigs) and mine. The highest feat that we attained to, and that wanted a lot of stirring, was to dissolve a threepenny-piece in nitric acid. Then there was photography; I think a godfather gave me a camera, and we made our own wet plates which was very difficult, and began with pouring collodion (was it collodion?) smoothly over a piece of glass. Then nitrate of silver—we might have used the dissolved threepenny-bit, I suppose—must be applied. The plates usually recorded nothing whatever, but once an image remarkably like the yew tree outside the nursery window did certainly appear there. Arthur began collecting butterflies and moths, which eventually became a very important asset to a museum which now overflowed into all our bedrooms. There was an extraordinary abundance of clouded yellows (*Colias Edusa*, and why do I remember that?) one year and he used to return, profusely perspiring, with captives in chip boxes, to which Maggie and I were anæsthetists, for Nellie took no part in this collection, as she objected to killing butterflies.

Small strips of blotting-paper—this was our procedure —were taken, and moons of chloroform, quite similar to the eau-de-Cologne moons, were made on them from an unstoppered bottle of chloroform. These were inserted in the chip boxes while Arthur, the executioner, got the oxalic acid and a nib. With this lethal weapon he speared their unconscious thoraxes, and out came the setting-boards. Nocturnal expeditions for purposes of "sugaring" tree-trunks were even more exciting. We mixed beer and sugar, heating them together, and at dusk pasted trees in the garden with the compound which Watch found so delicious that if the jug containing it was left on the ground for a moment, he began lapping it up. On such sugaring nights I was allowed to sit up later than usual, and about ten o'clock the excited procession again started with more chip boxes, and a dark lantern, which was turned on to the sugared patches. There were the bright-eyed creatures of the night, drunkenly feasting, and Arthur enriched his pill-boxes with Silver Y and an occasional Golden Y, and rejected the Yellow Underwing, and grew taut over the Crimson Underwing, while I carried a butterfly net, and swooped with it at wandering moths which were attracted by the unveiled lantern carried by Maggie, and Watch wagged his tail and licked up gratefully the droppings from the sugared tree and any moths that might be on them. And then Beth would come out and say that "my Mamma" said that I must go to bed at once, and I usually didn't. O happy nights!

I think every day in those holidays must have lasted a week, and every month a year, for when I consider it, we surely spent the whole afternoons in playing "Pirates" in the garden. Theoretically now, as well as practically then, I believe that "Pirates," a game evolved by the family generally, and speedily brought to its perfect and stereotyped form, was the best sporting invention, requiring no material implements, of modern time. What powers of the mind, what refinements of cunning, compared to which deer-stalking is mere child's play, were brought into action! For here we were up against each other's wits, and awful were the results of any psychological mistake. I must describe that game for the benefit of families of energetic children who like thinking and running and scoring off each other.

At the top of the garden there was a summer-house, and that of course was "home." There was a lateral laurel hedge to the left of it which screened a path that led by the copse outside the nursery windows, and communicated by means of a garden door with the abysses of the stable copse, and the stable yard. The henyard, an outlying piece of kitchen garden, and the other copse, excellent hiding-places in themselves, were outside the range of pirates, and the touch-line, so to speak, beyond which neither pirates nor trophy-seekers might go passed on the hither side of these. Straight in front of "home" was an open space, safe in itself but hedged in with peril, for there were climbable trees, from which a pirate might almost drop on your head, and thickets. To the right was a most dangerous door, because the latch was stiff and if you were pursued from outside by the pirate you were almost bound to be caught before you could kick it open. In the middle distance, straight ahead were beehives; beyond, kitchen garden and orchard. Never was there anything so trappy.

So much for the theatre: the *dramatis personæ* were five (occasionally six when my mother played, once seven when my father played), and of this number there were chosen in rotation two pirates, but my father and mother, of course, were never pirates, because they would not have had a chance, as you will see. The pirates, being chosen, went away together, and were given five minutes law to hide wherever they chose within the assigned limits. During these five minutes a captain was chosen from among the blockade runners, who directed his side as to what trophy each of them was to bring from his cruise. One had, for instance, to bring back a croquet hoop from the lawn, another an apple from the third tree in the orchard, another an ivy-leaf from the stable-yard. With their trophies in their hands they had to return in safety to the summer-house without being caught by a pirate.

So far all is simple, but now there comes in the great

point of the game. *No pirate could catch you, until you had your trophy, whatever it was, about you.* Thus if your trophy was the curry-brush, you might (and did) if you were seen by a pirate and knew it, hastily pluck up a croquet hoop and begin running. Then the pirate, supposing that this was your trophy, ran like mad after you, and when he caught you, you merely assured him that the croquet hoop wasn't your trophy. That was a score, it also winded the pirate a little, and perhaps Nellie, going cautiously towards the croquet-lawn where her real mission was, would have observed this, and plucking up a croquet hoop (which was her true trophy) begin to run. On which the slightly winded pirate would leave you and run after Nellie, who generally screamed, thus giving away the fact that she had her trophy. Meantime you would proceed with caution towards the stable-yard, seize up a curry-brush and instantly hear a crash from the copse and find the second pirate in pursuit. Even as deep called unto deep the pirates would then shout to each other, and though you thought you could get away from one, the other, having captured Nellie, would appear in front of you. . . .

There were infinite psychological problems. Supposing your trophy had been an apple, you would, if you were very cunning, put it in your pocket, and continue a pleasant stroll, without hurry, more or less in the direction of "home." Then if a fast pirate like Arthur sighted you, you would not run away at all, but ask him sarcastically if he had caught anybody yet. There was a good chance that he would think you had not yet got your trophy and would continue to follow you, till he saw another blockade runner looking guilty. On the other hand, he might conceivably suspect you had it already and clap an

awful hand on your shoulder, and say, "Caught." But
probably he preferred to watch you, for that made more
sport, and then you would suddenly sprint for home, while
he was off his guard. There was a bay tree round which a
skilful dodger could score off a heavier and faster craft,
but under no circumstances might you jump over flower-
beds, because that led to running through them instead,
which was ruinous to petunias.

In the same summer-house which was "home," we also
held a mystical "Chapter," of which Arthur was warden, Nellie, Maggie and myself, sub-warden, secretary
and treasurer, and Hugh was Henchman. The word
"Chapter" was no doubt of Cathedral origin, and denoted
a ceremonious meeting. We all subscribed to the funds
of the Chapter (my mother, who was an honorary member, subscribed most) and the money was spent in official
salaries, and in providing decorations, chains and crosses
and ribands for the officials. The largest salary, which I
think was half a crown, was drawn by Arthur as warden;
he also wore the most magnificent jewel, while Hugh,
the menial, drew but the salary of one penny, and had
a very poor gaud to console himself with. As Henchman, his duty was chiefly to run errands for the rest
of the Chapter, to summon my mother when she was
allowed to appear, to kill wasps, and to fetch the warden's straw hat. He was the only member of the Chapter
who dared to dispute the will of the warden, and was
known to exclaim, "Why shouldn't Fred?" (the treasurer) when he was tired of running about. Even more
subversive of canonical discipline was his assertion one
day that he would not be a member of any more societies,
in which he was only deputy sub-sub-bootboy. But I
secretly (though treasurer) rather sympathized with him,

for I considered then, and consider still, that the Chapter was rather a soft job for Arthur. It is true that he invented it, that he covered our symbols of office with sealing-wax lacquer—what has happened to sealing-wax lacquer all these years?—and that he wrote out in exquisite black-letter hand the patents whereby we held office, signed by himself, but a salary of half a crown was excessive. At the meetings we had to present these patents to him before we took our seats, and then had a short formal conversation in which we were "Brother Subwarden, Brother Secretary" and so forth, and read the minutes of the last meeting, and when the presence of the Honorary Member was requested, Brother Henchman had to go to find her. Donations were made, and salaries were paid, but I am confident that nothing else happened. The Chapter was then adjourned; the orders were put back in a box, and we played pirates. . . .

And yet though we played Pirates all day, and collected clouded yellows all day, and printed the most exquisite poems as well as writing them, and held Chapters, and did a certain amount of holiday-task, and rode with my father, and drove with my mother, there was always time for other excitements. There was bathing in the Fal, there were picnics at Perran, especially when a southwest gale had been blowing, and from seven miles inland there was audible the thump of Atlantic waves on that bleak beach. Then in Truro itself there were great things to be done, for the volcanic energy of my father had soon kindled the county into pouring out money for the erection of a new Cathedral, the first that had been built in England since the time of the Reformation. St. Mary's Church was the site of it, and to-day an aisle of St. Mary's (the rest of a wonderfully hideous church being demolished) forms the baptistery of the Cathedral. The ground was cleared and foundations were dug, and slowly the great stately building began to rise flower-like from the barren soil. I do not suppose that any of us cared independently two straws about a Cathedral, but to go down there with my father, and hear him talk to Mr. Bubb, the Clerk of the Works, infected us with his noble zeal, and the rising walls got pleasingly confused with the rebuilding of the temple by Nehemiah, and the vision of the New Jerusalem. Hugh, I am certain, was allowed to lay a stone himself, and Mr. Bubb presented him with the trowel and mallet with which he had laid it. Or did we all lay stones? I seem to hear my father say in an awestruck voice, "There, you have helped to build Truro Cathedral!" but I am not sure whether that was said to me or not, and my uncertainty is the measure, I am afraid, of the impression that the building of the Cathedral really made on me. . . .

I wonder if it could have been otherwise, and with regret I do not see how it could. As his own childish records show, my father at my age then was a zealous ecclesiastic, for did he not when ripely eleven obtain the use in his mother's house of an empty room, which he converted into an oratory? There was an altar there, and it was hung with rubbings he had made from brasses in churches. This piece of childish piety was certainly natural to him, and as certainly there was no kind of priggishness in it, for he set a booby-trap over the door, so that his sisters should not be able to enter "his" oratory in his absence without being detected. He did not want his sisters praying there: and the booby-trap over the chapel door was certainly an admirable device to keep them out. But in none of us, nor indeed in my mother, was there implanted an ecclesiastical mind, not even in Hugh. He took orders it is true, in the English Church, and subsequently the Catholic Church claimed him, and to it and its service he gave his whole love and energy. But the ecclesiastical mind in him was a later development, for it must be remembered that before taking orders at all he had tried and failed to get into the Indian Civil Service. (He and I, at that time, used to dress up in nightshirts, with trousers over our shoulders to represent stoles, and celebrate the "rite of the Silver Cow" in our sitting-room at Addington. I feel sure that there was not any solid profanity in it: we but parodied, and that with great amusement, the genuflexions, the bobbings and bowings, the waving of a censer, considered merely as ridiculous pieces of ritual, but such a rite could not be held indicative of a reverent attitude towards ritual as such.) But my father's mind, even as a child, was strongly ecclesiastical; only his children did not share it, nor did my mother. Of all men and women that I have ever known, she was the most deeply religious in her realization of the pervading presence of God, but the garb, the habiliments of her religion were not the same as my father's. To him the Church and its ceremonies were a natural self-expression, and in that he gorgeously clothed his love of God. To none of us was such expression natural, and thus his enthusiasms though they infected us to some extent were things caught from him, not cathedraically developed. That he missed this in all of us, I think could not be helped, but I do not think, at that time at any rate, that he missed it much, for he was Elijah in the whirlwind of his enthusiasms, and caught us all up, as in the fringes of a dust-cloud, to subside again when he had passed.

What estranged was my continued fear of him, which now yields easily to analysis and dispersal, but was in those days regarded by me merely as an instinct, as natural and as incontrovertible as hunger or thirst. I understood neither him nor any part of him. I did not grasp the fact that the root in him as regards his children was his love for them, and that it was his love and nothing else that, at bottom, was accountable for his quickness in putting his finger on a fault and his sternness in rebuke. It was out of his love that he regarded himself so strictly as responsible for our mental and moral education, and what I thought his readiness to blame was only the watchfulness of it. For instance, if, as I so well specifically remember, I appeared with an umbrella huddled up anyhow in its confining elastic, he saw in that a tendency towards slovenliness, and he made, in the fervency of his wish that I should not grow up to be of slovenly habit, no allowance for the natural frailty of tender years. Trivial carelessness and unpunctuality in the same way were pounced upon with a severity that altogether overbrimmed the cup of the occasion; he saw in them (and his love hastened to correct) instances of a dangerous tendency. In consequence he brought great and formidable guns to bear on small faults, which could just as efficiently have been visited with a light instead of a heavy hand. Sometimes, too, he was utterly wrong in his interpretation of our motives, and this gave us a sense of injustice; etchingly recorded on my memory, for instance, is a Sunday afternoon walk when Maggie and I pranced and ran ahead, from the mere exuberance, as far as I can judge, produced by a heavy meal and a fine day. But my father put the gloomiest interpretation on our antics, telling us that we were behaving thus in order to excite the admiration of passers-by at our agility. "You are saying to yourselves, 'I am Hercules, I am Diana,' " he witheringly observed; whereas, nothing was farther from our thoughts. But it was unthinkable to argue the point, to assure him that no similitude of that kind had ever suggested itself. The only course was to walk soberly and sedately instead of running. And since the lives of young children, especially if they are at all vividly inclined, are a chessboard of small faults, this fear of the rebuke, in the absence of comprehension of its root-cause, became a constant anxiety to us, making us mere smooth-faced, blue-eyed dolls in his presence, with set fixed movements and expressions; and when released from it, we scampered off as if from an examination under a magnifying-glass.

I do not mean to convey the idea that my father was continually pulling us up, for nothing is further from the truth. Continually we played to him, and he danced the most fascinating measure; continually he played to us, and our dancing strove to keep time with his enchanting airs. He could render us speechless with laughter at his inimitable mirth, or breathless with suspense at his stories. But all the time there was this sense that at any moment the mirth might cease, and that a formidable rebuke might be visited on an offence that we had no idea we had committed. But it was never any joy in fault-finding that prompted it: the real cause was the watchfulness and responsibility of his love. How often our fear was ill-founded, passes enumeration, but one way or another, it had become a habit with all of us, except perhaps Nellie, for she, out of a remarkable faculty of not knowing at all what fear meant (except when playing

Pirates) arrived at a much completer comprehension of my father than any of us.

Still less did the rest of us understand those fits of black depression which from time to time assailed and overwhelmed my father, not grasping the fact that when they were on him, he really ceased to be himself, and was under a sort of obsession. They were, I imagine, as purely physical as a cold in the head or an ache of indigestion, but during the two or three days that they lasted he was utterly unapproachable. He would sit through a meal, or take us out for a walk in a silence which if broken at all, was broken only by blame or irony. If we spoke to him, there would be no reply; if, under the intolerable heaviness we were silent, he would ask if there was nothing that interested us which he was worthy of hearing. . . . And all the time, as we knew later, he was struggling with this demoniacal load, longing to be rid of it, yearning to burst out of it, but possessed by it to the point of helplessness. While the fit was on him, and he was in this abnormal state, the most innocent of words and actions would evoke a formidable censure, and I suspect that three-quarters of our fear for him were derived from our belief that these attacks were a part of him, always there, and always liable to come into play. That was an entire mistake, though it was a natural one. As it was, these black fits were not incapsulated by us, but suffered to mingle with and make part of our estimate of him. That we should so have feared him, that we should so have made ourselves unnatural and formal with him, when all the time his love was streaming out towards us, makes a pathos so pitiful that I cannot bear to think of it. But there it was, and long it lasted, and all the time I never got a true perspective of him. We saw ourselves as a nervous row of pupils before a school-master, and all the time it was his very strictness which was a manifestation of his love, and his love hungered for ours. Our troubles and our joys, the worst of us and the best of us, went like homing pigeons to my mother, and she gave the same welcome to the one and to the other, and for ever treasured both.

The relationship of each one of us to her was unique as regards any other of us, for each of us found exactly and precisely what we desired, though how often we did not know what we desired till she gave it us! All her life she was wiser and younger than anybody else, limpid and bubbling, and from the first days when any of us began to understand what she was, she never had any blank surprises in store, for it was always quite obvious that she would understand and appreciate, and would never condone but always forgive. Never from first to last did I repent having opened my heart to her; never did I not repent having shut it. I do not think she ever asked any of us for a confidence, but the knowledge, conveyed in the very atmosphere of her, that she was ready, toeing the mark, so to speak, to run to us when the pistol fired, gave her that particular precision of sympathy. Did she scold us? Why, of course; but how her precious balms healed our heads!

Love is a stern business, and about hers there was never the faintest trace of sentimentality. She loved with a swift eagerness, and she had no warm slops to comfort us. But there was always the compliment of consulta-tion. "Now you've behaved very badly indeed," she would say, "Don't you think the first thing to do is to say you're sorry?" . . . And then with that inimitable breaking of her smile, "Oh, my dear, I *am* glad you told me." . . . And did ever any other mother at the age of forty run so violently in playing that strenuous game called, "Three knights a-riding," that she broke a sinew in her leg? Mine did. And did ever a mother so encourage an extremely naughty boy of thirteen after a really dreadful interview with his father, as by giving him a prayer book and saying, "I shall write in it 'Wherewithal shall a young man cleanse his ways?'" Being called a young man at the age of thirteen was enough in itself to make him realize what an exceedingly tiresome child he had been. Tact! Beth used to call it "tac," and when I got my shoes wet through three times a day, or fell backwards into one of those Cornish streams she said, "Eh, Master Fred, but you've got no tac'!" No more I had.

CHAPTER VI

AFTER that first brilliant year at school, when I
got so many prizes without taking any trouble,
there ensued two extremely lean years, during which I
took just as much trouble as before, and got nothing at
all. For just as, physically, growing children spurt and
are quiescent again, storing force for the next expansion,
so mentally they have in the intervals of development
periods of utter stagnation. I had swept, a prodigious
infant, through all the other forms, leaving Geege and
Davy and Daubeny mere dim fixed stars across the path
of the comet, and then the unfortunate comet gave one
faint "pop" and went completely out. Other boys
straggled and struggled up to the first form, which I had
so easily stormed, and I continued sinking through them,
like a drowned rag, to my appointed place at the bottom.
Agitated letters were exchanged between Waterfield and
my father, of which I found the other day several of
Waterfield's; he clung to a certain forlorn optimism about
me, but seemed puzzled to know why without positively
neglecting my work I invariably did it worse than anybody in the form. He still believed me not to be stupid.
In that quiescent period I could not assimilate any more;
all that I was fed with merely gave me indigestion, and
the mental stuffing was liberally supplied to the poor
goose, for at the end of that year I was to try for an

Eton scholarship, with regard to which my prospects grew
ever less encouraging. A drawer in Waterfield's study
adjoining the room where the first class was tutored was
entirely devoted to the dreadful copies of Greek and
Latin prose and Latin elegiacs which I produced. Week
after week these grew and collected there, each of them
thickly scored by Waterfield's red ink. Of one of them
I can recall the image now; scarcely a word remained
that was not underscored in red. But I gather that Waterfield must have concluded that some blight other than
carelessness and inattention was responsible for my failures, for he never threatened me with rulers or birchings
for them. Mentally, during those three atrocious terms,
the only thing in which I can remember taking the slightest interest was hearing him read out the piece of English verse which it was our task to turn into Latin elegiacs.
His reading was altogether beautiful; often his voice
broke, as when he read us "Home they brought her war-
rior dead," and, though he quite failed to instil in me
the desire to put such verses into beautiful Latin, he intensely kindled my love of beautiful English. Similarly,
when the Sunday divinity lesson was over and such storms
as had raged round St. Paul's missionary journey were
stilled, he would tell us all to make ourselves comfortable, and for the rest of the hour entranced us with *The
Pilgrim's Progress*. His delightful voice melodiously
rose and fell; he asked us no inconvenient questions to
probe the measure of our attention; his object, in which he
strikingly succeeded, was to let us hear magnificent English magnificently read, and to leave us to gather our own
honey.

A great event of the summer term was Waterfield's
birthday. The whole school subscribed to give him a

birthday present, which must have been of some value, for the sum of five shillings or ten shillings (I forget which) was charged up to every boy's bill. But we certainly got that back again, for the birthday, kept as a whole holiday, was celebrated by everybody being taken to the Crystal Palace for the day and furnished with half a crown to spend as he pleased, so decidedly Waterfield was not "up" on the transaction. A few of the more favoured were invited to spend the day on the Thames with him and his family; they embarked on a steam launch at Richmond and had luncheon in some riverside wood. Now, above all things in the world I longed to see the Crystal Palace, of which I had formed the image as of some ineffable glittering constellation, a piece of real fairyland fallen from the sky and now at rest on Sydenham Hill, and it was with a black despair that I received the distinction of being bidden to the family picnic instead. But a *dea ex machina* came to the rescue in the person of Mrs. Waterfield, who quite ironically said to me, "I suppose you would much sooner go to the Crystal Palace?" Throwing "tac" and politeness to the winds, I unhesitatingly told her that I certainly would, and I was given my half-crown and joined the proletariat. . . . Or was Mrs. Waterfield's enquiry not ironical at all, but a piece of supreme "tac"? Had some hint reached her that I really wanted to go to the Crystal Palace? I cannot decide. In any case, that kind-hearted woman would have been rewarded for making the suggestion, could she have realized with what rapture I beheld that amazing edifice glittering in the sun, and went through its Palm Court and its Egyptian Court and its Assyrian Court, and beheld all that the Prince Consort had done to educate the love of beauty in these barbarous islanders.

All day I wandered enchanted, and laid out most of the half-crown in a glass paper-weight with a picture of the Crystal Palace below, and the remainder in a small nickel ornament in the shape of an ewer, undoubtedly made in Germany. Indeed, I was wise to fasten on the opportunity given me by Mrs. Waterfield, for thus I secured the wonderful experience of being absolutely bowled over by the beauty of the Crystal Palace, which has not happened to everybody. All the same, I suffered a few years later a crushing and double disillusionment, for I was taken there again to hear *Israel in Egypt* at the Handel Festival. On that occasion my main impression was that I thought the Crystal Palace a very suitable place for that monstrous performance. The scale on which the one was built and on which the other was performed served not to conceal but to accentuate the essential meanness of each. . . .

I weave this into a digression not unconnected with the first of these lean years. Though mentally, as regards the metres of foreign verse and the inexorable grammar of Greek and Latin, I was as idle "as a painted ship upon a painted ocean," I gorged myself not only on the readings of Waterfield, but on music. That frail widow, Mrs. Russell, is probably unknown to fame as a teacher of the piano, but I owe her an undying debt of gratitude. I begged to be released from the study of such works as those of Mr. Diabelli, whom I had long ago judged and found wanting, and from "arrangements" of the *Barber of Seville*, and even from the sugared melodies of "Songs without Words" (over which, especially No. 8, an occasional tear used to drop from Mrs. Russell's eyes), and to be allowed to entrap my awkward fingers in Bach, whom I had heard rendered by the "Farmer

Society" at Lincoln. My request was granted, and I was permitted to make a rapturous hash of slow Sarabands and more rapid Gavottes and Minuets out of the *Suites Anglaises*. Never was there so enthralled a bungler; for I could hear (this I positively affirm), through the crash of my awkwardness, what was meant. Bach then and there and ever afterwards was my gold standard in the innumerable coinage of music. There was good silver, there was good copper, there was promissory paper. All these, in a loose metaphor, might temporarily be depreciated in the exchange of my mind, or might have a rise, but Bach remained gold. Out of my "taste," whatever that was, I was quite prepared to put Beethoven (in slow movements) in his place, and to give Mozart, as judged by his "Variations on a Theme in A," a very distinguished position, and to concede a neatness to "The Harmonious Blacksmith." Brahms I had never heard of. But all these, then as now, were, at the most, distinguished gentlemen, equerries or grooms or chamberlains in attendance round about the court, and having speech with the King.

By the time I heard *Israel in Egypt* at the Handel Festival, I had also heard the *St. Matthew Passion* at St. Paul's, and I quite definitely compared them. Probably it is a mistake ever to compare one achievement with another even if they are built on an appeal to the same sense: it is no more use comparing Handel with Bach than it is comparing a sunset with the view of the Bernese Oberland. But, taken by itself, that performance of *Israel in Egypt* seemed to me a monstrous attempt to cover up a common invention by inflating it with noise. The fact that there were four thousand (or perhaps four million) singers all bawling, "He gave them hailstones for rain," did not essentially make the hailstorm one whit the stormier, though the immensity of the row pleasantly stunned the senses. It would be as unreasonable to take a carte-de-visite photograph of a man with a stupid mouth and a chin-beard, and hope to make it impressive by enlarging it to the size of the Great Pyramid. Indeed, the bigger the enlargement, the sorrier would be the result. But by that time I had the sense to see how delicate and delightful an artist is Handel when he confines himself to the limits of his true territory. For sweetness and neatness of melody, in the violin sonata in A, the piano sonatas, and songs from countless operas, I knew he had no rival—in the silver standard. But no one, with the one exception of Bach, has ever defeated the awful limitations of the "form" of oratorio, and, as a rule, the larger the orchestra, the more stupendous the body of voice, the more shaky becomes the credit of the composer. Indeed, the very fact that so gigantic a representation as a Crystal Palace Handel Festival was ever desired or enjoyed postulates not only a complete want of musical perception on the part of the public, but a corresponding want of musical achievement on the part of Handel. No one would deny that the "Hailstone Chorus" sounds better when a huge band and an immense chorus all produce the utmost noise of which they are capable. We all like hearing a quantity of voices and a Nebuchadnezzar-band thundering out commonplace melodies, because a loud and tuneful noise has a stimulating effect on the nerves, and because we like our ears (occasionally) to be battered into a hypnotized submission. But we submit not to the magic of the music, but to the overpowering din of its production. And when "the feast is over and the lamps expire," when we have had "the louder music and the stronger wine" of noise, our hearts steal back to the spell of Cynara. . . .

Soon after that first enthralling day at the Crystal Palace came the scholarship examination at Eton, which, as far as I was concerned, produced no prize whatever. I spent a delightful three days there, basking in the effulgence of Arthur, then just eighteen and demi-godlike, and came back to Temple Grove after a pleasant outing. And at the end of that term Waterfield retired, and I went back in September to be tutored again for more scholarships.

The new headmaster, Mr. Edgar, previously conducted a boarding-house, and was hitherto distinguished for a very long clerical coat, two most amiable daughters, a gold-rimmed eyeglass which he used to clean by inserting it in his mouth and then wiping it on his handkerchief, and the most remarkable hat ever seen. The nucleus of it, that is to say the part he wore on his head, was of hard black felt, like the ordinary bowler, but it was geometrically, quite round, so that he could put any part of it anywhere. That I know because I have so often tried it on myself. Outside that circular nucleus came an extremely broad black felt rim, far wider than that of the shadiest straw hat, and turning upwards on all sides in what I can only describe as a "saucy" curve. As worn by Edgar, it produced an impression of indescribable levity, just as if he was, say, Mr. George Robey posing as a parson. His amiability was unbounded, and his driving-power that of a wad of cotton-wool. Indeed, he was so pleasant that for his sake it became the fashion to fall in love with either of his two daughters, whose mission was to influence us for good. They gave us strawberries, and tried to get between us and the soft spring-showers of their father's disapproval, like unnecessary umbrellas.

Under Edgar's beneficent sway, I managed to get into the most complicated row that ever schoolboy found himself immersed in, for I committed three capital (or rather fundamental) offences in one joyous swoop. In the first place, I concealed five shillings of sterling silver about my person, though all cash derived from "tips" had to be given up to the matron, and by her doled out as she thought suitable. This clandestine millionaire thereupon bribed a fellow-conspirator to break bounds and go into Richmond, there to spend four of those shillings in Turkish delight, and keep the fifth for his trouble. He got back safely, and three friends had a wonderful feast in the dormitory that night, all sitting on my bed, and cloying ourselves and the bedclothes with that delicious sweetmeat. Unfortunately there was amongst those midnight revellers one stomach so effete and spiritless that it revolted at the administration of these cloying lumps, and, prostrated with sickness, the owner of it confessed to an unusual indulgence, while the state of my sheets completed the evidence. The chain went back link by link from his sickness to my bed, and from my bed to the finding of the empty Turkish delight box, and from the Turkish delight to the place it came from, and from the place it came from to the money wherewith it was purchased, so that I was left in as the unrivalled culprit in the reconstructed story. But though I should have swooned with anxiety and probably confessed all, had Waterfield been the Sherlock Holmes, I never gave a moment's thought to Edgar's unravelling. He said I had been very naughty, and sucked his eyeglass, and hoped I wouldn't be naughty again. It was all very polite and pleasant, and I knew I had nothing to fear from him. But even at the time I had a secret misgiving as to the Judgment Book that should soon be opened at this page. The best thing, probably, that I could have done would have been to write home instantly and tell my father all about it, for that would certainly have seemed to him the proper course, and also he would have blown off part of his displeasure in a letter. But I continued to procrastinate, and before many weeks the term mildly ebbed away. Then with a sudden *crescendo* my misgivings increased, and it was a very unholiday-minded urchin who went back that December for Christmas at Truro.

About now my fear of my father was at its perihelion, and morning by morning I used to come downstairs, a quarter of an hour before breakfast time, to look at the post which had arrived, and see if among the letters for him there was one with the Mortlake postmark and the "Temple Grove" inscription on its flap. Some morning soon, I knew, my report on the term's work and my conduct generally would come, and in it, no doubt, would be an allusion to this escapade. Edgar had treated it so lightly that it was still just possible that he would not allude to it in his report, but that possibility was not seriously entertained. Morning by morning I turned over the letters, while my father was at early service, and then one day, while Christmas was nearly on us, I saw with a sinking of the heart that the fatal letter had arrived. What added to the terror of it was that my father was in a fit of black depression.

He did not open his letters at breakfast, and afterwards I went out into the garden in pursuit of an entrancing game just invented, that concerned a large circular thicket of escalonia which grew near the front door. There was an "It," who at a signal started in pursuit round the bush to catch Hugh and me, and "It" on this occasion was Nellie. She came running round the curve of the bush and set us flying off in the opposite direction, still keeping, by the rule of the game, close to the bush. Then, when she had got us really moving, she would double back with the design that we should still, running in that direction, rush into her very arms and be caught. Full speed astern was the only thing that could save us. . . . In the middle of this out came the butler, who said that my father wanted to see me at once. "Come out again quickly," called Nellie.

My father was sitting in his study with an open letter in his hand. I think he gave it me to read; in any case, Mr. Edgar had been sufficiently explicit, and in all my life I have never been so benumbed with fear. . . . Had I committed the most heinous of moral crimes my father could not have made a blacker summing-up. He said that he would not see me among the rest of his children. I was to have my meals alone and disgraced upstairs, and to. take no part in their games or in their society, and away I went battered and yet inwardly rebelling against this appalling sentence. Then I think my mother or Nellie must have pleaded, for I was allowed to go out for a walk with Nellie alone that afternoon, but was segregated from the others. I was still bewildered with the fierceness of my father's displeasure, and took it for granted that I must have done something unintelligibly wicked, for I asked Nellie if she had ever done anything so dreadful as the crime of which I had been guilty. She said she had not, so I drew the inference that her theft of dried plants from my collection (which, after all, was a violation of one of the commandments) was venial. But it was precious on that black afternoon to receive sympathy at all, which certainly she gave me, and I did not risk the loss of it by enquiring about the comparative wickedness of the "Affair Turkish delight" and theft.

Then on Christmas Eve, which I think must have been next day, came one of those unutterable brightnesses which my father always had in store. Again he sent for me, and I went stiff and resigned, not knowing whether there was not to be some renewal of his anger. . . . Instead, he put me in an armchair close by the fire and wrapped a rug round my knees, and asked if I was quite comfortable, and shared with me the tea that had been brought in for him, since he was too busy to come into the nursery as usual and have it with the rest of us. And then he somehow gave me a glimpse, sitting tucked up by the fire, of the love that was at the base of his severity. How, precisely, he conveyed that I cannot tell, but there was no more doubt about it than there was about the heaviness of his displeasure.

The remaining two terms at Temple Grove passed along pleasantly. In school work I continued my slow placid gravitation to the bottom of my form, as other boys were promoted into it and took their places below me. I sank gently through them and came calmly to rest at a position where no fresh sinking was possible. There I went in for a little more sleep, "a little slumber, a little folding of the hands in sleep," and resisted with the passive force of mere inertia any attempt to raise me. But probably vital forces were beginning to stir again, for I got free of the successive childish ailments which had been afflicting me—colds, sore throats, earaches and tooth-aches—all of which no doubt added their contribution to

E. F. BENSON, ÆT. 19

[Page 119

my general apathy, and also I woke to a violent interest
in friendship, steam-engines, and poetry. The last of
these I take to have been due to the fructification of the
seed sown by Waterfield's readings, and, with Carring-
ton's translation of the "Æneid" to help, it is a fact that
I produced in an American cloth-covered notebook a
complete and rhymed and rhythmical rendering of the
third "Æneid" which we were working at in school, without caring one jot for the merits of the original Latin.
What I wanted to do was to compose a quantity of English myself, and compose it I did, glorying in the speed
of its production, quite careless about the faithfulness of
the rendering or the accuracy of the grammar, and the
only merit it can possibly have had was that it was a
labour of love. Other poems dashed off in the intervals
of this epic were connected with friendship, for I conceived a violent adoration for a boy of the same standing
as myself, romantic to the highest degree in that I gave
him a whole-hearted devotion, but quite devoid of mawkishness or sentimentality. To him I addressed rhymed
odes, and then we quarrelled and made it up again, with
more odes, for he addressed me also in flowing stanzas.
Then there was a parody of Hood's "Song of the Shirt,"
held to be a devastatingly comic piece; and not less comic
I suspect was a blank verse lament by a mother over the
death of her only son.

Not very far behind poetry and friendship as objects of
existence came steam-engines, my fellow-engineer sitting
next me, bottom but one of the form. We got illustrated
catalogues from the makers of models, and copied and
recopied diagrams of slide-valves, waste pipes, and ec-
centrics with a zeal and accuracy which, if devoted to
lessons, must speedily have pulled us out of the humble

positions we so contentedly occupied. A certain geo-graphical jealousy was mixed up in this, since, though we both condemned the engines on the South-Western, on which line was Mortlake, as very poor and flimsy mecha-nisms, he, whose home was reached by the Great Northern, considered the engines on that line far superior to any-thing that the Great Western, which took me to and from Truro, had to show. He drew pictures of the Great Northern express engines, and I retorted with sketches of the "Flying Dutchman" (11.45 a.m. from Paddington), which went to Swindon without a stop and ran on a broad gauge, while the Great Northern was only a narrow gauge. Against that he set the fact that Peterborough was a mile further from London than was Swindon. . . . He was the happy possessor of a model locomotive with slide-valve cylinders and a waste-pipe going up the chim-ney, and though I could not run to that, by dint of saving up and of my mother's anticipation of my birthday, I became possessor of another model with a copper boiler and a brass chassis called the "Dart." The "Dart" had only oscillating cylinders, which, as all the world knows, do not discharge their waste steam up the funnel, but from small holes at their base, and have this further in-firmity, that they only have one steam-driven stroke in each revolution of their fly-wheel, whereas a slide-valve cylinder has two. The slide-valve engine, therefore, was of a different class altogether from the "Dart," but I found that I could get up a very powerful head of steam in the "Dart" by stuffing small pellets of blotting-paper up the safety-valve, so that she held her breath while her rival was letting off steam. Then, when for fear of a burst boiler I said the "Dart" was ready, and turned on the tap that conveyed the steam to the cylinder, she would start off like mad, and for a few yards easily outrun her more powerful rival. But long before she got to the end of the open-air cloisters where these races took place she would be overhauled; and, indeed, the "Dart" usually failed to run a complete course, and had to be bottled up again to develop fresh energy. But inferior as the "Dart" was in staying power, it must be accounted unto her for righteousness that she never burst when her safety-valve was stopped up. There was also a stationary engine (oscillating cylinder) belonging to one of us, but we unfortunately burned its bottom out by neglecting to put any water in the boiler.

Friendship, engines, and poetry, then, were the safety-valves—not choked with blotting-paper like that of the much-enduring "Dart"—through which my growing vitality discharged itself, and I used to lie awake at night, making rhymes and phrases and thinking of the friend of my heart, and trying to devise some plan by which the "Dart" should generate a more abundant supply of steam. To these objects of existence, when the summer term began, was added cricket, but never did my school work arouse one ounce of latent energy, even though scholarship time was coming near again. If I can recollect my attitude rightly, I was entirely without ambition as regards winning a scholarship, in the sense that I chose to devote myself to Latin and Greek with a view to subsequently obtaining one. It is true that I wanted, rather, to go to Eton, and knew that I should not be sent there unless I got a scholarship, but for that end I did not divert my energies from friendship, steam-engines, and poetry. I think I am correct in this recollection, for in all the years that have passed since then I cannot remember ever being nearly so much interested in the future as in the present.

The actual interest blazing within me (and there were often several respectable conflagrations going on) has always seemed to me of far vaster importance than a remoter goal. I do not mean that I was fitful in my intentions, because I certainly pursued the same object for years together; only it was not for the ultimate achievement that I pursued it, but because I was continuously interested in the same thing. That the opposite line of action is the most effective and brings the biggest results I do not deny, but, on the other hand, think of the wild and fugitive acquisitions that fall to the lot of the short-range strategist. . . . But I am not defending my conduct, in any case, but merely describing it.

My own lack of effective ambition must have been terribly disappointing to the elders who had formed and, in a material sense, directed this scholarship campaign. Mr. Edgar and my father agreed on a tremendous programme, which I was to carry out, and the "general idea" was this. There was a scholarship examination at Marlborough in June or perhaps early in July, in which there were offered for competition some half-dozen scholarships, with a great plum at the top called the "House Scholarship." The House Scholarship was worth, I think, £80 a year, the next six £50, and my father in a letter he wrote me shortly before the event said that he did not think the great plum was out of my reach. His main desire, I know, was that I should achieve a distinction, but I am also sure that he felt I ought to do something to help towards the expenses of my education, since he believed that I was capable of so doing. He was not a rich man; hitherto his sons Martin and Arthur had won scholarships which made their education at Winchester and Eton a matter of small expense, and he did not mean to send me to Eton, as the event proved, unless I got a scholarship, but to a much cheaper but in no way less excellent school. I was, therefore, in the examination at Marlborough to get a scholarship of some sort—the House Scholarship for choice—and then, a few weeks later, to go up for Eton. If I got a scholarship there, I was to be sent there instead of Marlborough, but, failing that, to accept the laurels which Marlborough would no doubt have offered me.

So first I went off to Marlborough and competed there. I didn't carry off the House Scholarship, nor did I carry off any other scholarship, nor was my name mentioned as having approached to distinction, and so Eton was given its chance without any back-thought at having wiped Marlborough's eye. Once again, therefore, I competed sadly at Eton, and Eton had precisely the same opinion of me as it had had a year before. The plan of campaign had completely failed, and it was settled that I should unconditionally surrender to Marlborough. I did not in the least want to go there, because I wanted to go to Eton, as far as I wanted anything at all apart from friendship, steam-engines, and poetry. Certainly I did not want to remain at Temple Grove any longer, for my greatest friend had won a scholarship at Winchester, and the steam-engine friend was off to Harrow, and another person who mattered had been successful at Eton. But the idea of Marlborough was not without charm, for a year before another friend had gone there, and I looked forward with a certain excitement to seeing him again. We had met during the days of the scholarship examination, and he had aroused in me some shy sort of adoration. He had grown tall and handsome, and asked condescendingly about Temple Grove and the odious habit of keeping stag-beetles, yet with a certain personal interest that he veiled behind a splendid manly brusqueness. I wondered whether he would appreciate a short ode, but decided that he would not. But he called me a "decent little kid," which I liked as coming from so magnificent a being.

Temple Grove ended very soon after that in a general *dämmerung* of failure. *Faute de mieux* I was to be sent to Marlborough, and throwing a Latin dictionary carelessly into my locker, I squashed my gigantic stag-beetle quite flat, and he was as Og the King of Bashan. On the last day of the term I played cricket against a team of Old Templegrovians and lost the match by failing to hold the easiest catch ever spooned up amid a wildly excited circle of contemporaries, having previously got out first ball (or second). But Mr. Edgar was kind, and said that it didn't matter, though his frenzied sucking of his eyeglass and his dropping it into my lemonade indicated tact rather than sincerity.

So the poor ugly duckling who had failed to accomplish anything went home to its family of swans, who, dazzlingly white, cut circles in the air above it on the pinions of their various accomplishments. There was Arthur, now nineteen, who had got an Eton scholarship at King's College, Cambridge, and was going there in October, whose scholastic success was only equalled by his volleys with an Eton football and his wholly untakeable service at lawn-tennis. He could do everything with ease, was listened to by my father with attention when he talked, and yet remained unconscious of his sovereignty, and was altogether kind and faintly pitiful to my all-round shortcomings. There was Nellie, who annexed every distinction that could be annexed at the Truro High School, except when Maggie butted up against her, who could play Schumann's first novelette and had been pronounced to have a "veiled" contralto voice in which she sang melodies by Marzials and Molloy, and who, on the occasion of Redruth High School or some inferior congregation of females challenging Truro High School for a match at cricket, bowled out the entire side of those misguided young ladies with lobs that cut the daisies from their stalks and were admired even by the vanquished for their paralyzing swiftness. Then there was Maggie, who took the rest of the prizes at the High School and painted ravishly not only in water-colours, but in oils, with McGuilp (was it?) as a medium, and tubes that squirted rainbows on to her palette. She was not athletic, but she had the great physical distinction of having been knocked down by a cow whose calf had been taken from her, and lying prone on the ground held on to the animal's horns and with perfect calmness continued to scream loudly and serenely until rescued by Parker the butler. After these dazzling swans there came the ugly duckling, who had failed in games and in scholarship, who had not achieved the smallest intellectual distinction, but who in some queer manner of his own was quite as independent as any of the swans.

And, finally, there was Hugh, on whom at this time my father's hopes were centred, for I think he regarded him as the one who was going to take Martin's place. If he listened with respect to Arthur, he hung on Hugh, who, for independence, for knowing what he wanted, and for a perfectly fearless disregard of other people's opinions, was, for a boy of nine, wholly unique. If his reason was convinced, he would adopt a plan different from the one he had chosen, but it was necessary to convince him first, and no amount of bawling or insistence would make him alter his mind if he did not agree. He adored Beth, but if he chose to walk through puddles, neither affection for her, nor respect for her authority, would make him cease to do so, unless she convinced him of the greater suitability of the dry places. He was so dreadfully funny that nobody could possibly be angry with him for long, and when he had reduced a sister, who was teaching him his lessons, to distraction by his disobediences and inattention, he would anticipate the final threat the moment before it came, and, with shut eyes and a face inexpressibly solemn, would chant, "Mamma shall be told!" Arthur alone out of us all could deal with him. Once, when in some theatrical rehearsal, Hugh, with soft paper round a comb, had to supply orchestral accompaniment to the piano, and wouldn't stop, Arthur observed in an awful voice, "If the orchestra isn't quiet, it shall be sent out of the room with several hard slaps." . . . Hugh had a habit, when things were breezy, of writing insulting remarks in round hand on a piece of paper, and then doubling it up and throwing it at the object of his scorn, and while you were reading it he ran away. A further development of this was that, when pursuit was hot behind him, he would pull a small ball of paper out of his pocket and surreptitiously drop it, as if fearing to be caught with it. Naturally, the pursuer stopped to smooth out the paper and see what fresh insult was recorded there, and would find a perfectly blank half-sheet. But by that time Hugh would be at the top end of the garden path and have had time to conceal himself anywhere. Clad in pasteboard armour, covered with silver paper, with a shield and a helmet and greaves, he would hide in the shrubbery and hurl paper lances at you. Then a hot pursuit followed, until one of the greaves dropped off, and, still flying, he would pant out "Pax, until I've put on my greave again!" He and I lived in a perpetual high-tension atmosphere of violent quarrels, swift reconciliations, and indissoluble alliances with secret signs and mysteries to which even Maggie was not admitted. We had a cypher language of our own which consisted in substituting for each vowel the one that came next in the alphabet; it was easy to write, but difficult to speak and even more difficult to understand when spoken. What we communicated to each other in it I have no conception, nor can I now remember the aims and objects of the mystic club called "Mr. Paido." One of the rites consisted in walking in the garden with bare feet, which, after all, was an adventure in itself.

The great excitement of this summer holiday, after which I was to go to Marlborough, was an expedition to Switzerland. All that any of us knew about Switzerland was a remarkable picture that hung in the nursery in which rows of dazzling summits crowned cerulean lakes. Above that panoramic view, in which the Jungfrau and Mont Blanc somehow appeared together, were little vignettes, one of a Swiss châlet, one of the Staubbach, one of the castle at Chillon. We journeyed viâ Southampton and Havre, five children, Beth, my father and mother, and sat upright in a second-class carriage all the way from Paris to Berne, by what route I have no idea. Our objective was a village called Gimmelwald, a few miles from Murren, and we spent a day and a night at Berne, and from Berne, on the terrace in front of the church, I had my first glimpse of snow mountains. Perhaps because I had been sitting bolt upright all night, perhaps because I had thought that the brilliant blues and dazzling whites of the pictures in the nursery would be collectively unveiled on an enormous scale, I was more disappointed than words can fairly convey. Low on the horizon were a few greyish jagged hills beset with streamers of mist, and that was all. Nellie drew a long breath and said, "Oh, isn't it wonderful!" and I labelled her the most consummate hypocrite.

Next morning we started again, and came out on the lake of Thun, the shores of which we traversed in some sort of train like an omnibus, with an open top, and in due proportion to the bitterness of the disappointment at Berne came that day's rapture. We passed below the Niesen, which wore a snow-cap, and my mother told us that the Niesen was nothing particular. Summits gleamed from the other side of the lake, and they were nothing particular; but oh! for the lake itself, while we awaited other incredible developments. It was bluer than the picture in the nursery, and it was trimmed with a translucent bottle-green that showed the shallow water, and sharp as the edge of a riband laid against it came that deep clear blue. From Interlaken we proceeded in carriages, between meadows tall with gentians, and over them there skimmed Apollo butterflies with orange spots on each under-wing, and Camberwell Beauties no less (foreign variety, with a yellow instead of a white border to their wings). And then we turned a corner (I was on the front seat), and Nellie opposite said, "Oh!" and I thought she had been a hypocrite again and didn't look round, because I was observing a pale clouded yellow. And then she said, "Oh, look!" and I was kind enough to forgive her her hypocrisies and look, and there, straight in front, was the Jungfrau, and the holy maiden was unveiled white and tall above her skirt of dark pine woods, and my heart went out to the snow mountains, and has never yet come back. Much did I suffer at their lovely hands during the next ten years, for that same Jungfrau treated me to an excruciating climb of many hours through soft snow; and the Matterhorn kept his worshipper interminably standing with one foot planted on exiguous icy steps as each was hewn out by the leading guide and the fragments went clinking down the precipice; and the Rothorn (Zienal) gave me a very awkward moment on the edge of a *bergschrund;* and the Piz Palu came within an ace of causing Hugh to die of syncope owing to the icy wind with which she enwrapped her arête, and the Matterhorn for the second time threw a large quantity of boulders at me because I inconspicuously crossed her eastern face on my way towards the Théodul Pass; and the Dent Blanche directed so damnable a blizzard at me that I could not make her further acquaintance. But, as David said, "though all these things were done against me," yet has my heart never returned to me from the keeping of the great mountains, nor yet from the keeping of the sea which I first saw at Skegness, and if I could choose the manner of my death it would be that I should, above some eminent ice-wall, fall asleep in the immaculate purity of starlit frost, or sink in the sea-caves round about the island of Capri, and, as I sank, see from far below the glitter of the southern sun above me in the clear dusk of deep waters. . . . If God pleases, I will be frozen or drowned when the time comes for me to have done with this body of mine. I do not covet for its last moment a comfortable bed, and pyjamas, and a medicine bottle on the washstand. . . . Not that it matters; only I should like the other mode of passage.

We passed the Staubbach somewhere near Lauter-brunnen and came in the hour of sunset to the little inn at Gimmelwald. And then there was no more spirit left in me, for Eiger and Monck and Jungfrau and Ebneflu and Silberhorn were aflame with the salute of the evening. Maggie sat down to sketch, and was prodigal of rose-madder; but whereas she put rose-madder on to a draw-ing-block, it was the sun that dyed the snows. And we had bilberries and cream at dinner, and cows went home, swinging bronze bells as they cropped a wayside morsel; and there was a noise of falling torrents and a scent of pasturage, and the exitement of being "abroad" and the knowledge that the Jungfrau would be there in the morn-ing.

I wish I could estimate even in the roughest manner the amount of luggage which accompanied that month in Switzerland. My father had a heavy box of books and manuscript, for he was working, then as always, when he saw leisure ahead of him, on his *Life of St. Cyprian*, which he began at Wellington and completed only shortly before his death. Cyprian alone took up a large box, and, apart from that in the way of books, there must have been a great library. There were certainly half a dozen copies of Shakespeare, because of an evening after din-ner we read Shakespeare aloud, each taking a character; and there was a quantity of Dickens, which my mother read to us before dinner. Then each of us had some kind of a holiday task, except Arthur. Nellie had something about logic, and Maggie had her political economy, and I had a large Latin dictionary and a large Greek diction-ary to elucidate Virgil and the "Medea" of Euripides, and Hugh had, at any rate, a Latin grammar and a volume called "Nuces," which means "nuts," and hard they were for him to crack. Everybody, individually, had a Bible and prayer-book and hymn-book, and I am sure there must have been some Sunday books as well. Then the materials for "collections" came along also: there were presses for each of us in which to receive and to dry the flowers we picked, and there were killing bottles for butterflies (not chloroform and oxalic acid any more) containing cyanide of potassium, which killed after you had screwed the lid on, and when you took it off next morning, they were all dead bodies, like Sennacherib's hosts; and setting boards for the laying out of the slain, and large cork-lined boxes for their exhibition, and packets of pins for their impalement, and many butterfly nets for their original capture. Then there were packs of cards for diversion, and my mother had a great medi- cine-chest in case of illness. There were cool clothes for all of us in the blaze of the Alpine day, and warm clothes for the chill of the Alpine evenings; and each of us had a paint-box and a "Winsor and Newton" block, and Beth never moved without rolls of flannel and mustard plasters and cylinders of cotton-wool. Each one of us had an alpen-stock and huge hob-nailed boots, and when you consider that there were eight persons, each marvellously equipped for mental, physical, and artistic enterprises, you must only wonder that some mode of conveyance, if not all, was not fit to bear the strain of this transportation. But arrive at Gimmelwald we did, and while Maggie was prodigal with rose-madder this train of equipment somehow got inside the inn. Beth swooped on her flannel and her mustard plasters, my father established his Cyprian library in our sitting-room, my mother clutched her medicine-chest, and there was left an enormous pile of books, apparatus for botany,

climbing, and entomology, which remained in a passage
and was gradually broken up between its owners. I think
that the last pressing-case for dried flowers, the last kill-
ing-bottle for the extinction of butterflies, can hardly have
been clawed from that common heap before it was time
to pack it all up again.

Of that month certain indelibly vivid impressions remain. One was the ascent of the Schilthorn, popularly
supposed to be 10,000 (ten thousand) feet in height, and
to possess the witching attraction of owning "everlasting"
snow. It was not, unless it has abbreviated itself very
much since, anything near ten thousand feet high, and,
as for the everlasting snow, we climbed through torrid
uplands and finished by a mild rocky ascent without ever
setting foot on any snow perishable or everlasting. True,
there were patches of it on the northern face, and perhaps those may be there still. But it was an enchanting
expedition, for we carried our alpen-stocks and the guide
had a rope round his shoulders, and we started at five
in the morning. My father had a guide-book with a
Schilthorn panorama, and we sat on the top and rejoiced
in the fact that we were ten thousand feet up in the
air and that small quantities of everlasting snow were
below us, and we followed his guiding finger as he pointed
out the jewels in the crown of mountains that surrounded
us. . . . We passed through Murren on the way down,
and there saw English people playing lawn-tennis on one
of the hotel courts, and never shall I forget my father's
upraised eyebrows and mouth of scorn as he said, "Fancy,
playing lawn-tennis in sight of the Jungfrau!"

But if there was some subtle profanity in playing lawn-
tennis in sight of the Jungfrau, I thought it much more
blasphemous to study "Medea" and the "Æneid" in the

same sacred presence. I had a considerable spell of these, because it had been discovered that, although I was going to Marlborough without a scholarship, there was yet another of those odious competitions which I could enter for after I had got there. I had fondly thought that after this trinity of failures I had thoroughly be-dunced myself and need make no more efforts, but it appeared that I was wholly mistaken, for next December there would be a chance of going in for Foundation Scholarships at my new school, and in that there would be less competition, for they were open only to sons of clergymen. So, after a few days' holiday, out came the Greek dictionary and the Latin dictionary and the "Medea" and the "Æneid," and I had a couple of hours every morning under my father's tuition. I think he was very strict with me, for he still believed in the existence of my brains, and was determined that I should use them. But it is impossible to get good results from a small boy unless somehow interest is kindled, and there was often despair on the part of the teacher and resentful gloom on the part of the taught. Things came to a climax on one particular wet morning, when we were all seated in the sitting-room, Nellie with her logic, and Maggie with her political economy, and Hugh going swimmingly with his "nuces" under my mother's instructions. One by one they all finished their tasks, and there was I left with a chorus in the "Medea" which I could not translate at all, getting more muddled and hopeless every minute, and making fresh mistakes as we went over it again, and my father getting exasperated with my stupidity. Stupid I was, but my chief ailment that morning was that I was frightened and addled and dazed with his displeasure. Right up till lunch time was I kept at my task that day,

and in the afternoon there was a walk in the rain, and I
got into some further disgrace for hitting Hugh with my
umbrella in mere retaliation. I was "done to a turn" by
this time, and I think my mother must have pointed that
out, for next morning, anyhow, instead of that just and
terrible thunder-cloud, when I brought up the weary
chorus again for retranslation, my father was enchant-
ingly encouraging, and slipped in little corrections when
I made mistakes, as if I had corrected myself. There was
no allusion to yesterday's trouble, and under his approv
my wits rallied themselves, and at the end he shut up the
book with a delicious smile and told me that it was the
best lesson I had ever brought him. . . .

CHAPTER VII

THE WIDENING HORIZONS

MY father took me in person to Marlborough. I did not much relish that, since I thought, with private school ideas still hanging about me, that it would be a handicap to be known as the son of a man who wore black cloth gaiters, an apron, and a hat with strings at the side. That was all very well in Cornwall, where he was bishop, but here I should have preferred a parent who looked like other parents. He seemed to have no consciousness of being unusually dressed himself, and one incident in the few hours he stayed much impressed itself on me, for he came with me into some class-room or other where a lot of boys were sitting, talking and whistling, with their caps on. My father took off his hat when he entered (which again I thought showed a slight want of knowledge), and then, to my surprise, every boy in the place did the same. The whistling ceased, nobody laughed, and I went out again rather proud of him. He seemed to have done the right thing. . . .

Outside the College buildings there were two or three small boarding-houses and three large ones containing forty to fifty boys each, into one of which I should have gone if I had got the famous "House Scholarship." As it was, I was put into B House, a square brick building of three stories, each of which constituted an in-college house. The edifice itself was like a penitentiary:

a big open space from the skylight to the basement occupied the centre of it, with two class-rooms and a boot-room in the basement. Round this open space ran three floors of stone passages, connected by stone stairs; these passages were lit by arches opening on to the central space, and defended from it by tall iron bars; and out of these three tiers of passages opened four dormitories on each floor, a class-room, one bathroom with three baths, a sitting and bedroom belonging to the house-master of each house, with corresponding accommodation for a second house-master at the opposite corner, and a study next to the bathroom for the head of the house. Ten to fifteen boys slept in each of these dormitories, which were lit by day from three or four small windows, and for purposes of going to bed and getting up in the dark from one small gas-jet. Down the centre of each dormitory stood a board punctuated with basins, one for each boy, and furnished with a corresponding number of crockery mugs to hold water for tooth-washing. A narrow shelf ran round the room above the beds, where brushes and combs were kept. There was a chest of drawers underneath the gas-jet belonging to the prefect of the dormitory, and he had a chair by his bedside where he could put his clothes. As half the beds were directly below the windows, the occupants naturally objected to having their immediate windows open during inclemencies, so on cold or rainy nights they were all shut. There were no partitions between the beds; all operations were conducted in wholesome publicity, and there was no objection to anybody saying his prayers. Each dormitory was known by a letter of the alphabet; the houses were called B 1, B 2, B 3, and every boy had his school number. Thus my dry description was Benson, E. F., 234, B 1, L.

The day was a strenuous one. A clanging bell per-ambulating the passages murdered sleep at half-past six, and there was chapel at seven. If you chose to get up at half-past six, you had time for a cup of water-cocoa on the ground floor and for a bath. Usually you got up on the first sound of chapel-bell at 6:50, and, cocoa-less and with bootlaces flying, sped down the stairs and across the court to get within the gates outside chapel before a single fateful stroke of the bell announced that you were late. By the gate were stationed two masters who on the stroke put their arms across the entrance and prevented further ingress. If there were many boys outside at that critical moment they used to charge the masters and get in some-how, bearing down all opposition, and it was delightful on such occasions to be safely and legitimately inside and see a sort of football scrimmage going on. Usually, how-ever, there would only be a few stragglers, who attempted no violence. Punishments for being late varied: on the first occasion there was no penalty, but if you persevered in tardiness, the penalties became unpleasantly heavy. But if you were late, you could at least do up your boot-laces and get a cup of cocoa.

There was a lesson from about a quarter-past seven on the conclusion of chapel till a quarter-past eight. A wholly insufficient breakfast was then provided, consist-ing of tea ready mixed out of a tin can, a circular inch of butter, and bread; on certain mornings there was por-ridge. If you wanted anything beyond this fare, you had to buy it yourself at school-shop. But you took your pri-vate milk-jug in to breakfast and were given, I suppose, about a quarter of a pint of milk, which you kept for a purpose. During the morning there were two hours' school and one hour's preparation and an hour and a half leisure. There was meat and pudding for dinner at half-past one, and thereafter the total provender provided was another inch of butter, with tea and bread, at six, and supper consisting of hard biscuits, a piece of cheese, and a glass of beer after evening chapel, about 8.45. I had an allowance, originally, of sixpence a week, which was soon increased to a shilling; and, quite rightly, the whole of that used to be spent in getting things to eat. These were consumed at that daily love-feast called "brewing," which was a joyful affair and merits its own paragraph.

"Brewing" was a social function; you brewed in your class-room with your friend, for everybody had a friend of some kind, and nobody brewed alone. This function took place at varying hours in the afternoon, as dictated by the hours of school, and rendered unnecessary the scanty affair called "tea" provided by the college commissariat. In fact, as a rule, nobody went into college tea at all, so bloated was he with liquid when poor, and with liquid mixed with cake when rich. Brewing had never anything to do with beer, for in winter you brewed tea or coffee, and in summer lemonade in large earthenware bowls, with straws or india-rubber pipes to drink it from. The tea itself you certainly brought from home (and when that was used up Beth would send me some more), sometimes you had sugar, and sometimes you hadn't, and the milk was provided, as aforesaid, by the college commissariat, and thus the whole of your money could be devoted to cake. And there we sat each fellow by his friend, when football was over, with kettles interminably filled at the college pump, and put to boil on public gas-stoves, jealously watched in turn by you or your friend, and the fresh kettle-full of water was poured on the tea-leaves, and the last crumb of cake was devoured, and the last drop of milk was coaxed out of the jug, and you enjoyed the full fellowship of not quite enough to eat, scrupulously divided, and the romance of being fourteen or fifteen thickened and fructified. You quarrelled and made it up, and indeed there was very little quarrelling, and you looked round the class-room, and intrigued and wondered and loved, and spliced a broken squash-racket, and uncurled the interminable folds of felt of a burst fives-ball, down to the heart of cork that lay in the centre of it, and made fresh plans. Then if you were very prudent you washed out the teapot and the cups and saucers, and especially the milk-jug, because if you didn't, it stank appallingly next morning, and in the morning you could not get any hot water. Cold water was of no use with a milk-jug: it had to be rinsed with hot water, unless you wanted to find dreadful curds when, next day, the fresh milk was poured into it. Bloated with tea you went to chapel again, and didn't want any beer or cheese, and wished it was brewing-time again. Then there was an hour's preparation in the house class-room, and if you had not had a bath in the morning very likely you had one at night, and the other boys drifted into your dormitory where already you lay warm and sleepy in bed, and perhaps the head of the house gave you a piece of hot buttered toast, as he came in, for pre-fects had the privilege of taking bread and butter away from hall, and you ate it sumptuously and wiped your greasy hands on the bedclothes. If there was a boy with the gift of narrative in the dormitory, he often told a story as soon as lights were put out (or rather the one gas-jet) until he or his hearers got sleepy, and the story faded into silence. A slippered footstep would be heard along the passage, and the house-master, candle in hand, made his round of the dormitories. . . .

In each dormitory there was a big boy, not in sixth form, who was captain of the dormitory, and a prefect in sixth form. On the character of these and the two or three other big fellows depended the character of their dormitory. Bullying, as far as I know, was non-existent; but in all other respects, they had far more power for good or ill in their hands than the whole staff of masters put together, for the house-master went his rounds soon after lights were put out, and it was pretty certain that he would not intrude again. Even if he should take it into his head to come out of his rooms a second time, his approach could be signalled by the boy who occupied the bed opposite the door, which was always left open; he would be told to "keep cavé," and stories or bolster-fights or any other irregularity could safely be committed, for the young Brangaene from the watch-tower of a bed would whisper, "cavé," and the white-robed had plenty of time to steal back to their nests from wherever they might be and be plunged in profound sleep before the master traversed the passage. Practically, then, there was no superior supervision; the elder boys and prefects of dormitories moulded the material committed to their charge as they chose, and certainly there was no secret detective-work or encouragement of talebearers on the part of the masters. The decency, the morality, the discipline that result from such a system, where these virtues are the result of public opinion, are of far more robust quality than if they are merely the forced product of the fear of detection. With the hideous ingenuity that is peculiarly characteristic of boys, it would have been perfectly easy to have evaded detection, if the knowledge that there was secret detective-work going on on the part of masters had challenged our wits and roused us to invention for the sake alone of "scoring off" masters. As it was, a well-behaved dormitory behaved well because it was "bad form" to behave otherwise, while a dormitory naturally ill-behaved, would have invented some system of sentries which would certainly have defeated all surprise night-attacks on the part of masters, and not, as Plato says, have "advanced one whit in virtue." Boys are far more ingenious than grown-up men, and the challenge on the part of the authorities implied by creeping about at strange hours of the night in slippers would certainly have been delightedly accepted. But there was no such challenge and well-conducted dormitories, by far the majority, grew, so to speak, on their own root, and were not grafted on to any stem that fed them with the sap of authority.

Meantime, the fatal foundation-scholarship examination, to be held in December, was approaching, and I awaited its advent with an unruffled consciousness of another failure imminent. To prepare for it, I had certain private tuition out of school hours, and by a much more oppressive piece of legislation, I was not allowed to have anything to do with music except in so far as it was musical to contribute a muscular treble to the choir in chapel. That deprivation I still deplore, for I had at that time an odd and quite untrained faculty for visualizing, by some interior process, tunes that I heard, and being able to "see" them, so to speak, without any direct exercise of will. Thus, a term or two later, when an accompanist failed, I took his place at some sing-song, and transposed at sight Handel's "Where'er you walk," which I did not previously know, from the key of B flat into G, without any sense of effort, thanks to this little "kink" of internal visualization. Whatever that kink was, it was not the result of training, but, I suppose, some small natural aptitude towards the science of sound which now I dearly wish that I had been allowed to water and cultivate without break. It must have been a feeble and under-vitalized growth, for when I was at liberty again to waste as much time as I chose at the piano, it was certainly less vigorous than it had been, and never afterwards recovered, when I could stray and strum as I pleased in melodious pastures. The soil in which it grew was there, for all my life music has been to me as a celestial light, shining in dark places for the mitigation of their blackness, and flooding the serene and sunlit with its especial gold, but from that soil there withered a little herb that once grew there, a nest with incubated eggs was despoiled, and the bird came not back. But I expect that the wisdom of the edict was fully justified in the judgment of the prohibitionists, when on one snowy morning in December the list of the winners of foundation-scholarships was promulgated, and there was my name incredibly among them at a decent altitude.

By one of Nature's most admirable devices our memories always retain a keener sense of such experiences as have been enjoyable, than those of the drabber sort, and to-day I find nothing that I can pick out of the bran-pie that was not bright and alluring. There were friendships and hero-worships, the initiation, in a blue and black striped jersey, into the muddy mysteries of Rugby football, and the dizzy heights (soaring far above the sordid business of the foundation-scholarship) of playing in the lower team of the house. There was a school concert at the end of that first term, and it gave me a complacent thrill to remember that I was a foundation-scholar when the "Carmen" was sung. But it gave me a sense of stupefied astonishment to hear the organist, Mr. Bambridge, play as an encore to his piano-solo, his own original variations on the theme of "Auld Lang Syne." Never (except in the case of Miss Wirtz) was there such a finger, and speaking purely from the impression then made, I should be obliged to confess that for matter of pure brilliance of execution and mastery of technique, Mr. Bambridge must have been a far more accomplished performer than any pianist whom I have heard since. Why did he not take London by storm with those amazing pyrotechnics of his own invention, and throne himself higher than ever Paderewski or Carreno or Busoni soared? I cannot even now bring myself to believe that any of those lesser lights ever shone like Mr. Bambridge, when with flying fingers and any quantity of the loud pedal he swooped up and down in pearly runs and tremendous octaves, while all the time that powerful thumb of his, relentless and regular as the stroke of a piston, beat out simultaneously (there was the wonder of it) the original air. I wanted the piano to comprise an extra octave or two that so he might have a larger arena for his melodious magic. I wanted to have more ears, so that they should all be glutted with the beautiful banging and netted in the gossamer of Mr. Bambridge's chromatic scales. Even Bach—but it is always idle to make comparisons between the supreme: who judges between the various peaks that face the dawn, or cares to plumb the sea, so long as the sun glitters on its surface, and in the shadow of the rock there glows the translucent blue of Tyre? . . .

Straight from that concert I made my honourable return to Truro, and found that my spurs were won, and

with a light heart played Pirates again, and under the
short reign of Byron's supremacy (for we had been learning "Childe Harold" by heart in the English repetition
lesson) deluged the chaste pages of the *Saturday Magazine* with amorous innocence. Soon, too, the butterfly
collection began to assume the virile toga, for though
music was forbidden as a study, natural history, as encouraged at Marlborough by the society known as the
"Bug and Beetle," was a legitimate pursuit, and my father
strongly approved of my entering for the "Staunton
Prize," awarded to the best collection of butterflies and
moths, to be made that spring and summer, and to be
adjudged in the autumn. In the warm early-maturing
spring of Cornwall, the downs and lanes were lively with
lepidoptera at Easter, and those second holidays, passing
in a whirl of butterfly nets and a corking and uncorking
of killing-bottles, were a sort of canonization of the collections. Brimstones and garden whites, and holly blues
and small tortoiseshells took on a more serious aspect,
and the pins that eventually fixed them in cork-lined
boxes were indeed as nails driven in by masters of as-
semblies. The collection must be a strictly personal one:
I had to catch the victims myself, and kill and set them,
but Maggie, even more wildly enthusiastic than me,
might, without a violation of conscientious scruples, in-
dicate a yellow-tip enjoying the sunshine, or among nib-
bled leaves discover a geometer caterpillar turning itself
into a measuring-rod.

Cricket, therefore, on the return for the summer half
took a subordinate place, and obtaining "leave off" from
it as a compulsory game, I spent the long summer afternoons in the enchantment of Savernake Forest. Here it
was that the Staunton Collection began to lay more preg-

nant eggs in a receptive soil, for I trace to those sunny hours the betrothal of my soul to the goddess of trees and solitary places, to whose allegiance I have ever been faithful. Net in hand, and bulging with nests of chip-boxes I used to climb the steep down fringed with the secular beeches that form the outer wall of that superb woodland, pausing perhaps for a "blue" or a "small copper" on the way, but eager for entry into the temple of trees. Here underneath those living towers, the earth would be bare, but from the coverts where the sunlight fell only in flakes and shower-drops of gold, you passed into open glades of bracken and bramble, through which ran smooth grass-walks of short downland turf. In these sunny lakes of forest-enfolded open, a few hawthorns stood like snowy and sweet-smelling islands, and along the edges of the grass-rides hovered the speckled fritillaries. Then came a group of hazel trees to be beaten, with net spread beneath to catch the dropping caterpillars, and grey-trunked oaks, whose bark was to be diligently searched for slumbering dagger-moths, difficult to find owing to their protective colouring. Red-spotted burnets clung to thistle-heads, green hair-streaks (especially in Rabley Copse) must be put up from their resting-places before they were visible, and there too marble whites rustled their chequered wings in my net. Deeper and deeper into the forest would I go, and though I had every conscious faculty alert for pursuits and captures, yet all the time—and this is precisely why I have lingered with such prolixity over the Staunton Prize—the honey-bees of my subconscious self were swarming in with their imperishable gleanings. Cell after cell they constructed within me, and filled them with the essences that they culled from beech and fern and all the presences that subtly haunted the great forest aisles. There first did I hear the music of Pan's flute with the inward ear, and with the inward eye did I see the dancing satyrs, and the dryads of the woods; and if, as most surely I believe, my disembodied spirit shall some day visit the places where I learned to love the beauty of this peerless world, how swiftly will it traverse the thyme-tufted downs of Wiltshire to breathe again the noble and august serenity of the forest, and see the fritillaries poise on the bracken at the edge of the grass-rides.

The Staunton Prize (with how much more derived from those excursions!) fluttered pleasantly into my butterfly net, and with the flaming of the autumn leaves, and the hibernation of my quarry, another interest, that of athleticism, asserted its supremacy over its eager subject. Much has been written by many wise men as to this robust autocracy in schools, deploring its paramount sway, and suggesting nobler ideals than muscular swiftness and accuracy of eye for youth's pursuing, but what, when all is said and done, can be proposed as a substitute while the nature of the average boy remains what it is? Love of learning, intellectual ambitions at that age are natural but to the few, and while we all respect the youth who at the age of fifteen is really more attracted by history or philosophy than by fives and football, who can believe that there would be any great gain to the nation at large if every schoolboy was like him? It is frankly unthinkable that the average boy should choose as his heroes those members of the sixth form who have a tremendous aptitude for Iambics, or applaud, with the fanatic enthusiasm with which he hails a fine run down the football field, the intellectual athlete who this morning showed up so stunning a piece of Ciceronian prose.

Full opportunity in school hours and in voluntary study is given to the few who, from physical disability or mental precocity, actually prefer intellectual pursuits to athletics, but the English fifteen-year-old is naturally a Philistine, and Philistia had much better be glad of him. For as a rule he is not a prig, and while he cannot quite understand how anyone should prefer reading to playing games, he does not despise the student, but generally refers to him with a certain vague respect as being "jolly clever." But if it was possible to implant firmly in the soil of schools the intellectual banner, and to succeed in making the whole body of boys rally enthusiastically round it, it is difficult to repress a shudder at the thought of what that school would be like. Germany, perhaps, alone among the modern nations has succeeded in imbuing its youth with a passion for learning and discipline, and it would appear, now that we have been able to appreciate German mentality, that this triumphant achievement has been won at an appalling cost; at the cost, that is, of precisely those virtues which games, generally speaking, are productive of. And in the long run, and on the large scale that type seems to come to a bad maturity.

It is right then that for small boys games no less than work should be compulsory, for if work produces the man of letters, the man of science, the artist, the educated individual who can take his place in a progressive nation, not less do games produce a certain general hardihood, a sense of fair play, lacking which we should fare badly as a nation. To most boys with growing limbs and swelling sinews, physical activity is a natural instinct, and there is no need to drive them into the football field or the fives court: they go there because they like it, and there is no need to make games compulsory for them. But it is for those who, whether from a lazy habit of body or from a precociously active habit of mind, do not naturally gravitate to those pleasant arenas, that this compulsion is necessary, and to make them, for the sake of their health, go for a walk instead, does not produce at all the desired effect. They can go for any number of pleasant walks when they are fifty: at fifteen (given they have not got some corporal disability) it is far better for them to run and to kick and to hit and to sweat. Not their bodies alone partake in these benefits: their minds learn control of all kinds; they must keep their tempers, they must remain cool in hot corners (such as they will assuredly experience in their offices in later life), they must maintain a certain suavity in the midst of violence; and it is just this discipline here roughly summed up that gives games their value. Presently, when the studious are a year or two older, they will have attained to scholastic altitudes where athletic compulsion is no longer put upon them, and then they can please themselves. By that time, too, the normal young Philistine will have awoke to the importance of other things than games, and, unless he is a sheer impenetrable dunce, have come to regard the studious with far more sincere respect. But for both, this year or two of compulsion is wholly beneficial. As for the supposed inflexibility of this athletic autocracy, it is founded on a complete misapprehension: it should with far more accuracy be described as a democracy, for its heroes and legislators are undoubtedly elected by the people, and until the nature of boys is subjected to some radical operation, so long will they continue (though with infinite indulgence for the "jolly clever") to make heroes after their own hearts.

That which above all gilded and glorified these delights, that which was the stem from which their green leaves drew nourishment, was friendship. All these were the foliage that was fed from that stem, though the sun and the clear windy air and the rain fortified and refreshed them and swelled the buds that expanded into flowers. For what man is there, surrounded though he be with the love of wife and children, who does not retain a memory of the romantic affection of boys for each other? Having felt it, he could scarcely have forgotten it, and if he never felt it he missed one of the most golden of the prizes of youth, unrecapturable in mature life. In many ways boys are a sex quite apart from male or female: though they take on much of what they are and of what they learn, strengthened and expanded, into manhood, they leave behind, given that they grow into normal and healthy beings, a certain emotional affection towards the coevals of their own sex which is natural to public-school boyhood, even as it is, though perhaps less robustly, to girlhood. For twelve or thirteen weeks three times a year they live exclusively among boys, and that at a time when their vigour is at its strongest, and it would demand of them a fish-like inhumanity, if they were asked to let their friendships alone have no share of the tremendous high colours in which their lives are dipped. Naturally there is danger about it (for what emotion worth having is not encompassed by perils?) and this strong beat of affection may easily explode into fragments of mere sensuality, be dissipated in mere "smut" and from being a banner in the clean wind be trampled into mud. But promiscuous immorality was, as far as I am aware, quite foreign to the school, though we flamed into a hundred hot bonfires of these friendships, which were discussed with a freedom that would seem appalling, if you forgot that you were dealing with boys and not with men. Blaze after blaze illumined our excited lives, for without being one whit less genuine while they lasted, there was no very permanent quality about these friendships. Your friend or you might get swept into another orbit; diversity of tastes, promotion in school, conflicting interests might sever you, and in all friendliness you passed on, with eyes eager to give or to receive some new shy signal which heralded the approach of another of these genial passions. For me the sentimentality that coloured the choir-boy affair, or that not less misbegotten case of Mrs. Carter had quite faded from my emotional palette, which now was spread with hues far more robust and healthy. My signals were all made for the strong and the masculine, and I quite put out my lights and showed a stony blackness to flutterings from one of mincing walk or elegant gestures or a conjectured softness of disposition. I loved the children of the sun, and the friends of rain and wind, who were swift in the three-quarter line, and played squash with me in the snow; but still, by some strange law of attraction, too regular for coincidence, they were most of them musical, and once more, though now without sentimentality, chapel services, as in the case of the choir-boy and Lincoln Cathedral, were entwined with my volatile but violent affections. One such friend sang tenor and I intrigued my corn-crake way back into the choir in order to sit next him: another led the trebles. He must have been quite two years younger than myself, which is a gulf wider than two decades in mature life. But we bridged it with a structure that carried us safely to each other; there was music in that bridge, and there was the wonder in young eyes of the fact that you had found (and so had he) a passionate pilgrim, voyaging through fives-courts and glades of Savernake, because of whom those external phenomena shone with a new brightness, so that now the sweep of the forest, and the fives-courts, and the mire in the football fields, and the inadequate bound-ing of balls in an open squash court, owing to the snow that lay soddenly melting, grew into scenes and settings for the jewels of human companionships and boyish af-fections.

Intellectual kinship, community of tastes had very little part in those friendships: they were founded on a subtle instinct, and they were born of a blind mutual choice. Often your tentative scouting was quite still-born: you would hope for a friendship, and perhaps he would have no signals for you, but wait wide-eyed and expectant, for somebody quite different. Or again you could have a "culte" (to adopt an odious phraseology for which, in English, there happens to be no equivalent) for someone, who in the sundered worlds of modern and classic schools, might be miles away, and then with a sudden and wondrous reward, the idol would give some such signal of glance (that would be a direct method) or more indirectly, he would say something to his compan-ion as he happened to pass you in the court, which you knew was really meant for you, and on your next meet-ing you would perhaps get a glance, which was at least an enquiry as to whether you were disposed towards friendship. And then as you waited in the clear dusk of some summer evening for the sounding of the boring chapel-bell, you would sit down on one of the seats round the lime-trees in the court outside, and he would stroll by, still linked by an arm to some other friend, and you rather dolefully wondered whether, after all, there was to be anything doing. The two would be lost in the crowd beginning to collect round the chapel gate, and then perhaps the figure for which you were watching would detach itself, alone now, from the others, and with an elaborate unconsciousness of your presence he would stroll to the seat where you waited, and with the implacable shyness that always ushered in these affairs still take no notice of you. As he sat down it may be that a book dropped from under his arm, and you picked it up for him, and he said, "Oh thanks! Hullo, is that you?" knowing perfectly well that it was, and you would say, "Hullo!" . . . So after each had said, "Hullo," one said, "There's about three minutes yet before stroke, isn't there?" and the other replied, "About that," and then taking the plunge said:

"I say, I've got a squash court to-morrow at twelve. Will you have a game?" and the answer, if things were going well would be, "O ripping; thanks awfully!"

Then a precious minute would go by in silence and it was time to get up and go into chapel, with a new joy of life swimming into your ken. Never did Cortez stare at the Pacific with a wilder surmise than that with which he and you looked at each other as together you passed out of the dusk into the brightly lit ante-chapel, thinking of that game of squash to-morrow, which perhaps was to lay the foundation-stone of the temple of a new friendship. There would be time enough after that for a dip at the bathing-place, and a breathless race not to be late for hall. . . .

The ardent affair, if the squash and the bath had been satisfactory, blazed after that like a prairie fire, and the two became inseparable for a term, or if not that for a few weeks. But to suppose that this ardency was sensual is to miss the point of it and lose the value of it altogether. That the base of the attraction was largely physical is no doubt true, for it was founded primarily on appearance, but there is a vast difference between the breezy open-air quality of these friendships and the dingy sensualism which sometimes is wrongly attributed to them. A grown-up man cannot conceivably recapture their quality, so as to experience it emotionally, but to confuse it with moral perversion, as the adult understand that, is merely to misunderstand it.

For a year I sat solid and unmovable in the form in which I had been placed when I came to Marlborough, and was then hoisted into the lower fifth, and began a rather swifter climbing of the scholastic ladder, because I came for the first time under a master who woke in me an intellectual interest in Greek and Latin. This was A. H. Beesly, who was by far the most gifted teacher I ever came under either at school or at the University. Not for me alone but for his whole form he made waters break out in the wilderness, and irrigated the sad story of Hecuba with the springs of human emotion. He had translated it himself into English blank verse, with a pro- logue that told how some Athenian slave, carried off to Rome to serve in the household, read to fellow-captives this song of Zion in his captivity. What the intrinsic merits of the translation were, I can form no idea, but of the effect of it on his form, as read by the author, I cherish the liveliest memory. For three or four Hecuba lessons we would get no reading, and then Beesly would turn round to the fire when we had stumbled through another thirty lines, and say, "Well now, you boys don't know what a fine thing it is. Let's see what we can make of

your last few lessons. I'll read you a translation: follow
it in your Greek. We'll begin at line 130." Then he
would read this sumptuous jewelled paraphrase, which
rendered in English blank verse the sense of the passages
we had droned and plodded through, and gave them the
dramatic significance which we all had missed when we
took the original in compulsory doses of Greek. For a
long time we never knew who was the author of this
English version, and then one day Beesly brought into
form a whole bale of copies, printed in sheets, unfolded
and uncut, and gave one to each of us. There was the
name on the title page, as translated by A. H. B., with
the heading, "The Trojan Queen's Revenge." Never in
bookshop or in second-hand bookstall have I seen a copy
of that work, and I rejoice in that for perhaps I might be
disillusioned as to its merits, if I had seen it subsequently.
Certainly "The Trojan Queen's Revenge" was printed,
but I suspect (and bury the suspicion) that it fell still-
born from the press, and that the author bought up the
unbound copies. As it is, it has for me the significance of
some equerry who introduced me to the presence of royal
Greece, making the Greeks from that day forth the
supreme interpreters of humanity. Under the influence
of "The Trojan Queen's Revenge" I passed through the
portals into the very throne-room of that House of Art,
so that to this day I must secretly always employ a certain Greek standard to whatever the world holds of
beauty. Greek gems, Greek statues, became for me the
gold standard, compared to which all else, though noble,
must be of baser stuff. There were to be many idle terms
yet before I cared one atom about the Greek language
intrinsically: as far as the literature went I only cared for
the spirit of it revealed in "The Trojan Queen's Re-

venge." And before I quitted that form we had pieces of *Œdipus Coloneus* brought to our notice, and once again Beesly read out some translation—I suppose of his own —of the great chorus.

"But if you want the spirit of it," he said, "listen to this. It's by a man called Swinburne, of whom you have probably never heard. Shut your books."

I can see him now: it was a chilly day in spring and he put his feet up on the side of the stove that warmed the classroom. He had closed his book too, and his blue merry eyes grew grave as he began:

> "When the hounds of spring are on winter's traces,
>   The mother of months in meadow and plain
>   Fills the hollows and windy place
>   With lisp of leaves and ripple of rain,
>   And the bright brown nightingale, amorous,
>   Is half assuaged for Itylum,
>   For the Thracian ships and the foreign faces,
>   The tongueless vigil and all the pain."

Beesly held the thirty boys under the spell of that magic: we were all quite ordinary youngsters of fifteen and sixteen, and lo, we were a harp in his hand and he thrummed us into melody. There was stir and trampling of feet outside, for the hour of school was over, and I remember well that he waited at the end of one stanza, and said, "Shall I finish it or would you like to go? Any boy who likes may go."

Nobody got up (it was not from fear of his disapproval), and he went on:

> "For winter's rains and ruins are over,
>   And all the season of snows and sins,
>   The day that severs lover from lover,

The light that loses, the night that wins.
And Time remembered is grief forgotten,
And frosts are slain and flowers begotten,
And in green underwood and cover
Blossom by blossom the spring begins."

He came to the end of the chorus and got up.

"You can all be ten minutes late next school," he said, "because I have kept you."

Just as I must always think of "The Trojan Queen's Revenge" as being among the masterpieces of blank verse in the English language, so I cannot believe that Beesly was not the finest racket-player who has ever served that fascinating little hard ball into the side-nick of the back-hand court. There was a new racket court just built in the corner of the cricket-field, and here at twelve o'clock on three mornings of the week, Beesly and another master played the two boys who would represent the school in the Public Schools racket competition at Easter. The court, anonymously presented to the school, was announced, when Beesly retired a few years later, to be his gift, and he provided practically all the balls used in these games. Hour after hour I used to watch these matches and began to play myself with the juniors. Beesly often looked on from the gallery, in order to detect new talent, and on one imperishable day, as we came out of the court he said to me, "You've got some notion of the game: mind you stick to it." If I had wanted any encouragement that would have determined me, and I began to think rackets and dream rackets and visualize nick-services and half-volley returns just above the line. Beesly kept a quiet eye on me, and after I had left his form, he would often ask me to walk up towards his house with him, if I was going that way, and would ask me to breakfast on

Sunday mornings, and what feasts of the gods were these! Perhaps there would be one of the school representatives there, and Beesly, when the sausages and the kidneys were done, would show us the racket cups he had won, or he would read us something or tend the flowers in his greenhouse. All this sounds trivial, but he never produced a trivial effect, and gradually he established over me a complete hold, morally and mentally, which was as far as I can judge entirely healthy and stimulating. If he had seen me often with someone whom he considered an undesirable companion he would fidget and grunt a little and pull his long whiskers, and then with a glance merry and shy and wholly disarming he said, "Now there are plenty of people it's good to see a little of, but not too much of." He would mention no name, but he never failed to convey the sense of his allusion. On the other hand if he thought I was devoting myself too much to games (and in especial rackets) he would say, "Nothing makes you enjoy a game of rackets so much as having done a couple of hours hard work first." Or if, having watched me playing, he thought I wasn't taking the game seriously enough, he would stroll away with me from the court, and à propos of nothing at all, he would casually remark, "Better do nothing than do a thing slackly. You'll find your games fall off, unless you play as hard as you can." . . . And then up at his house on one ecstatic morning when I was getting on for seventeen he suddenly said, "You'll be playing for the school next year if you take pains." Next moment he had a volume of Browning in his hand and said, "Browning now: ever read any Browning? I thought not. Listen to me for a couple of minutes," and he read "The Lost Leader." Once, I remember, I had been to his house in the evening, and he walked back with me across the cricket-field after night had fallen. The sky was clear and a myriad frosty stars burned there. For some little way Beesly walked in silence, then, in his low distinct voice he began:

"See how the floor of heaven
Is thick inlaid with patens of bright gold."

I insist on the apparent triviality and fragmentariness of all this, for it was just in these ways, not in heavy discourses or lectures on morality and studiousness and activity, that Beesly gained his ascendency over me. He was never a great talker, but these *obiter dicta* stamped themselves on my mind like some stroke of a steel die on malleable metal. He was never in the smallest degree demonstrative: he might have been speaking to a blank wall, except just for that glance, merry and intimate, which he occasionally showed me, but for all that I divined a strong affection, which I for my part returned in a glow of hero-worship. The very fact that he never asked for a confidence prompted me to tell him all that perplexed or interested me, in the sure knowledge that he would always throw light in some brief curt sentence. "Stupid thing to do," was one of his wise comments when I had told him of some row I had got into with my house master. "Go and apologize, and then don't think anything more about it." There was the root and kernel of the matter: down came that steel die, sharply impressing itself, whereas discursive and laboured advice would have merely been boring and unconvincing. Off I went, trusting implicitly in his wisdom, and finding it wholly justified.

And then, alas and alas, I wholly and utterly disappointed Beesly. I had, as he prophesied, attained to the dignity of playing for the school at rackets, and had yet another year before I left, and he made up his mind that I and my partner were going to win the challenge cup for Marlborough, where it had never yet been brought home. Certainly two terms before that final event we were an extremely promising pair, but after that we scarcely improved at all, and fell from one stagnation of staleness into another. Beesly took the wrong line about this, and in the Christmas holidays that year I went to stay with him at Torquay, in order to get more practice, whereas what I needed was less practice. Even then we made a close match in the semi-final or thereabouts with the pair who eventually won, and Beesly, who up till the last day, when he urged me to take a heroic dose of Hunyadi water, continued to cling to the idea that at last Marlborough would win, had all his hopes dashed to atoms. Well do I remember his waiting for me outside the court, when we came out; he could hardly speak, but he patted me on the shoulder and blurted out, "Well, I know you did your best: I know that," and walked quickly away. He wrote me that night the most charming letter, trying to console me who really cared far less than he did; for it was, I am perfectly convinced, the main ambition of his life that Marlborough should win this cup, and for a whole year he had believed that now at last we were going to, and that I was the chief of the instruments through whom that ambition was to be realized.

He combined his two passions for rackets and poetry, in some such way as Pindar, who wrote the most magnificent odes the world has ever read in honour of boys who won victories at Olympia, and it was this Pindaric affection which he felt for those on whom his hopes centred at Queen's. The affection I certainly returned, but woe for the manner in which I failed to fulfil the rest of the contract.

I suspect he was an unhappy man, and he was certainly a very lonely one, and his loneliness no doubt was accentuated to him by his shy reticence. He kept himself largely apart from other masters; to the best of my knowledge I never saw him speak to a woman, and all the time he was stewing in the affection which he was incapable of expressing. But he had, out and away, by far the most forcible and attractive personality of any tutor I came across either at school or the University: he was one of those reserved demi-gods whom a boy obeys, reverences, and loves for no ostensible reason.

CHAPTER VIII

LAMBETH AND ADDINGTON

WHILE I was still in my second year at Marlborough a thoroughly exciting and delightful thing happened at home, for my father was appointed Archbishop of Canterbury, and up trooped his pleased and approving family to take possession of Lambeth Palace and Addington Park with, so far as I was concerned, a feeling that he had done great credit to us. Delightful as Truro had been, we all welcomed the idea of these expanded grandeurs, and felt colossally capable of taking advantage of them to the utmost. How great a man my father had become was most pointedly brought home to me by the fact that, when he came down to Marlborough soon after his appointment for my confirmation, I could, then and there, measure the altitude of his pinnacle by the fact that there appeared on the school noticeboard next day an inscription to the effect that His Grace had asked that a whole holiday should be given to the school in honour of his visit. He had just asked for it, so it appeared, and in honour of his visit, it was granted. "Can't you be confirmed again?" was the gratifying comment of friends. "I say, do be confirmed again."

To me, personally, all the splendour and dignity of his office signified nothing: what concerned a boy in the orgy of his holidays, was the new sumptuousness of his surroundings.

Stupendous though my father had become, we knew but little of his work and of its national significance, and it was my mother who to us, far more than he, was exalted into the zenith. Often since has she told me how shy and inadequate she felt on entering London, as she now did for the first time, in such a position, but never can I conceive of her otherwise than as filling it with the supremest enjoyment, which, after all, is the first of a hostess's qualities. Her wisdom, her conversational brilliance, above all her intense love of people, just as such, nobly filled and fitted the new sphere. The management of the great house, with the added concern of the second house at Addington, appeared in her a natural and effortless instinct: she took the reins and cracked her whip, and the whole equipage bowled swift and smooth along the road. The stables were under her control as well; she arranged all the comings and goings of my father: out rolled his landau with its tall black high-stepping horses and gilded harness to take him to the House of Lords, and scarce had the great gates below Morton's tower clanged open for him, than Maggie and I set out on our horses for a ride round the Row, very stiff in top-hats, and riding habit and strapped trousers, and then round came my mother's victoria, and woe be to the carriage-cleaner if the japanned panels failed to reflect with the unwavering quality of glass. She would be going to pay a couple of calls and visit a dentist, and while she was there, the victoria would take Hugh and Nellie to the Zoo, and drop them with strict injunctions that in an hour precisely they were to pick her up at a fatal door in Old Burlington Street, and so proceed homewards to tea. Meanwhile the carriage that deposited my father at the House could take Arthur to some other rendezvous, and once at any rate, the hansom containing the Archbishop was prevented from entering the Lambeth Gate, because the Archbishop's carriage (containing Hugh and me) must be admitted first. Never were children so indulged in the matter of equine locomotion, for the riding horses clattered in and out, and Hugh returning from a straw-hatted visit to the Zoo must in three minutes hurl himself into the top-hatted and black-coated garb which in those days was current in the Row, in order to ride with my father on his return from the House. One of the five of us, at any rate, was kept on tap for a rather stately ride with him whenever during the busy day he found an hour to spare, and it was a pompous pleasure to see the traffic stopped at Hyde Park Corner, so that we might ride past saluting policemen through the arch. Physically I suppose we enjoyed our fraternal scampers more, but it could not help being great fun for a boy of fifteen to steer a rather fretful horse that went sideways across the street and behaved itself unseemly, while tall buses waited for his esteemed progress. After all, if you happened to be riding with your father, for whose passage in those days all traffic was stayed, you might as well enjoy it. . . .

All such arrangements, all such "fittings in" were a pure delight to my mother. She revelled in her dexterity, and revelled no less in the multitude of her engagements. She loved, after a busy day, to dine at some political house, and hear the talk of the hour, and follow that up with some party at the Foreign Office, for though she cared very little if at all about political questions themselves, she delighted in the froth and bustle and movement. She was great friends with Mr. Gladstone, though she cared not one atom about the Home Rule question, and he in turn had the greatest appreciation of her wit, her humour which would strike a spark out of the most humdrum of happenings: and I believe it is authentically told that when once at Hawarden there was discussion as to the identity of the cleverest woman in England, and someone suggested my mother as the fittest candidate for the post, he said in that impressive voice, reinforced with the pointed forefinger, "No, you're wrong: she's the cleverest woman in Europe." Quite unfatigued, she would be up and dressed in her very oldest clothes before seven next morning, and walk for a full hour before breakfast, since the rest of the day held for her no leisure for exercise. Never was there anyone so acutely observant as she, and at breakfast there would be some grotesque or comic side-show of the streets for narration. Parks and open places were of no use to her at all in those rambles; Lambeth Walk, or the humours of Covent Garden Market were her diversion, and refreshed by these humours she tackled her new and delightful day. Never by any chance did she go out to lunch, but never by any chance did we lunch *en famille;* guests were invariably there. Even more to her mind were her dinner-parties, in the selection and arrangement of which she took an infinity of rapturous trouble, and the bigger they were the more I think she enjoyed them. There was, of course, a great deal of clerical entertainment, but half a dozen times in the season she gave more secular dinner-parties of about thirty guests, when literature and science, and art and politics, and the great world magnificently assembled. And when the last guest had gone, a piece of invariable ritual was that she with any of us children who were at home, executed a wild war-dance all over the drawing-room in a sort of general jubilation. I remember Lord

Halsbury coming back unexpectedly to tell my mother some story which he had forgotten to mention, and finding us all at it.

But however full was the day, my mother seemed possessed of complete and unlimited leisure for talk with any of us who wanted her. I can remember no occasion on which she was too busy for a talk. Her letters could wait; anything could wait, and she would slew round from her writing-table, saying, "Hurrah! Oh, this is nice!" She would listen alert and eager to some infinitesimal problem, some critical observation, and say, "Now tell me exactly why you think that. I don't agree at all. Let's have it out." It seemed that nothing in the world interested her nearly as much as the point in question, and verily I believe that it was so. She projected her whole self on to it: she desired nothing so much, just then, as to put herself completely in your place, and realize, before she formed an opinion of her own, precisely what your opinion was. Then invariably the magic of her sympathy seized on any point with which she agreed, "Quite so: I see that, yes I feel that," she would say. "But how about this? Let me see if I can put it to you."

It was no wonder that the closeness of her special, particular relation to each of us was ever growing. The primary desire of her heart was to give love: when it was given her (and who ever had it in larger abundance?) she welcomed and revelled in it, but her business above all was to give. And her love was no soft indulgent thing: there was even an austerity in its intenseness, and it burned with that lambent quality, which was so characteristic of her. Never was anyone so like a flame as she: her light illuminated you, her ardour warmed and stimu-

lated. Withal, there was never anyone who less resembled
a saint, for she was much too human to be anything of
the kind; she had no atom of asceticism in her, and without being at all artistic she adored beauty.

Spiritual beauty came first, for she loved God more
than she loved any of His works, but how close to her
heart was intellectual beauty, things subtly and finely
observed, things humorously and delicately touched!
How, too, she hated spiritual ugliness, as expressed by
priggishness with regard to the Kingdom of Heaven, and
mental ugliness as expressed by conceit or narrowness, and
hardly less did she dislike physical ugliness.   Her tones
would rise from a calmness which she found quite impossible to maintain, into a *crescendo* of violent emphasis
and capital letters as she said something to the following
effect:

"Yes, I know: I'm sure he's a very good man, and
that's so trying, because he is such a prig, and always
does his duty, and, my dear, that awful mouth, and the
Beautiful sentiments that come out of it.   Besides he's
so Very, Very Plain!"

No one was ever more beset with human frailties.   She
was afraid of getting stout, and in her diary recorded
solemn vows that she would *not* eat more than two dishes
at dinner, nor take sugar.   Then came an entry, "Soup,
fish, pheasant and soufflé.   What a Pig I am!" . . .
Or again if she found herself in some difficulty, where a
precise statement of what had really occurred would make
things worse, she would say, "I shall have to be very
diplomatic about it," and a perfectly well justified chorus
went up from her irreverent family, "That means that
Ma's going to tell a lie about it."   With all her intense
spirituality, she had no use for conventional worship,

"His Grace"

Sep. 91

"HIS GRACE" (A DOMESTIC CARICATURE)

and I can hear her say, on an occasion when my father was out, "We won't have prayers to-night for a treat." Similarly she could never take any emotional interest (and I think gave up trying) in Synods and Pan-Anglican Conferences, and Bishops' meetings, though she knew that her tepidity about these things that concerned my father so intimately was a distress to him. But while he drove on his fervent way along the roads of organization, tradition, ritual and ecclesiastical practice, her religion was on quite other lines: prayer and meditation were the solitary methods of it, and in the world which she delighted in, love and sympathy. And whatever she sought for and gathered there, with all her own temptations and fallings and new resolves, she brought with humble confident hands and laid them at the feet of Christ.

Though the beauty of living and sentient beings—whether in the region of the soul, the mind or the body—made so irresistible an appeal to her, she never really cared for the beauty of plants or trees or skies or scenery. Just there a firm frontier-line was drawn round the territory of her real sympathies, and it accorded very fitly with her lack of touch with mere organizations. Just as she cared not two straws for the Pan-Anglican Conference, yet delighted in the human members of it, so, when standing in front of the west façade of, say Rheims Cathedral, or looking across from the Riffel Alp to the Matterhorn, her real attention would not be devoted to these silent sublimities, but much rather to a cat blinking in the sun, or a sparrow building in the eaves. Things must move or think or form opinions or commit voluntary actions to enchant her, and in the Swiss holidays which often followed the end of the London season, I doubt if she ever looked with eagerness or wonder at the Matterhorn, except on the day when she knew that one of her sons was somewhere near the summit in the early morning. On such another day her eye was glued with enthusiasm on the Rothhorn because two of us were making the ascent, but towards the Rothhorn in itself, or towards the waving of poplars, or the flame of a sunset, she never felt the emotional heart-leap. Thus, when August in Switzerland or elsewhere was over, the ensuing five months or so at Addington, with its delights for us of shooting and riding and all the genial thrill of country life, made no appeal to her. As far as they affected us, she threw herself into them, but at any moment, she would have chosen to be in the swim and the thick of things again, and have taken those early morning walks down the Lambeth Road with the interest of fishshops and costermongers to enlighten her, rather than walk under the flaming autumn beech trees, or see the frail white children of the spring beginning to prick through the thawing earth of January. There had to be a beating heart in that which enchained her; she could not bother about primroses. That may have been a limitation, but such limitation as that merely stored her force of sympathy and discernment towards the rest. She did not attempt to let it dribble out in exiguous channels, but conserved the whole vigour of it for the supply of the mansions where her treasure and her heart lay. In the country also, she was a far more defenceless victim against the one strong foe of her triumphal banners, and that foe was fear.

In real trouble, especially when the trouble was concerned with those she loved best, she walked boldly; no one faced the large sorrows and bereavements that fell to her destiny with a more courageous front. The magnitude called forth the faith which unwaveringly supported her, but when all seemed peaceful and prosperous, she was often a prey to acute imaginative apprehensions. She could not bear, for instance, to see us all start out riding together, and when the announcement came that the half-dozen of riding horses were at the front door, she went back to her room on the other side of the house. Certainly she had some slight basis for her feelings, for among those steeds there was a bad bucker and a rearer. None of the riders minded that in the slightest, and away went the cavalcade at a violent gallop up the long slope of turf in front of the house with "Braemar" in the shape of a comma, and "Quentin" playing the piano in the air with his forelegs, and "Ajax" kicking up behind, and "Peggy" going sideways, just because my father had mounted first and smacked "Columba" over the rump while the rest of us were betwixt and between the gravel and the saddle.   There were hurdles stuck up on the slope, and Braemer, shrilly squealing, bucked over the first and Ajax ran out, and Peggy trod solemnly on the top of one, and Quentin still hopping on his hind legs refused and was whacked, and my father went pounding on ahead as we rocketed after him.   He was not a good horseman, but he had no knowledge of fear, and, though he avoided the hurdles, he went tobogganing down the steep sides of Croham Hurst with Columba slipping and sliding on the pebbles and putting her foot into rabbit holes, while her rider with slack rein enjoyed it all enormously.   In the meantime my mother had dreadful visions of two or three of us being brought back on hurdles, and carried into the house.   But exactly at that point her essential courage knocked her nervousness on the head, for she would not at any price have had any one of us *not* go out riding.   Only, she didn't want to see the start.

It was this vague fear that was her enemy all her life, and it could pounce on any quarry. She did not really believe that the corpses of her children were soon to be brought back to her, any more than she really believed that when my father had a bad cold, it was speedily to develop into double pneumonia, but she was prey in imagination to these disastrous possibilities. Hardly ever did she suffer under them as regards herself; once only do I remember her conjuring up a personal spectre. On that occasion she got the idea that she was going to die before the end of the month, a prognostication which she unfortunately made public. Thereupon, as the days went by, some one of her children hurried from the tea-table every evening, and stood spectre-like in the corner of the room, and in a sepulchral voice said, "Nine days now": or "Eight days now," until the fatal and last evening of her prophetic intuition arrived. The "To-night" was received with roars of laughter, and she was in brilliant health and spirits next morning, when she ought to have been a corpse. She laughed at her fears herself (which is just the reason why I treat them humorously now) but, for all her laughter, they were year after year a miserable bugbear to her, mostly and mainly during the leisurely months at Addington. Oftenest they were quite vague, but couched to pounce on any excuse for definiteness: if my father had a cold she would evoke the image of pneumonia, if he was tired she would conjure up visions of a breakdown. She kept these groundless imaginings to herself, and no one could ever have guessed how often she was a victim to them, or how heavily they rode her. They did not, except quite occasionally, get between her and the sunlight, for she forced them into the shadow, caught them and shut them in cupboards, steadily and continually disowned them. And when any real trouble came they haunted her no more; she rose serene and faithful to any great occasion, welcoming it almost, as she had done with Martin's death, as a direct dealing from God, receiving it sacramentally.

I wonder if children ever ran so breathless a race in pursuit of manifold interests and enjoyments as did we in those years when our ages ranged from the early twenties to the early teens, and the Christmas holidays in particular, brought us together. One year, about 1884, a snowfall was succeeded by a week's frost, and that by another week of icy fog, and the foggy week I look back on as having given us the fullest scope of hazardous activity in hopeless circumstances, for shooting and riding were impossible. We made a toboggan-run which soon became unmitigated ice, down a steep hill in the park among Scotch firs that loomed dim and menacing through the mist. Half-way down the hill, just where the pace was swiftest, and the toboggan skidding most insanely, grew one of these firs close to the track, and on the other side was a bramble-bush. From the top you could not see this gut at all, and with eyes peering agonizedly through the thick air you waited for the appearance of this opening somewhere ahead. Sometimes you saw so late that the bramble-bush or the Scotch fir must inevitably receive you, and there was just time to slide off behind, be rolled on the hard glazed snow, and hear the plunge of the toboggan in the bramble-bush, or its crash against the Scotch fir. If you got through safely, a second and more open slope succeeded and you pursued your way across the path between the church and the house, and bumped into the kitchen-garden fence. Bruised and

unwearied we took the injured toboggans to the estate
carpenter, whose time at Christmas must have been chiefly
occupied with repairing these fractures, and played golf
over the nine holes which we had made along the slope
in front of the house, on the snow and in a fog. The
greens, which were about as large as tablecloths, had
been swept, and the boy who had the honour whacked his
ball in the conjectured direction, and ran like mad after
it. When he had found it, he shouted and his opponent
drove in the direction of his voice. If he sliced or pulled,
he too ran like mad in the conjectured direction; if he
drove straight his ball was probably marked by the first
driver. The thrillingest excitement was when, driving
first, you topped your ball or spouted it in the air, for
then you crouched as you heard the crack of the second
ball, which whizzed by you unseen. Football in the top
passage with bedroom doors for goals ushered in lunch
and after lunch we skated on dreadful skates called
"Acmes" or "Caledonians," which clipped themselves on
to the heels and soles of the boot, and came off and
slithered across the ice at the moment when you proposed
to execute a turn. Hugh despised my figure-skating (and
I'm sure I don't wonder) and christened himself a speed
skater. The pond was of no great extent and fringed on
one side by tall rhododendron thickets, into which he
crashed when unable to negotiate a corner.

The evening closing in early was the dawn of the intellectual labours of the day. *The Saturday Magazine*
made frequent appearances, burgeoning like Aaron's rod
into miraculous blossom of prose and poetry: between-
whiles Arthur composed voluntaries to be played on the
organ in the chapel at prayers, Nellie studied the violin,
Hugh produced a marionette theatre, and wrote a highly

original play for it, called *The Sandy Desert; or, Where
is the Archbishop?* and Maggie made oil pictures of her
family of Persian cats. Once at least during Christmas
holidays we all jointly wrote a play: it was *The Spiritual-
ist* one year, in which there was a slashing exposure of
mediums; another year we dramatized *The Rose and the
Ring* in operatic form with original lyrics set to popular
tunes. With the exception of Nellie, our voices were
singularly inefficient and completely untrained, which
was part of the fun of it. To these plays the neigh-
bourhood was invited, and all the servants and lodge-
keepers formed a solid mass at the back. At one of them,
Arthur for some reason, must be disguised as a young
woman, six feet two high, with a yard or so of trousers
showing below the skirt. This impersonation made a
kitchen-maid laugh so hysterically, that the play had to
pause while she was taken out by two housemaids, and her
yells died away as she retreated down the back-stairs.

Life in those holidays was an orgy, celebrated in an
atmosphere of absolutely ceaseless argument and discussion. Every question rose to boiling-point: for while
we regarded each other with strong and quite unsenti-
mental affection we were violently critical of each other.
We drew biting caricatures of my father going to sleep
after tea, of my mother keenly observant above and not
through her spectacles, of Hugh falling off Ajax, of any
ludicrous and humorous posture. But above all it was
writing that most enthralled us, and innumerable were
the quires of sermon-paper that yielded up their fair white
lives to our scribblings. These were now beginning to
enter a more professional arena than the *Saturday Magazine;* Nellie, then at Lady Margaret's Hall in Oxford,
had, before she was twenty, published an article on

Crabbe in *Temple Bar;* Arthur, a year or two older, had written his first book, *Arthur Hamilton*, in the form of an imaginary memoir, and Maggie and I were in the throes of a joint story, in which I can perceive the infancy of a novel called *Dodo*. This was abandoned before completion, but in a moraine of forgotten dustinesses, I came across some few pages of it the other day and really felt that there was some notion in it, some conscious attempt anyhow, to convey character by means of conversation rather than by analysis, an achievement in the direction of which, in spite of dispiriting results, I am still grubbing away. There certainly, in that heap of ancient manuscript fortuitously preserved, was the conscious striving after psychical dialogue, in which the interlocutors revealed themselves. Trivial as might be the personalities revealed, the idea of the excited authors was to avoid narrated analysis, and to convict and justify their characters out of their own mouths. There was a crisis of creativeness in the writing of it, for we firmly and designedly intended that a certain middle-aged lady, at whose feet everybody else fell flat in adoration of her tact and her sympathy and her comprehension, should "be" my mother. But, such is the waywardness of idealistic portraiture, we found, about Chapter VI, that though she was already supposedly installed on the throne of tact and comprehension, before which everybody else bowed the knee, she had not justified the part which we had cast for her, for she really had said little more than "I feel so deeply for you," or "Pass the mustard." We were determined that she should reveal her incomparable humanity by the sympathetic dialogues in which we engaged her, but she was so tactful that she never said anything at all that bore on the problems which were submitted to her. In the book to which I have alluded, she certainly appears as "Mrs. Vivian," who, as may faintly be remembered, is supposed to be possessed of super-human tact and insight, taking painful situations with calming and yet exhilarating effect. For the satisfaction of the curious, it may be stated that Mrs. Vivian was the one live model in the book and was completely unrecog-nisable. When first we enthusiastically scribbled at its earlier incarnation, my sister and I were at the ages of nineteen and seventeen, and for the very reason, namely, that we thought of my mother in our adoring limning of her, the presentment is not only unlike her, but unlike anybody at all.

We went to Addington for a few weeks at Easter, and the sojourn then was, according to my mother, of the nature of a picnic. As a matter of fact there was not really anything very picnicky about it; the drawing-room, it is true, was not used, but we managed with the ante-room, the Chinese room, the schoolroom, my father's study and her own room, by way of sitting-rooms, and perhaps part of the household remained at Lambeth. But to her vivid sense, to her delight of using all things to the utmost, this constituted a very informal way of life, for when she was running a house, everything must be, in its own scale, spick-and-span and complete. You might, for instance, dine on bread and cheese and a glass of beer, but the cheese must be the best cheese, the bread of the crispest, and the beer must be brimmed with froth. Short of completeness and perfection, whatever your scale was, you were roughing it, you were picnicking. She did not at all dislike picnicking, but It Was picnicking, and why not say so? For herself, with her passion for people (like Dr. Johnson she thought that one green field was like another green field, and would prefer a walk down Fleet Street) she would sooner have stopped in London, but my father needed this break in the six months of his busy London life. But to his volcanic energy and vitality, such a holiday was of the nature of a compulsion and a medicine rather than an enjoyment. In the long run he was refreshed by it, but the getting out of the shafts was always trying to him, and usually resulted in a fit of depression, such as I have described before. When he was very hard worked, he never suffered from this; it was when he was obliged to rest that these irritable glooms descended on him, and I particularly connect them, during these years, with the Easter holiday. All the time, as he once told me when talking of them, he would be struggling and agonizing to get his head out of those deep waters, but was unable to until the nervous reaction had spent itself, and the pendulum swung back again. By now we children had begun to understand that, and though this mood of his was a damper on mirth and generally an awful bore, we no longer feared him when he was like that but "carried on," very sorry for him, and sincerely hoping he would be better next day. The person who felt it most was undoubtedly my mother: he was miserable and she knew it, and knew the pathos of his futile strivings to get rid of it, and her picnic was a melancholy and anxious one till that cloud lifted. Often, however, she and my father went to Florence for Easter, where they stayed with Lady Crawford at the Villa Palmieri, and of all the holiday sojournings it was that which he enjoyed most keenly. He was absolutely indefatigable where churches or sacred art were concerned, because of the cause which had inspired painter and architect. To him the achievement for which the architect builded,

the sculptor chiselled, the musicians composed, and the
artist painted, must be the palpable and direct service
of God, and just as he would gaze in genuine rapture at
a second-rate Madonna, whereas a portrait or even a
Primavera would leave him cold, so, without any knowledge or appreciation of music he would listen to Handel's
Messiah, while a Wagner opera, or a symphony by
Beethoven, had he ever listened or heard such, would have
been meaningless to him. Of ecclesiastical architecture,
again, its periods or its characteristics, he had a profound
knowledge, but whether a house was Elizabethan or
Georgian was a matter of much smaller interest to him.
He did not truly care, to put it broadly, who built a
column and when and how, or painted a picture and when
and how, so long as those monuments of art were only
directed towards human and æsthetic enjoyment. The
natural works of God, the woods at Addington, the mountain ranges of Switzerland, he admiringly loved as being
in themselves direct divine expressions, but if the work
of man insinuated itself, he liked it in proportion as
it was religious in its aims.

One exception he made, and that was in favour of
Greek and Roman antiquities and the language of the
classics, and I am sure he enjoyed making a translation
of some English poem into Virgilian hexameters or
Sophoclean iambics fully as much as he enjoyed the original version. Latin and Greek, especially Greek, were to
him only a little below the Pentecostal tongues: of all
human achievements they were the noblest flowers. To
him a classical education was the only education: he rated
a boy's abilities largely by his power to translate and to
imitate classical lore, and to wander himself in these
fields was his chiefest intellectual recreation. He loved

to unpack, so to speak, some Greek word compounded with prepositions, and insist on the value of each, overloading the dissected members of it with meanings that never conceivably entered into the mind of its author, and his own style in weighed and deliberate composition was founded on the model of these interpretations; the sentences were overloaded with meanings beyond what the language could bear; he packed his phrases till they creaked. But highest of all in the beloved language, with a great gulf fixed below it and above the masterpieces of classical literature, came the New Testament, which he studied and interpreted to us as under a microscope. That eager reverence was like a lover's adoration: his interpretations might be fanciful, and such as he would never have made in any other commentings, but here his search for hidden meanings in simple phrases had just that quality of tender and exquisite scrutiny. The subject of this study was his life, and the smallest of its details must be searched out, and squeezed to yield a drop more of sacred essence. . . . On any other topic he would have criticized the Hellenistic Greek, as falling far below classical standards, but, as it was, he accepted it as verbally inspired, and no enquiry was too minute. Rather curiously, collations of differing texts did not engage him, nor did he touch on Higher Criticism. The text of his own Greek Testament was all that concerned him, there was the whole matter, and on to it he turned the full light of his intellect and his enthusiasm, without criticism but minutely and lovingly poring over it, as it actually and traditionally was.

From Monday morning until Saturday night these weeks at Addington, especially at Christmas, were to us a whirl of delightful activities from the moment that

chapel service and Bible lesson were over in the morning,
till evening service at ten o'clock at night. But Sunday
was a day set so much apart from the rest that it hardly
seemed to belong to Addington at all. There was early
communion in the chapel, unless it was celebrated after
the eleven o'clock service in church; morning service in
church was succeeded by lunch, lunch by a slow family
walk during which my father read George Herbert to us;
the walk was succeeded by a Bible reading with him, and
then came tea. After tea was evening service in church,
and after Sunday supper, he read the *Pilgrim's Progress*
aloud until we had compline in chapel. To fill up intervals we might read certain Sunday books, the more mature successors of Bishop Heber and *The Rocky Island*
and *Agathos*. No shoal of relaxation emerged from the
roaring devotional flood; if at meals the conversation became too secular, it was brought back into appropriate
channels; there was even a set of special graces before
and after meals to be used on Sunday, consisting of short
versicles and responses quite bewildering to any guest
staying in the house. No games of any sort or kind were
played, not even those which like lawn-tennis or golf
entailed no labour on the part of servants. However
fair a snow covered Fir Mount, no toboggan that day
made its perilous descent, and though the pond might be
spread with delectable ice no skates profaned its satin on
the Day of Rest. The Day of Rest in fact, owing chiefly
to this prohibition on reasonable relaxation, became a
day of pitiless fatigue. We hopped, like "ducks and
drakes," from one religious exercise to another, relent-
lessly propelled.

To my father, I make no doubt, with his intensely devotional mind, this strenuous Sunday was a time of re-

freshment. It is perfectly true that he often went to sleep in church, and if on very hot Sundays, the walk was abandoned, and we read aloud in turns from some saintly chronicle, under the big cedar on the lawn, not only he, but every member of the family, except the reader (we read in turn), went to sleep too. But he dozed off to the chronicle of St. Francis and came back to it again; nothing jarred. Thus ordered, Sunday was a perfect day for one of his temperament; no work was done on it, no week-day breeze ruffled its devotional stillness, but his appreciation of it postulated that all of us should share to the full in its spiritual benefits. He did not believe that for himself Sunday could be spent more profitably, and so we were all swept, regardless of its private effect on us, into the tide. What he did not allow for was that on other temperaments, that which so aptly fulfilled the desires of his own produced a totally different impression. That day, for us, was one of crushing boredom and unutterable fatigue. Certain humorous gleams occasionally relieved the darkness, as when the devil entered into me on one occasion when *Lives of the Saints* came to me by rotation, for reading aloud. There was the serene sunlight outside the shade of the cedar, positively gilding the tennis court, there was the croquet lawn starving for the crack of balls, and there too, underneath the cedar was my somnolent family, Hugh with swoony eyes, laden with sleep, Nellie and Maggie primly and decorously listening, their eyelids closed, like Miss Matty's, because they listened better so, and my father, for whom and by whom this treat was arranged, with head thrown back and mouth nakedly open. . . . And then came Satan, or at least Puck. . . . I read four lines of the page to which we had penetrated, then read a few sentences out of the page that had already been read. Deftly and silently, but keeping a prudent finger in the proper place, I turned over a hundred pages, and droned a paragraph about a perfectly different saint. Swiftly turning back I read some few lines out of the introduction to the whole volume, and then, sending prudence to the winds, found the end of the chapter on which we were engaged. I gave them a little more about St. Catherine of Siena, a little more from the introduction, then in case anyone happened to be awake read the concluding sentences of the chapter about St. Francis and stopped.

The cessation of voice caused Nellie to awake, and with an astounding hypocrisy, subsequently brought home to her, she exclaimed:

"Oh, how interesting!"

Her voice aroused my father. There we all were sitting under the cedar, reading about St. Francis. Hugh had awoke, Maggie had awoke: it was a peaceful devotional Sunday afternoon.

"Wonderful!" he said. "Is that the end, Fred?"

"Yes, that's all," said Fred.

Fred was also a passive actor in another Sunday humour. My father had noticed in me a certain restlessness at readings, some twitching of the limbs at a Bible lesson, or whatnot, and in order to confirm me in the right practice of the day, had looked out a book in his library about Sunday, which he recommended me to read, without having sufficiently ascertained the contents of it himself. Judge of my rapture when I found a perfectly convincing chapter, showing how the sad, joyless, unrelaxed English Sunday was purely an invention of Puritan times. My father had given me the book to convince me of the antique sanctity of the Addington use: the book told me that from the patristic times onwards, no such idea of Sunday as we religiously practised had ever entered into the heads of Christians, or had ever dawned on the world until the sourness of Puritans robbed the day of its traditional joy. It had been a day of *festa*, of relaxation from the tedious round of business, and all the faithful dressed themselves in their best clothes for fun, and village sports were held, and hospitality enlivened the drab week. Sure enough they went to church in the morning, and after that abandoned themselves to jollity. With suppressed giggles I flew to my mother's room to tell her the result of this investigation, and she steered a course so wonderful that not even then could I chart it. Her sympathetic amusement I knew was all mine, but somehow she abandoned no whit of her loyalty to my father's purpose in giving me the book. I had imagined myself (with rather timorous glee, for which I wanted her support) pronouncing sentence on his Sunday upon the very evidence which he had given me to judge it by, but some consummate stroke of tact on my mother's part made all that to be quite out of the question. How she did it I have no idea, but surely the very test of tact lies in the fact that you don't know how it is done. Tact explained ceases to be tact, and degenerates into reason on the one hand or futility on the other. Certainly I never confronted my father with this evidence, and Sunday went on precisely as usual. Sometimes Hugh and I played football in the top passage, but you mightn't kick hard for fear of detected reverberations through the skylight of the central hall.

There is a play by some Italian dramatist, which I once saw Dusé act: perhaps it is by D'Annunzio, but I cannot identify it. In the second act anyhow, the curtain went up on Dusé, alone on the stage. She wrote a letter, she put some flowers in a vase without speech, and still without speech, she opened a window at the back, and leaned out of it. She paused long with her back to the audience, and then turning round again said, half below her breath, "Aprile." After that the action of the play proceeded but not till, in that long pause and that one word, she had given us the magic of spring. . . . Not otherwise, but just so, were those Addington holidays, when I was sixteen and seventeen, my April, and thus the magic of spring in those seasons of Christmas and Easter and September came to me. Bulbs and seeds buried in my ground began to spike the earth, and the soft buds and leaves to burst their woolly sheaths. It was the time for the rooting up, in that spring-gardening, of certain weeds; it was the time also of planting the seedlings which should flower later, and of grafting fresh slips on to a stem that was forming fibre in the place of soft sappy shoots. Above all it was the time of receiving more mature and indelible impressions, and there is scarcely anything which in later life I have loved or hated, or striven for or avoided that is not derivable from some sprig of delight or distaste planted during those seasons of first growth. Childhood and earlier boyhood were more of a greenhouse, where early growths were nurtured in a warmed windlessness; now they were pricked out and put in the beds, where they had to learn the robustness which would make them resist the inclemencies of a less sheltered life. Some died, scorched by the sun or battered by the rain; the rest, I suppose, had enough vitality to make sun and rain alike serve their growth. Above all it was the time of learning to enjoy, no longer in the absolutely unreflective manner of a child, but in a manner to some extent reasoned and purposed. Some kind of philosophy, some conscious digestive process began to stir below mere receptivity. I looked not only at what the experiences with which I fed the lusty appetites of life were at the moment, but at the metabolism they would undergo when I had eaten them. But of all mental habits then forming, the one for which I most bless those lovely years, was the habit of enjoyment, of looking for (and finding) in every environment some pleasure and interest. That habit, no doubt, with all our games, our collections, our scribblings had long been churned at: about now it solidified. And by far the most active and assiduous of external agencies that caused this—the dairymaid, so to speak, who was never weary of this magnificent churning—was my mother.

CHAPTER IX

THE FALL OF THE FIRST LEAF

THE dreadful "season of snows and sins" was already beginning to approach again: in other words more scholarship examinations at Oxford and Cambridge began to pile their fat clouds on the horizon. These were the snows: the sins were my own in not taking any intelligent interest in the subjects which would make them "big with blessing." Certainly I had been sent to school to learn Latin and Greek among other things, but the other things were so vastly more interesting. I was usually about tenth in any form where I happened to be, and I remember a very serious letter from my father (after a series of consecutive tenths) saying that he had always observed that boys who were about tenth, could always do much better if they chose: boys lower in a form were those who often tried very hard, but were deficient in ability. I do not think I was so diabolically minded as to consider this a reason for doing worse, but certainly I declined from that modest eminence where boys who could do better pleasantly sunned themselves, and sank half a dozen places lower. By one of those wonderful coincidences which from time to time nourish starving optimists, it so happened that in the summer of 1884 an unusually large number of the sixth left school, and thus seventeen promotions were made out of the fifth form, the very last of which consisted of myself. With all the dignity and decoration of sixth form upon me, I had somehow justified my existence again, and the stigma of being seventeenth was swallowed up in the glory of being in the sixth. I had a study of my own, instead of being one of a herd in a classroom. I could make small boys fill my brewing kettle for me and run errands, and I could, without incurring criticism, wear my cap at the back of my head.

Something, I fancy, in an address which the headmaster gave to the new sixth form at the beginning of the September term, was said about duties and responsibilities: if it was, it must have rebounded out of one ear without penetration. For the average schoolboy is, I believe, waterproof to such suggestions, if they come from without: he will get his idea of his duties and responsibilities purely from his own instinct, or rather from the collective instinct of his contemporaries, and his notion of proper behaviour in himself and others is practically entirely built on what he and they consider to be "good form." These commandments are the most elusive and variable of decalogues, but usually wholesome, and completely autocratic. Immorality, for instance, at that time was bad form, though language which would have blistered the paint off a sewer, was perfectly permissible, if you wished to indulge in it: bullying was hopelessly beyond the pale, gambling and drinking, which figure so menacingly in those lurid histories designed to make mothers tremble for their innocent lambs, were absolutely unthought of. We (the sixth form generally) were a set of genial and energetic pagans, caring most of all for each other, next for games, but doing quite a decent amount of work; indeed, it was rather the fashion, and became more so, to be industrious in certain well-defined patches.

Nobody took the very slightest interest in such subjects as French or mathematics, and considering the way in which they were taught, it would have been truly remarkable if we had. An aged man, mumbling to himself, wrote out equations and made pictures of Euclidian proposition on a blackboard, apparently for his own amusement, without any reference to his audience. When he had had enough of it, he told us to close all books, and write out the proposition he had demonstrated. Sometimes you could, sometimes you couldn't, and if you couldn't very frequently, you had to do it twice and show it up next school. If the aged man remembered to ask for it, you had forgotten to do it, but usually he forgot too. But what it was all about was a blank mystery, until it became necessary to find out, because elementary Euclid and algebra formed a part of the Oxford and Cambridge certificate examination. When that approached, we put our heads together and found out for ourselves.

French was equally hopeless: once a week we prepared a couple of pages of some French history for the head-master. Whatever French he knew he certainly did not impart: of the spoken language I had picked up enough abroad to be aware that he would have been practically unintelligible to a Frenchman. I believe that both these subjects were admirably taught on the modern side; on the classical side the study of them was a mere farce. But at Latin and Greek we worked quite reasonably and intelligently: it was "good form" to take an interest in them, and it was not thought the least odd if somebody was found reading the *Apology of Socrates* (in a translation) out of school hours, though it had nothing to do with class-work, or that I treasured a piece of white marble which my sister Nellie on a foreign tour had picked up on the Acropolis.

The real interest of life centred in "the Alley," a passage running above a couple of classrooms in the school buildings, out of which on each side opened minute studies inhabited by sixth-form in-college boys. Some of these were double studies shared by two occupants, but most were single; inviolable castles if the owner chose to shut the door. Inside there was room for a table, a hanging bookcase, and perhaps three chairs if you sat close; but who would dream of measuring Paradise by cubic contents? Never surely was there a more harmonious democracy, and it was seldom that doors were shut; the inhabitants, unless tied to their books, drifted up and down and round and round like excited bubbles in some loquacious backwater. Within the limits of "good form" every freedom of action and opinion was allowed, and those limits were really very reasonable ones. It must not be supposed that "good form" was ever discussed at all: it was merely the unwritten, unspoken code, which held things together, and undoubtedly the gravest offense against it was a hint of condescension or superiority. If you were so fortunate as to get into the school fifteen or achieve any distinction, "the Alley" pooled the credit, and woe be to any who showed "side" to the Alleyites. If you liked (hardly anybody did) to be extremely neat in dress, to get yourself up to kill, to wear buttonholes, you were perfectly at liberty to do so; but if you showed the least "swank" over your rosebud, the witnesses of your enormity would probably stroll thoughtfully away and return embellished with dandelions and groundsel. That was sarcasm, popularly called "sarc," and was a weapon ruthlessly employed towards the superior person. No one could stand a conspiracy of "sarc" for long: it was better to mend your ways and reduce your swollen head. Only one member of the Alley was ever known to resist a continual course of "sarc," and he, poor fellow, was goaded by the shafts of love, for he adored to distraction one of the masters' daughters who appeared unaware of his existence. This was unusual conduct, but he was at liberty to squander emotion on her if he wished; what roused the Alley to arms, so that they loaded themselves with "sarc," as with hand grenades, was that he affected to despise all who were not enslaved by some pretty-faced maiden. Then, as was right, he found hairpins mysteriously appearing on his carpet, and heard his Christian name called in faint girlish falsetto from a neighbouring study, and discovered notes with passionate declarations of love and a wealth of suggestive allusions that I would no longer "pollewt" my pen with describing nestling in his coat-pocket. But such was the innate depravity of his amorous heart that he really didn't seem to mind the most withering "sarc." . . . Games were not compulsory in the sixth, and in consequence, though athletes were in the majority, athleticism was no longer automatic, and now a boy would suffer no loss of esteem, or offend any sense of decency, if he chose not to play any game whatever. A wide tolerance for your fellows was the first lesson of the Alley; liberty, equality, and fraternity were its admirable guides to life.

Next year, when, by another intervention of Providence, I suddenly found myself head of my house, with a magnificent apartment next the bathroom for my habitation, the snowstorm of scholarship examinations burst over me. For a suitable inducement in the shape of a scholarship or exhibition, I was prepared to go to New,

Magdalen, or Worcester at Oxford, or to King's College, Cambridge; but not a single one of these ancient (or shall we say antiquated?) seats of learning would, after examining me, put their hands in their pockets in order to secure me. I was very busy at the time, for I was editing *The Marlburian* and conducting the school "Penny Readings," and playing football for them and rackets, and not being able to find time for everything I let my schoolwork slide altogether and, when the depressing results came out, bore failure with admirable fortitude. In other words, I did not care at all; if anything, I was rather pleased, because I began dimly to conceive the possibility of being allowed to stop at school for an extra year, whereas I should normally have left in the summer. But Marlborough was now to me the most amiable of dwellings; there were friends there whom I could not bear the thought of parting with; there were schemes that I could not bear to leave unfulfilled, and I directed all the ingenuity of which I was capable to secure my remaining here for an unheard-of year longer. From being resigned to failure I passed, as my plans matured, into being enraptured with it. A false step, a misplaced interview, might spell ruin, and after much thought I went to the headmaster with a homily all about myself. It was clear that I had not attained a decent standard of scholarship yet; surely my coming years at the University would be more profitable if I was better prepared to take advantage of them? My father was bent on my having a career of some distinction there, and would not he be far more likely to find his ambitions for me realized if I made there the better start that another year at school would give me? Another year now of undiluted classics. . . .

This scheme enlisted his sympathy, and he said he

would talk to my house-master about it, who might not, however, want to keep me in such august seniority. But as to that I had no doubt whatever, for this gentleman had only just come to the house, and his seat in the saddle was at present remarkably uncertain. He used to ask members of the sixth, and in especial the head of the house, to go the rounds for him when it was the hour for him to parade the dormitories at night; he would do anything to shirk disciplinary contact if a senior member of the house could accomplish this for him. No senior member of the house felt the slightest nervousness at what so terrified the house-master: we visited the dormitories, sat on a bed here and there, talking to friends, helped a straggler who had not finished a construing lesson for the morning, and eventually went back to the house-master's room to say good night and report that all was well. Then he gave you a slice of cake, and tried to conceal his pipe, and hoped that nobody in the house smoked (which, as a matter of fact, they didn't), and everything was very pleasant and comfortable. The house was behaving quite well, because prefects and senior boys had it well in hand; but if I left, my successor as head of the house was bound to be a very mild, spectacled youth, and, without conceit, I felt sure that my house-master would prefer to keep me, who during this last year had managed it quite nicely for him. His attitude came off according to plan, and we had quite an affecting interview.

Then came the clincher to this careful spade-work, and I got both him and the headmaster to write to my father urging him to allow me to stop another year, not only for my own good (interview A), but for the well-being of the house (interview B). The double appeal was successful: it was settled that I should stay for another year,

and then go up to King's College, Cambridge. As I
would be over nineteen when the next scholarship examination came round, I was ineligible on account of advanced age, and thus, while the snowstorms were next
vexing my contemporaries, I should sit serene and calm
on the sunny slopes of antiquity. I had no notion of
using this extra year of life (for so it appeared then) for
idle or unedifying purposes. I meant to work hard at subjects that would eventually "tell." I meant also, with
a suspicion of priggishness, to make the house streak a
meteor-like path across the starry sky of school. We were
going to be a model of enlightenment (this was the ambition); we were to win the racket house-cup, and the
fives cup, and the gymnasium cup, and the football cup,
and the singing cup (for, like the Meistersingers, every
house competed in singing), and two vocal quartettes,
triumphantly performed, gave a fifth challenge cup.
There it was—forty boys were to be drilled into winning every event of this immense pentathlon. A sixth
cup, possibly within the range, was the cricket cup; but
in the matter of cricket the house generally was no more
than a company of optimistic amateurs. The other five
cups seemed within the limits of probable achievement,
and who knew but that a breezy eleven, rather ignorant
of cricket, except for the presence of the best left-hand
bowler in the school, might not effect some incredible
miracle? Never has anybody's head been so stuffed
full of plans as was mine when I went back a year later
than was reasonable for this series of inconceivable excitements.

The head of the school this year was Eustace Miles.
We had already been great friends for many terms, and
now this friendship ripened into a unique alliance; from

morning till night we were together, and seethed in projects, failures and accomplishments. There was no sport or industry in which we were not associated. No matter came up within the jurisdiction of either of us in which each did not consult the other. He was going up for a classical scholarship at King's, Cambridge, for we had quite settled not to have done with each other when school was over. I had to get to learn some classics somehow, and so together we concocted the most delightful plan, namely, that we should neither of us do any French, mathematics, or history, but should be excused coming into school altogether while such lessons were in progress, devoting ourselves in the privacy of our studies to classics. The headmaster most sensibly saw and sanctioned our point, and consequently we had a whole holiday one day a week, and on two other days only one hour in school. For me that voluntary unsupervised reading, that browsing at will in Attic and Roman pastures, gave me precisely all I had lacked before; the two dead languages stirred and lived, the dry bones moved, and the sinews and the flesh came up on them, and the skin covered them, and the winds of the delicate Athenian air breathed upon them. Four years ago Beesly had awakened in me the sense of the Greek genius for beauty, but not till now had the flame spread to the language. That for me had always smouldered and smoked under the damp of grammar and accents; now, when I could learn as I chose, it flared up. Prosody and inflexions, moods and cases, all that was tedious to acquire, need no longer be learned by rule; the knowledge of rules began to dawn on me merely by incessantly coming across examples of them, and I began to learn under the tuition of admiration. The same thrilled interest invaded Latin also, and it was no longer what could be made of the languages in English that attracted me, but what they were in themselves. Such study did not lead to accurate scholarship, but it gave me what was of much greater value to one who did not mean to spend his life in editing school-books, namely, an inkling of the infinite flexibility of language and joy in the cadences of words, while from the scholastic standpoint it added the stimulus which enabled me not to remain at Cambridge such a hopeless dunce at classics as I had hitherto always been. All the teaching I had ever received had failed to make me apply such intelligence as I was possessed of, directly and vividly: there had never been any sunshine, as regards language, in the earlier grey days of learning, for the sky had always pelted with gerunds and optatives. . . . With that illumination a great light shone on English also: in the galloping race of composition at home I, at any rate, had much preferred to run than to read, but now I plunged headlong into the sea of English literature, reading fast, reading carelessly, but reading rapturously. I bought the six-volume edition of Browning out of the money I won over school-fives, which should have been devoted to the purchase of a silver cup; a successful competition in rackets landed the works of Dickens, and in the hours when I should naturally have done mathematics and French and history, these shared with Juvenal and Aristophanes the honey of the flying minutes. Then came the need to imitate which always besets the budding author, and if you searched in the proper pages of *The Marlburian* you would surely disinter some specimens that aimed at Addison and stanzas which could never have found their printer, had there not been in my study a well-thumbed copy of Tennyson's early lyrics.

There was another by-road for the literary pilgrim: four of us were joint editors, producers, and proprietors of that school paper. Who the two others were I have no idea; it is certain that Eustace and I wrote the greater part of it, and that, with some fine journalistic flair, he, and he alone, caused it to pour money into the pockets of its four editors. Domestically he knew something about printing and pulls and proofs, which had escaped the experience of his friend and the family printing press, and that year *The Marlburian*, as I hope it is now, was a paying concern. Eustace interviewed an astonished tradesman, paid the printing bills, audited the accounts, and flowed back to his collaborators a Pactolus of large silver pieces. We wrote indignant letters signed "A Parent," and answered them with withering rejoinders signed "Another Parent"; we invented abuses, and firmly denied them; we cut down the habitual drowsy accounts of house matches to the smallest paragraphs and spread a table of Socratic dialogue, proving that football was the same as cricket and that masters were the slaves of boys; or imagined that a hundred years hence a fragment of "The Princess" was dug up and edited and amended by Dry-as-Dust; or recommended the school generally, when a two-mile run was ordered by the football captain of their houses, to buy a hoop and bowl it along the road, in order to enliven the stupid act of purposeless running. In this latter point we set the example ourselves and bowled nice wooden hoops down the Bath road, thereby for some reason infuriating the staff of masters. Once, I remember, Eustace and I, going out for a run with our hoops, passed the open door of a class-room at an hour when the lower school was at work, on which a demented master sent out two junior boys with orders to capture the hoops and bring them in to him. Now, there was nothing immoral about hoops, nor was there any school rule that forbade their employment, and so we went very briskly along down the Bath road for a mile or two, with two small boys in pursuit, and when they could run no longer we sat down on a gate. They panted up, and said they had been told to take away the hoops and bring them back to Mr. Sharpe, and so, very politely, we said, "Come and take them." Naturally they could make no serious attempt to take away the hoops of the head of the school and the captain of the Rugby fifteen, and so, after a little conversation, we all came back together. It was all very silly, but why did Mr. Sharpe send two small boys to take away the hoops of two big boys who happened to choose to bowl hoops? We soon got tired of the habit, but it was great fun to write indignant letters to *The Marlburian* about hoops signed "Magister," and scathing replies signed "Discipulus." It made excellent selling stuff for the paper, and boys who had never dreamed of buying a *Marlburian* before put their threepence down with a spendthrift recklessness, because they knew that there was a correspondence about hoops, with plenty of "sarc" in it. There were real letters as well from dignified Old Marlburians, beginning "Has it come to this?" . . .

To all these entrancing topics the editors gave their serious consideration. They herded together for consultation, and rejected each other's contributions with suave impartiality, and when they had settled what they wished to print, Eustace measured it, and usually said that there was too much. If it was all very precious a double number (price sixpence) was decreed; if not, a Socratic dialogue or some trifle of that kind was cut out.

Three out of the four would be very complimentary to the baffled author, and assure him that they found his contribution most amusing, and if that did not soothe the rejection of it, they would grow more candid, and say it was beastly rot. When that was disposed of there might perhaps be a few inches of column to spare, and we inserted an advertisement that a sixth form boy was willing to exchange his hoop (nearly new) for a set of false teeth. Luckily someone remembered that a mathematical master had false teeth, and would be liable to think that this was "sarc" directed at him, and some answers to non-existent correspondents were put in instead. By that time the cake would be finished and the teapot dry, and Eustace took the MSS. to the printers, and I went to conduct a rehearsal of Haydn's Symphony for the approaching Penny Reading, and ask Harry Irving what he was going to recite at it.

These Penny Readings which took place once a term were an entirely delightful institution. *Qui docebant jam docentur*, as the *Carmen* told us, for the whole of this musical and dramatic entertainment was got up, rehearsed (to whatever stage of efficiency), conducted and performed by boys without any help from masters. There were piano solos, part-songs, vocal solos or duets, and perhaps some reading or representation, say, of the trial scene in *Pickwick*. But this year the Penny Readings included grim and finished recitations by Harry Irving, who "drew" in a manner so unprecedented, that instead of holding them in the "Bradleian," a hall of but moderate dimensions, Upper School itself, capable of holding the entire body of boys and masters, had to be requisitioned. It fell to my lot to conduct the musical part of the entertainment, and this year we audaciously rehearsed and performed Haydn's Toy Symphony, in which, for a special treat, we allowed Mr. Bambridge to play the cuckoo. There he sat, rapturously cheered as he mounted to the platform with his little wooden tube, lean and grave with a steady eye fixed on the conductor's baton. It had been arranged that the cuckoo, otherwise so obedient and punctual in its flutings, should at one point run amuck altogether, and go on saying "cuckoo" in spite of the efforts of the conductor to silence it. On it went till the roars of the audience entirely drowned its voice, and when silence was restored, it gave one more "cuckoo," *pianissimo prestissimo*, just to show that it was quite unrepentant. . . . But more than anything did Harry Irving's recitations bring down the house. In appearance he was his father, young and amazingly good-looking, and he had all the assurance and grip of a mature actor: he stalked and he paused, he yelled and he whispered, and he withered us with horror in some appalling little soliloquy by a dying hangman, round whose death-bed the ghosts of his victims most unpleasantly hovered. Then in the manner of a parson he gave us a short sermon on the moral lesson "to be drawn from, dear brethren, that exquisite gem of English poetry, 'Mary had a little larm.' "

The athletic ambitions of the first of these three terms was of course to win the football cup in house-ties, and also all the school matches. Neither quite came off, for the house was beaten in the final, while the school only made a moderate show in its foreign matches. But there was little time for moaning. Close on the heels of that disappointment came the Lent term with its fives, rackets and singing cups, and there was then no cause for anything but jubilation. At Easter came the dreadful fiasco of the Public School rackets in London, and following on that, the house was again knocked out in the final at cricket. Never shall I forget the heaviness of heart with which I came down that day from the cricket-field, due, not to the fact only of defeat—for even if we had won, that sense of finality would have been there—but because for me all the zeal and the struggle, with its failures and successes, of these entrancing school games, was over. Not again could games, so I dimly and correctly realized, have quite that absorbing and pellucid quality which distinguished house matches: there was already forming in my mind, now that the last of these competitions was over, a certain dingy philosophy clouding the brightness, which recognized that games were amusements, to be taken as such. They might give exhilaration and enjoyment, but not again would they produce that unique absorption. I could not imagine again caring quite as much as I had cared during these last six years. Some hour had struck, and not alone for games, but for the multitudinous aims that had been bounded by the chapel wall on one side, the master's garden on another, the field where was the racket court and the football grounds in winter and the cricket pitches in summer, on the third and fourth sides. There was the *angulus terræ*, which, apart from brief holidays, had constituted the whole of life for the vision of a boy. Apart from Addington, there was nothing in the whole round world that mattered like those few acres, and the glory which exuded out of their very soil.

Dimly I conjectured that in a few months Marlborough would be withdrawn into some bright starry orbit of its own, as far as I was concerned, revolving there with a sundered light in which I should no longer share, and that soon I should peer for it through the fog of the years that drifted across it. Some other orbit was to be mine, which, when I began to move in it, would no doubt have a heaven of its own to scour through, but as yet it had no significance for me; it was dim and uncharted. Still incurably boyish, in spite of the nineteen years which were verging on the twentieth, I felt that I was being cast out of the only place that mattered. I suppose I knew in some dull logical way, that it was otherwise: that inexorable Time which sent me forth out of this mature infancy had something left in store, but to the eyes of nineteen, everyone who is thirty, at any rate, must clearly be a sere and yellow leaf, waiting for an autumnal blast to make an end of him in the fall of withered foliage. Life might be possible up to twenty-five or so, but then beyond doubt senility must be moribund and slobbering. "Thirty at least" was the verdict then: "Thirty at most" was so soon substituted for it. For the first time in my life I had the definite sense of a book read through and loved from cover to cover, being closed, the sense of an "end," a finished period. Hitherto, change of home or the leaving of a private school had been not an "end" but a beginning: though one experience was finished the opening of a new one, of fresh places, fresh conditions had made the old just slip from the fingers of a careless hand, without sense of loss. But now my fingers clung desperately to what was slipping away: they did not clutch at that which was coming, but tightened, as the smooth days hurtled by, on that which they still just held.

The last game that mattered "frightfully" had been already played, the last number of *The Marlburian* came out, and while one half of me would have chosen that the full moon of July should know no wane, the other would willingly have seen her turn to ashes, and fall like a cinder from the sky, to match the days from which the glow and the radiance were dying in the frost of the coming departure. Inanimate objects, beloved and familiar, like the row of lime trees in the court with the circular seats round them, my house study with the copies of Turner water-colours by my sister, the Alley and its noisy merry staircase, began to wear a strange aspect, for, so soon, they would have passed completely into other occupation. Drop by drop, like the sweet drippings from the limes, the honey was oozing from them, leaving empty cells and alien habitations.

In especial there was a certain covered columned passage, a paved and roofed pergola close to the sixth form class-room where so often I had waited for the advent of a friend. In stormy south-westerly weather the rain beat into it, but it was a good meeting-place, for the Alley, the Upper School, the sixth form room and the Bradleian made it a junction for passengers, and there was a board up with school-notices, promotions into the eleven and the fifteen and whatnot, to while away the waiting. A congregation of steps would come there as some form was released, but he was not there: then would come a few scattered steps, but not his. And then he would come round a corner, in a blustering hurry, and say, "Oh, sorry," and together we went up to the house-study madly alive, and sanely content. Those minutes of anticipation made the columned pergola more vivid than even the house-study or the Alley or the lime trees, and in so short a while it would all be dead, as a piece of scenery remaining on a stage, where others should play their friendly and wholesome parts. If I had had that which in the cant phrase is called "the corporate sense," I suppose the great thing would have been that generations of others should do as I had done, and I should have said my grace, and got up thankfully from the delicate and vigorous feast. Instead I was Oliver and asked for more, and every year since I have wanted more of some quality that is inseparable from the wonder and sunset of boyhood. But now the sun was notched by the hills over which I must soon climb, where lay the untravelled country: its last rays were level over the plain, and before this last week of July was over, only high up on the peaks of memory away to the east would the rose linger. That, too, so I dismally supposed, would fade presently, but there I was wrong. It has never faded nor lost one atom of its radiance.

There were rejoicings and jubilations to be gone through: the advent of Nellie for prize-giving, in which at last it was my lot to make several excursions to the table where morocco-bound books were stacked. There was a house-supper on the last day of all in celebration of the winning of those challenge cups, which was gratifying also, but below that was the sound of the passing-bell. All that day it sounded, except just at the moment when I should have expected it to be most unbearably funereal. For the friend for whom I had so often waited in the colonnade came up with me to the cricket pavilion, from which I had to take away blazers and bat and cricketing paraphernalia, and having got them stuffed inside my bag, we sat on the steep bank overlooking the field to wait for the first stroke of the chapel-bell. Other groups were straying about the grass, and some came and talked for a bit, and we wished they would go away, because nobody else was wanted just then. It was not that there was anything particular to say, for boys don't say much to one another, and we lay on the grass, and chewed the sweet ends of it, and when not silent, talked of perfectly trivial things. And at last the friend rolled over on to his face and said:

"Oh, damn!"

"Why?" I asked, knowing quite well.

"Because it will be awful rot without you."

"You'll soon find somebody else," said I.

"Funny," said he.

"Laugh then," said I.

He sat up, nursing his knees in his arms, and looking down over the field. Just below was the stretch of grass where house football-ties were played in the winter, to the left was Beesly's house, and at the bottom of the field the racket court. Beyond and below across the road the chapel and the red school-buildings. Then his eyes came back from their excursion.

"It's been ripping anyhow," he said. "Did two fellows ever have such a good time?"

Quite suddenly at that, when the passing-bell should have been loudest, it ceased altogether. The whole of my dismal maunderings about days that were dead and years that were past, I knew to be utterly mistaken. Nothing that was worth having was dead or past at all: it was all here now, and all mine, a possession eternally alive.

"But did they?" he repeated, as I did not answer.

"Never. Nor will. And there's chapel-bell. Get up."

He stood up and picked the grass seeds from his clothes.

"Psalms this morning," he said telegraphically.

"I know. 'Brethren and companions' sake.' Didn't think you had noticed."

"Rather. Good old Psalm."

I took up the cricket-bag, and he pulled at it to carry it. A handle came off.

"Ass," said I.

"Well, it was three-quarters off already," said he. "Come on; we shall be late. You can leave it at the porter's lodge."

"Oh, may I, really? Thanks awfully," said I.

"Sarc," said he.

There was Beesly on the platform next day when I got to the station, and I remembered he had asked me what train I was going by. He just nodded to me, and continued looking at volumes on the bookstall. But just as the whistle sounded, he came to the carriage door.

"Just came to see you off," he said. "Don't forget us all."

CHAPTER X

THE whole family went that summer holiday to the Lakes, where my father had taken the Rectory of Easedale, and in that not very commodious house five children, two parents and Beth all managed to shelter themselves from the everlasting rain that deluged those revolting regions. Had not steep muddy hills separated one lake from another, I verily believe that the Lakes must have become one sheet of mournful water with a few Pikes and Ghylls sticking up like Mount Ararat on another occasion that can scarcely have been more rainy. There was fishing to be had, but no fish: you might as well have fished in the rapids of Niagara as cast a fly on the streams, while the lakes themselves are noted for their depths of barren water. Out we used to go in mackintoshes, and back we came in mackintoshes, and I cannot suppose that thirty years later the Rectory at Easedale can have lost its smell of wet india-rubber and drying homespuns. As a special contribution to the general discomfort Nellie discovered and developed a grand sort of ailment called "pleurodynia," which I suppose is the result of never being dry, and I capped that by cultivating the most orange-coloured jaundice ever seen, and continued being violently sick when you would have thought there was nothing to be sick with.

But these atrocious tempests gave my father unlimited

scope for what his irreverent family called "The Cottar's Saturday Night." Best of all situations in the holidays he loved to have his entire family sitting close round him busy, silent and slightly unreal to their own sense, while he "did" his Cyprian. There he sat with his books and papers in front of him, at the end of a table in a smallish room, with all of us sitting there, each with his book, speaking very rarely and very quietly, so as not to disturb him, and everybody, alas, except him, slightly constrained. In these holidays, Hugh, owing to inveterate idleness at Eton (where, beating me, he had got a scholarship), had a tutor to whom he paid only the very slightest attention, and on these evenings he would have some piece of Horace to prepare for next day, and would work at it for a little, and then drop his dictionary with a loud slap on the floor. Soon he would begin to fidget, and then catch sight of Arthur reading, and something in his expression would amuse him. He drew nearer him a piece of sermon paper which Nellie's pen was busy devouring on behalf of the next *Saturday Magazine*, and began making a caricature. At the same moment perhaps I would observe below lowered eyelids that Arthur was drawing me, and so I began to draw my mother, and Nellie catching the infection, began to draw Maggie. (If you gave her pulled-back hair and a tall forehead, the family would easily recognize it.) And then perhaps my father, pausing in his work, would see Hugh with his tongue protruding from the corner of his mouth (for that is the posture in which you can draw best) and say:

"Dear boy, have you finished your preparation for to-morrow? What are you doing?"

Hugh would allow he hadn't quite finished his preparation, not having begun it, and my father would look at his drawing, and his mouth, the most beautiful that ever man had, would uncurl, until perhaps he threw back his head and laughed with that intense merriment that was so infectious. Possibly he might not be amused, and a little grave rebuke followed; he returned to his Cyprian and we all sat quiet again. But the criticism of the family was that this was "Papa's game, and he made the rules." For he, unable to get on with his Cyprian, or arriving at the end of a bit of work, would interrupt at will the mumness which was imposed on his behalf. But if Maggie or I finished what we were doing, we might not make general conversation. . . . And then the door would open, and Beth looked in, and said, "Eh, it's dressing-time," and her lovely old face would grow alight with love when she looked on my mother, her child of the elder family, and five more of her children of the second generation. From my father there would always be a delicious word of welcome for her, and he would say:

"Beth, you're interrupting us all. Go away. Your watch is wrong."

"Nay, sir, it isn't," said Beth—she always said "sir" to him, whatever his title was—"It's gone half-past seven." And she beamed and nodded, perfectly at ease in this solemn assembly. With her (who counted of course as one of it) there were eight in that little stuffy room, where we fidgeted and sat and read. And what would not I give, who with one other alone survive from those evenings, to have an hour of them again, in that inconvenient proximity, surrounded by the huge love of a family so devoted and critical of each other, with the two amongst them whom nobody criticized, my mother with her spectacles on her forehead, and Beth looking in at the door?

Then jaundice descended on me like the blur of a London fog, and through the depression of it, there seemed no ray that could penetrate. But my mother managed to effect that entry, as of course she always would, and she came back one dripping afternoon from Grasmere, with a packet in her hand.

"As it's all so hopeless," she said, "I bought some lead soldiers. Oh, do let us have a battle."

She poured a torrent of these metal warriors on to a table by my bed. There were cannons with springs that shot out peas, and battalions of infantry, and troops of cavalry. It was she, you must understand, who wanted to play soldiers, and to a jaundiced cynic of twenty that necessarily was quite irresistible. Who could have resisted a mother who *asked* you at her age to play soldiers? We shot down regiments at a time, for when you enfilade a line of lead soldiers with a pea, if you hit the end man, he topples against the next one, and the next against the next, till there are none left standing. The peas flew about the room, rattled against washing-basins and tapped at the window-panes, and I felt much better. Then we bombarded Beth who came to know if I wouldn't like some dinner, and as I wouldn't, it was time to go to sleep.

"A nice little bit of beef," began Beth.

"If you say beef again, I shall be sick," said the invalid.

"Nay, you won't," said Beth hopefully.

Then to my mother:

"Eh, dear, do go and dress," she said, "or you'll keep everybody waiting."

My mother shot a final pea.

"I won't be the conventional mother," she said, "and smooth your pillow for you. Nor will I peep in on tiptoe after dinner to see if you're asleep. But, my darling, I *know* you'll be better to-morrow! Won't you?"

King's College, Cambridge, whither my father accompanied me in October, had, scarcely twenty years previously, become an open College; for centuries before that, it had been, as was originally the intention of the pious founder, Henry VI, a close monastic corporation consisting of Eton scholars destined for the priesthood. If a boy, say, at the age of twelve, won a scholarship at Eton, and was thus on the Royal Foundation there, it followed that unless he was supremely idle or vicious, he obtained in due rotation, without any further examination, a King's scholarship, when he went up to the University. After that, often while he was still an undergraduate, he became a fellow of King's, and for the rest of his life the bounty of Henry VI supplied him with commons, lodging, and an income of £200 a year provided he did not marry, till he became a senior fellow, when his emolument was doubled. At the time of its foundation, the college was a regal and magnificent endowment for the encouragement of learning and the education of priests, but long before this Etonian sanctuary, consisting of fellows and scholars, was violated by the rude hordes of barbarians from other schools, the system had become one of those scandalous and glorious anachronisms, that take rank with such institutions as pocket-boroughs, where the local magnate could nominate his own friends to represent the views of the nation in Parliament.

The founder's idea had been that from year to year the band of scholars going up from Eton should keep the torch of learning alight, and grow old in celibate fineness and wisdom. No doubt there may have been some very minor Erasmuses thus trained and nurtured, and given stately leisure for the prosecution of their studies and the advancement of sound learning, but such a system was liable to many abuses, and as a matter of fact, acutely suffered from them. A Fellow of King's, thus supported for life by the bounty of the King, was under no compulsion to study; he was perfectly at liberty to be lodged, boarded, and supplied with a pocket-money of £200 or £400 a year, without doing anything at all to earn it. Strange crabbed creatures were sometimes the result of this monastic indolence, for (as would have been the case in a monastery) there was no abbot or prior to allot tasks and duties to the fellows. Some, of course, did tutorial work among the scholars, but for the rest, who might or might not, according to their own inclination, work at Greek texts and scholia, there was no rule; and a man with no ambition in his work, meeting his fellows only once a day at the high table in Hall, if he chose to go there, and otherwise living alone might easily turn into a very odd sort of person. One of them, who died not so long before I went up, was never seen outside his rooms till dusk began to fall: then he would totter, stick in hand, out on to the great grass lawn in the court, and poke viciously at the worms, ejaculating to himself, "Ah, damn you, you haven't got me yet!" After this edifying excursion, he would go back to his rooms and be seen no more till dusk next day. All his life since the age of twelve or so, the bounty of Henry VI had supported him, and until the worms finally did "get" him, nothing could deprive him of his emoluments. How far short of the intention of the Royal Founder the college fell may be conjectured from the list of the fellows, which from first to last contains no name of the slightest eminence or distinction as a scholar, except that of the late Walter Headlam, who was not an Etonian.

The reconstruction of King's took place some years before I went up, and no more of these life-fellows were appointed. Henceforth fellowships expired at the end (I think) of six years, though they could be prolonged if the holder was doing tutorial work in the college, or was engaged in such research as made it proper that his term should be extended. But such men as were already life-fellows were not shorn of their fellowships, and whether or no they were resident, whether or not they were engaged in any work which might, ever so faintly, be held to be congruous to the intention of the founder, they were still entitled for life to their income, their commons, and dinner, and if they chose to reside in the college to a set of fellows' rooms. At that time the college buildings would not nearly hold all the undergraduates, and freshmen, unless they were scholars, must have lodgings outside college; but in spite of this certain life-fellows still clung to their privileges, and continued to retain sets of rooms in Fellows' Buildings, which they never occupied. One of these, engaged in wholly unscholastic work in London, used to come up for a week or two at the end of the Christmas term, but for the rest of the year his rooms stood vacant, while two others, who to the best of my knowledge never appeared in Cambridge at all, had another set of rooms, which were used merely as guest-rooms by other fellows. A fourth specimen of survivals such as the founder never contemplated was ancient and dusky in appearance, and never left King's at all, though he took no part in the academic life of the place, appearing only in chapel and in Hall, and occupy-

ing himself otherwise with making faint wailings on a
violin. . . . But a friend of mine and I chanced on the
discovery that if you whistled as he crossed the court to
chapel, he stopped dead, and after a little pause, proceeded cautiously again.   A repetition of the whistle
would make him retrace his steps, and it was possible
by continuing to whistle, to drive him back to his rooms.
This was extremely interesting, but the cause baffled conjecture.   Later on, however, after years of eremite seclusion, he suddenly burst into activity, like a volcano long
believed to be extinct, gave tea-parties in his rooms with
a leg of cold mutton on the sideboard and a table laid
as for dinner, and was induced to play the violin at college concerts.   Then (Ossa piled on Pelion for wonder)
he married a girl in the Salvation Army, and disappeared
from these haunts of celibacy.   Again I cannot imagine
that the founder contemplated that the head of the college should resemble our Provost, for Dr. Okes, though
resident, was approaching or had already reached his
ninetieth year, and inhabited in complete seclusion the
Provost's Lodge.   I am sure I never set eyes on him at
all; he took no part whatever in college business, as indeed his advanced years prevented him from doing, but
there he had lingered on from year to year without a single
thought of resignation entering his venerable head.
Though totally past work, he was Provost of King's and
Provost of King's he remained, a drone apparently imperishable.

Others, however, of these life-fellows justified themselves by a busy existence; there was the Vice-Provost,
Augustus Austen Leigh, who performed all the presiden-
tial duties of the Provost; there was Mr. J. E. Nixon,
Dean of the college, lecturer on Latin prose to under-

graduates, and Professor of Rhetoric at Gresham College, London, who surely made up for these drones who abused the bounty of the founder, by his prodigious activities. In appearance he was the oddest of mortals, a little over five feet tall, wearing always, even when he went down to play lawn-tennis in the Fellows' Garden, a black tail-coat, and boots of immense length, of which the toes pointed sharply upwards. He had only one hand, and that the left; his right hand was artificial, covered with a tight black kid glove. He had also only one eye and that the right, but the other was marvellously sharp. He made a tennis-ball to nestle in the crook of his arm, and then by a dexterous jerk of his body flung it into the air and severely served it.

His mind was like a cage-full of monkeys, all intent on some delirious and unintelligible business. "Show me a man with a green nose," he once passionately exclaimed, "and I'll believe in ghosts." He had a voice as curious as his boots, in range a tenor, in quality like the beating of a wooden hammer on cracked metal plates, and every week he held a glee-singing meeting after Hall in his rooms, and refreshed his choir with Tintara wine, hot tea-cakes, and Borneo cigars. We sang catches and rounds and madrigals, he beating time with a paper-knife, which, as he got shriller and more excited, would slip from his hand and fly with prodigious velocity across the room. He always took the part of first tenor, and whoever gave the key on the piano put it up a tone or two, in order to hear Nixon bark and yelp at some preposterous C. If it was obviously out of range he would say (running all his words into each other like impressions on blotting paper): "Surelythatsratherhighisthatonly A?" .... Then the unaccountable mistake was discovered and we started again. Where he found all these rounds and catches I cannot conjecture: much music, certainly, that I have heard in Nixon's room has never reached my ears again, nor have I ever seen anyone, except those who attended these meetings, who was acquainted with the following catch. It started *Lento*, and, under the strokes of the paper-knife quickened up to *andante* and *allegro*, and ended *prestissimo possibile*. The words ran thus, starting with a first tenor lead:

> Mr. Speaker, though 'tis late,
> I must lengthen the debate,
> The debate.
> Pray support the chair!
> Pray support the chair!
> Mr. Speaker, though 'tis late,
> I must lengthen the debate.
> Question! question! Order! order!
> Hear him! Hear him! Hear him! Hear!
> (Da capo: da capo: da capo.)

Every moment it got quicker, the barks and yells over "Order! Order!" grew louder and louder, until the whole kennel was a yelp, and when everyone was quite exhausted, and the pandemonium no longer tolerable, Nixon brought down the paper-knife (if it had not flown out of his hand) with a loud bang on the table and wiped his face and laughed for pleasure. Then he poured out Tintara wine, and gave us Borneo cigars, while he tumbled an avalanche of music out of a bookcase and tried to find "I loved thee beautiful and kind."

Apart from glee-singing, lawn-tennis and Latin prose, his mind chiefly ran on argument and on what he called "starting a hare." He would advance some amazing

"Her Grace"

Nov 20 99

"HER GRACE" (A DOMESTIC CARICATURE)

proposition, such as "Why shouldn't we all—no, that wouldn't do, but why not play lawn-tennis and sing glees in the morning, and work in the evening?" He argued about the most casual topic: if you said, "It's a fine day," he cleared his throat raspingly, and dropped something he was carrying, and said, "It all depends on what you mean by fine. If you mean sun and blue sky, granted; but why shouldn't you call it fine if there are buckets of rain? It all depends what you mean by 'fine.' A fish now——"

"I meant an ordinary fine day," began his bewildered guest.

"Very well: but I say 'fish.' I'm a fish and you're a fish. To a fish probably the wetter it is, the finer it is, and there you are."

There you were: long before anybody else Nixon had invented the art of preposterous conversation, which Mr. Hichens wrongly attributes to Oscar Wilde. To Nixon it was not only an art, a product of instinct, but a science, a product of definite reasoning. He would not change the subject, when his argument had been burnt to ashes (often by himself), but would confidently blow on the cinders, expecting some unconjecturable Phœnix to arise from them.

By far the most notable of the life-fellows was Oscar Browning, without mention of whom no adequate idea of Cambridge life in the late eighties and early nineties can possibly be arrived at. Though King's was in large measure a college quite apart from the rest of the University, giving itself (so said the rest of the University) unwarrantable airs, Oscar Browning (whom it is simpler to designate as O.B. for he was never known otherwise) pervaded not King's only, but the whole of Cambridge, with his pungent personality. His was a perennial and rotund youthfulness, a love of loyal adventure not really challenged by the most devout of his competitors, for who except O.B. at the age of forty-five or so, ever bought a hockey-stick, and imperilled a majestic frame in order to have the pleasure of being hit on the shins by the Duke of Clarence, then an undergraduate at Trinity, and heir-presumptive to the English throne? I was still a junior at Marlborough when these Homeric events happened, but years afterwards, O.B. was still talking about the "awfully jolly" games of hockey he had with Prince Eddy. . . . Even the fact of his playing hockey at all, which he certainly did, affords a key to the intensity of his activities.

He rode a tricycle, and once, accompanying him on a bicycle with funereal pedallings, while he discoursed of Turkish baths and Grand Dukes, and Taormina and English history, I observed that he stuck fast in a muddy place, and prepared to dismount, in order to shove him out of it. But he obligingly told me to do nothing of the kind, for some casual youth was on the path beside his enmired tricycle to whom he said:

"Charlie, old boy, give me a shove. Ha! Ha!"

"Charlie old boy," with his face a-shine with smiles, gave the required push, and O.B. rejoined me, as I swooped and swerved along the road in order to go very slowly.

"Charlie is my gyp's son," he said. "Such a jolly boy. Thanks awfully, Charlie. Well, there I was, when the Grand Duke's yacht came into Taormina. And, by the way, do you know the Maloja? The Crown-Princess of Germany came there one year when I was in the hotel, so I dressed myself like a Roman proconsul, in a white toga of bath towels, ha, ha, and—and—really these ruts are most annoying—and a laurel wreath, and went out to meet her Royal Highness. I had a retinue of four young men who were staying at the hotel as lictors, with axes and sticks, and I read a short address to her to welcome her, and we had lunch together, and played lawn-tennis and it was all awfully jolly and friendly and unconventional. Why aren't we all natural, instead of being afraid of poor Mrs. Grundy, whose husband surely died so long ago? She has never married again, which shows she must be a most unpopular female. Most females, I notice, are so unpopular: they never know when they're wanted, and their hearts are always bigger than their heads. Not of course your dear mother—those charming Lambeth garden parties—and dear Lady Salisbury. I saw the Queen when I was at Balmoral last year—my bootlace has come undone, so careless of Charlie not to notice it—and how hopelessly benighted is Cambridge altogether! Lord Acton came to stay with me the other day —I think my tricycle wants oiling—and dined with me at the High Table. Nixon was sitting on his other side, propounding conundrums about bed-makers, and hoping that he would sing glees with him. Ha! Ha! Every boy ought to realize his youth, instead of wasting his energies over elegiacs. When the Grand Duke came into Taormina——"

It is really impossible to render the variety of O.B.'s general conversation, of which the foregoing is but a dim reproduction. His performances, too (the expression of himself in deeds), were just as various, and yet everyone in Cambridge was aware that behind this garish behaviour there was a real, a forcible and a big personality. His performances chiefly expressed themselves in tricyclings and bathings, in lectures on English history, which nobody attended, and in At-Homes on Sunday evening, which everybody attended. He had a set of four rooms (the first being a bathroom) which were all thrown open to anybody, and if you had said you wanted a bath in the middle of the party, O.B. would certainly have said, "Ha, ha! awfully jolly," have given you a sponge and a towel and have come in to help. Next to that came his bedroom, lined with bookshelves from floor to ceiling, with a bronze reproduction of the Greek "Winged Sleep" over his bed; then, not a whit more public than these apartments came two big sitting-rooms, in one of which was a grand piano, and four small harmoniums of various tones, one flute-like, one more brazen in quality, and two faintly resembling wheezy and unripe violins. On these —each with its performer and a miniature score—O.B. and Bobby, and Dicky and Tommy would execute some deliberate quartette, or with the piano to keep them all moderately together would plunge with gay, foolhardy courage into the Schumann quintette. Never was there a more incredible sight (you could hardly believe you saw it) than that of O.B. pedalling away at this Obeophone (for thus this curious harmonium was aptly named) with his great body swaying to and fro and strange crooning sounds coming out of his classical mouth to reinforce the flutings of his melody, while Bobby and Dicky and Tommy, nimble-fingered members of the Cambridge Musical Society, sat with brows corrugated by their anxiety to keep in time with O.B. They never learned that they were attempting an impossibility, but followed him faint yet pursuing as he galloped along a few bars ahead, or suddenly slowed down so that they shot in front of him. At the conclusion he would pat them all on the back, and say, "Awfully jolly Brahms is, or was it Beethoven?" and proceed to sing, "Funiculi, funicula" himself. . . . Groups formed and reformed; here would be a couple of members of the secret and thoughtful society known as "The Apostles" with white careworn faces, nibbling biscuits and probably discussing the ethical limits of Determinism; there the President of the Union playing noughts and crosses with a Cricket Blue; there an assembly of daring young men who tore their gowns, and took the board out of their caps, in order to present a more libertine and Bohemian appearance, when they conversed with the young lady in the tobacconist's. Dons from King's or other colleges fluttered in and out like moths, and the room grew ever thicker with the smoke of innumerable cigarettes. But O.B., however mixed and incongruous was the gathering, never lost his own hospitable identity in the crowd; waving bottles of curious hock he would spur on the pianist to fresh deeds of violence, making some contribution to the discussion on Determinism, and promise to speak at the next debate at the Union, as he wandered from room to room, bald and stout and short yet imperial with his huge Neronian head, and his endless capacity for adolescent enjoyment. Age could not wither him any more than Cleopatra; he was a great joyous ridiculous Pagan, with a genius for geniality, remarkable generosity and kindliness, a good-humoured contempt for his enemies, of whom he had cohorts, a first-rate intellect and memory, and about as much stability of purpose as a starling. His extraordinary vitality, his serene imperviousness to hostility, his abandoned youthfulness were the ingredients which made him perennially explosive. Everyone laughed at him, many disapproved of him, but for years he serenely remained the most outstanding and prominent personality in Cambridge. Had he had a little more wisdom to leaven the dough of his colossal cleverness, a little more principled belief to give ballast to his friskiness, he would have been as essentially great as he was superficially grotesque.

A small college as King's then was, splits up into far more sharply defined cliques than a large one, and it was not long before I found myself firmly attached to a small group consisting in the main of Etonians belonging either to King's or Trinity. The younger fellows of the college mixed very democratically with undergraduates of all years, and the head of this vivid group was certainly Monty James, subsequently Provost of King's and now Provost of Eton. Walter Headlam, perhaps the finest Greek scholar that Cambridge has ever produced, and Lionel Ford, now headmaster of Harrow, both of them having lately taken their degrees, were of the company, so too were Arthur Goodhart, then working for a degree in music, and a little later among junior members R. Carr Bosanquet, now Professor at Liverpool. We were all members of the Pitt Club, that delightful and unique institution where, to the end of your life, once being a life-member, your letters are stamped without any payment, and most of us were, or soon became, members of a literary society called "The Chitchat," in which on Saturday night each in rotation entertained the society at his rooms with an original paper on any subject as intellectual fare, and with coffee and claret-cup, anchovy toast, and snuff, handed solemnly round in a silver box, for physical stimulus. Sometimes if the snuff went round too early, awful reverberations of sneezing from the unaccustomed punctuated the intellectual fare, and

I remember (still with pain) reading a paper on Marlowe's *Faustus*, during which embarrassing explosions unnerved me. I had reason to quote (at a very impressive stage of this essay) certain lines from that tragedy, which with stage directions came out as follows:

Faustus.   Where are you damned? (*Sneezings.*)
Mephistopheles.   In Hell. (*Sneezings and loud laughter.*)
            For where I am is Hell (*Sneezing and more laughter*),
            And where Hell is (*Uproar*) there must I ever be.

On another occasion a prominent philologist whose turn it was to regale us, found that he had not had leisure to write his paper on "Manners" and proposed to address us on the subject instead. He strode about the room gesticulating and vehement, stumbling over the hearth-rug, lighting cigarettes and throwing them away instead of his match, while he harangued us on this interesting ethical topic, with interspersed phrases of French and German, and odd English words like "cocksuredom." As this ludicrously proceeded, a rather tense silence settled down on "The Chitchat"; its decorous members bit their lips, and prudently refrained from looking each other in the face, and there were little stifled noises like hiccups or birds in bushes going about the room, and the sofa where three sat trembled, as when a kettle is on the boil. Then he diverged, *via*, I think, the exquisite urbanity of the ancient Greeks, to Greek sculpture, and proceeded as a practical illustration to throw himself into the attitude of Discobolus. At that precise moment, Dr. Cunningham of Trinity, who was drinking claret-cup and trembling a great deal, completely lost control of himself. Claret-cup spurted from his nose and mouth; I should not have thought a man could have so violently choked and laughed simultaneously, without fatal damage to himself. That explosion, of course, instantaneously spread round the entire company, except the amazed lecturer, and Dr. Cunningham, finding he could not stop laughing at all, seized his cap and gown and left the room with a rapid and unsteady step. Even when he had gone wild yells and slappings of the leg came resonantly in through the open windows as he crossed the court. . . .

But the Love-feast of the Clan was on Sunday evening, when in rotation, they dined in each other's rooms. This institution (known as the "T.A.F." or "Twice a Fortnight") had been inaugurated by Jim Stephen, that brilliant and erratic genius, then in London, editing *The Mirror* and astounding the Savile Club, who a year or two later returned to Cambridge again, and, until his final and melancholy eclipse, diffused over everyone who came across him the beam of his intellect and personality. Of him I shall speak later: at present the clan of friends met, so to speak, under the informal hegemony of Monty James. Intellectually (or perhaps æsthetically) I, like many others, made an unconditional surrender to his tastes, and, with a strong prepossession already in that direction, I became convinced for the time—and the time was long—that Dickens was the St. Peter who held the keys of the heavenly kingdom of literature. When dinner at the T.A.F. was over, Monty James might be induced to read about the birthday-party of the Kenwigses, with a cigarette sticking to his upper lip, where it bobbed up and down to his articulation, until a shout of laughter on the reader's part over Mr. Lillyvick's glass of grog, cast it forth on to the hearth-rug. He almost made me dethrone Bach from his legitimate seat, and by a revolutionary movement place Handel there instead, so magnificent were the effects produced, when with him playing the bass, and me the treble from a pianoforte arrangement for two hands, we thundered forth the "Occasional Overture." He was a superb mimic, and at the T.A.F. and elsewhere a most remarkable saga came to birth, in which the more ridiculous of the Dons became more ridiculous yet. And when on these Sunday evenings the Dickens reading, and the "Occasional Overture," and some singing and Saga were done, a section of the T.A.F. would go to O.B.'s "at home," and mingle with inferior mortals.

Another society common to many members of the T.A.F. was the Decemviri Debating Society. To this, some time during my undergraduate days, I was elected, though I do not think I ever expressed any wish to belong to it, for when it came to making a speech, terror, then as now, invariably deprived me of coherent utterance, and a rich silence was all that I felt capable of contributing to these discussions. Knowing this I never attended any meeting at all, and as a rule of the society was that if any member absented himself for a term (or was it two?) from the debates, he should be deprived of the privileges of membership, I received one day a notice of the next debate, at which there was private business to be transacted in the matter of my own expulsion. Unjustifiable indignation, for this time only, put terror to flight, and I was allowed to open another debate in the place of that already arranged for, and to make a speech to show reason why I should not be expelled. My motion was triumphantly carried, and I never went to a meeting of the Decemviri again.

I suppose it must have been that belated year of voluntary reading at Marlborough, which enabled me to win an exhibition at King's at the end of my first term; after that for a year and a half I was utterly devoid of all interest in classical subjects. There was not the smallest spur to industry or appreciation provided by tutors or lecturers: if you attended lectures and were duly marked off as present, you had conformed to the rite, but nothing you heard could conceivably stimulate your zeal. The classical tutor under whose academic frigidity we followed Thucydides' account of the Peloponnesian War stood on a daïs at the end of the lecture room, and indecently denuded his subject of any appeal to interest. He put his head on one side and said, "Then came Sphacteria: I don't know what Sphodrias was about," and so nobody knew what either Sphodrias or Mr. X—— was about. He looked over exercises in Greek prose as well: on one occasion I was fortunate enough to drag in a quantity of tags from Plato and Thucydides, and received, for the only time, his warm approval. A piece of Greek prose, according to academic standards, appeared to be good, in proportion as it "brought in" quotations and phrases plucked from Thucydides or Plato; Baboo English was its equivalent in more modern tongues. Tags and unusual words and crabbed constructions from the most obscure passages were supposed to constitute good Greek prose, just as in the mind of a Bombay or Calcutta student, the memoir of Onoocool Chunder Mookerjee represented an example of dignified English. To quote from that immortal and neglected work, "Having said these words, he hermetically sealed his lips never to open them again. He became *sotto voce* for a few hours, and he went to God about 6 p.m." As this sublime deathbed scene appears to the ordinary Englishman, so would the prose which Mr. X—— approved have appeared to the ordinary Greek of the time of Pericles. . . . But he had been Senior Classic, and carried on the wonderful tradition, and in other respects was classical tutor and an eager but inefficient whist-player. Nixon, an equally traditional Latin scholar, trained us to produce a similar Latinity, and we got Monty James to imitate them both. Any dawning of love for classical language receded, as far as I was concerned, into murk midnight again, and having temporarily justified my existence by winning an exhibition, I deliberately proceeded for the next year and a half to follow more attractive studies. A year's hard work on the approved Baboo lines, I calculated, would be sufficient to secure success in the Classical Tripos, which was the next event of any importance.

Young gentlemen with literary aspirations usually start a new University magazine, which for wit and pungency is designed to eclipse all such previous efforts, and I was no exception in the matter of this popular gambit. Another freshman lodging in the same house as myself was joint-editor, and so was Mr. Roger Fry, two or three years our senior, and some B.A. whose name I cannot recollect. Mr. Roger Fry certainly drew the illustration on the cover of the *Cambridge Fortnightly*, which represented a tremendous sun of culture rising behind King's College Chapel. O.B. contributed a poem to it, so also did my brother Arthur, and Mr. Barry Pain sent us one of the best parodies in the language, called "The Poets at Tea," in which Wordsworth, Tennyson, Christina Rossetti, Swinburne and others are ludicrously characteristic of themselves. He also tried to galvanize the *Cambridge Fortnightly* into life by one or more admirable short stories, and Mr. G. Lowes Dickinson applied the battery with him. But the unfortunate infant was clearly stillborn, and considering the extreme feebleness of most of its organs, I do not wonder that it was, after the lapse of a term or so, quite despaired of. It had really never lived: it had merely appeared. My share in the funeral expenses was about five pounds, and I was already too busy writing *Sketches from Marlborough*, which was duly and magnificently published within a year, to regret the loss. Fearing to be told that I had better attend to my Greek and Latin, I did not inform my father of this literary adventure; then, when a local printer and publisher at Marlborough, to my great glee, undertook its production, I thought he would consider it very odd that I had not told him of it before and so I did not tell him at all. The book had a certain local notoriety, and naturally enough, the fact of it reached him, and he wrote me the most loving letter of remonstrance at my having kept it from him. There was no word of blame for this amateur expenditure of time and energies, but I divined and infinitely regretted that I had hurt him. And somehow I could not explain, for I still felt that if he had known I was working at it, he certainly would have suggested that I might have been better occupied. Already, though half-unconsciously, I knew to what entrancing occupation I had really determined to devote my life, and though I might have made a better choice, I could not, my choice being really made, have been better occupied than in practising for it. The book in itself, for the mere lightness which was all that it professed, was not really very bad: the ominous part about it (of which the omens have been amply fulfilled) being the extreme facility with which it was produced.

Of all the temples in the world, built by the wisdom of cunning artificers, and consecrated by the love of reverent hearts, none can surpass and few can equal the glory of that holy and beautiful house which the founder of King's decreed for the worship of God, with its jewelled windows and the fan-vaulting of its incomparable roof. Half-way up, separating choir from nave, is the tall oak screen stretching from side to side, on which stands the organ, a "huge house of sounds" with walls of gilded pipes, and, at the corners, turrets where gold angels with trumpets to their mouths have alighted. The nave on Sunday afternoons in the short days of winter would be nearly dark, but for the soft glow of the innumerable wax candles with which the choir was lit, flowing over the organ screen. At half-past three, the hour of those Sunday afternoon services, there would still be a little light outside, though that would have faded altogether before service was over, and just opposite where I sat was the window that I love best in all the world. The Saviour has risen on Easter morning, and before him in dress of sapphire and crimson Mary Magdalene is kneeling. She had been weeping and had heard behind her the question, "Woman, why weepest thou?" Her bereaved heart had answered, and he whom she supposed to be the gardener had said, "Mary." It was then, in that window, that she knew him, and turning, she bowed herself to the ground, with one hand stretched out to him, and said, "Rabboni!" In the garden of the Resurrection He stood, with the flowers of the spring about His feet, instead of the spikenard, very precious, with which she had anointed them for his burial. . . . During the Psalms for the twenty-seventh evening of the month, when she who sowed in tears reaped in joy, the window would grow dark against the faded light outside, and the wise and tranquil candle-light spread like a luminous fog to the cells of the vaulting above. At the end of the service, the red curtain across the arch in the screen was drawn back, and you peered into the dusk of the nave, and the dark of the night. . . .

Or else on week-days a consultation of the musical bill of fare on the chapel door would bring you, a little before anthem time, into the nave, for Wesley's "Wilderness" was soon to be sung. The choir, when service was going on, was behind the screen and the crimson curtain, but the candle-light there, aided by a few sconces here, made visible the roof, and the black silhouettes of the trumpeting angels on the organ. Then the solo bass began: there was the fugue of the waters breaking out, and the treble solo and chorus of the flight of sorrow and sighing. Perhaps you waited for the conclusion of inaudible prayers, on the chance that Dr. Mann would play a Bach-fugue at the end, after the crimson curtain had been drawn back and the white choir had gone into its vestries. There was this reward, let us say, that afternoon, for the *gamba* on the swell started the melodious discussion, and its soliloquy provoked an answer in the same words but with another voice. The duet "thickened and broadened," fresh voices joined; they found a second theme, and gradually step by step, the whole organ, but for one keyboard, silent as yet, took up the jubilant wrangling. What the *gamba* had stated, the diapason now proclaimed: what the diapason had shouted was thundered from the pedals. And then the last keyboard was in use, for what but the *Tubas* could so have imposed themselves and penetrated that immense and melodious rioting of sound? Perhaps the golden angels at the four corners of the organ, "opened their mouths and drew in their breath," and spoke through their celestial trumpets.

It is impossible to disentangle and reduce to chronology the infinity of interests that interweaved themselves with these three undergraduate years, and the reader must sympathetically partake of a *macedoine* of memories, that were the ingredients in the enthralling dish. Outside Cambridge, which daily became more absorbing, I had the emotional experience of seeing Miss Mary Anderson double the part of Hermione and Perdita in *The Winter's Tale*, and fell violently in love with her. Never surely was there so beautiful a Shakespearian heroine, never did another actress make such music of the tale of the flowers she had gathered. No sculptor's skill or whiteness of Pentelic marble ever approached the glory of that queenly figure, and with what amazement of joy I saw it stir and cease to be a statue when, with a waving of lovely arms, that sent up a cloud of powder, there was no statue any more but the queen, living and moving again. I bought a photograph of her, carried it about with me by day, and by night put it on a table by my bed, fearing all the time that my father would discover it, for he would not have cared much about this experience of mine. Not for nearly thirty years later did I meet my Hermione in the flesh and lay my belated homage before her.

Marlborough also was a lodestar, appearing already, as must needs be, of lesser magnitude, now that new constellations directed my voyagings, but, being granted an *exeat* of two nights in order to witness the opening of Truro Cathedral, I spent both in the train in order to get half a day at my school. Already the old order had changed; the values were different, and even as I had once suspected, a few months had sufficed to do that. Yet the other aspect was true also; I had absorbed and assimilated something from the Wiltshire upland which was imperishably part of my personality: my very identity would have been something other than it was, had I not lived and grown up there. But many ties which had seemed close had drooped and loosened, and now I saw which were the closest of all, and they, just one or two of them, were as taut as ever; that of Beesly, still merry-eyed behind the pince-nez to which he had taken, and that of the friend who on the last day of term had sat with me in the field waiting for chapel-bell. He absented himself from an hour of morning-school, and met me, dishevelled with a night journey, at the station. As we passed through the town we bought rolls and sausages, and while I had a bath, he came in and out, making breakfast ready in the study that had been mine, and for that hour it was as if the rind of the last months had been peeled off, and the old friendship glowed like the heart of the fruit. Otherwise, the little impression I had made on that shining shore was already washed by the advancing tide, and its edges were blunt, while, a little higher up the beach, the sand-castles of others were growing tall and turreted under vigorous spades. . . .

CHAPTER XI

THE CIRCLE IS BROKEN

EVEN away from Cambridge, which in those under-graduate years was necessarily the hot hub of the universe, life remained as highly coloured as at the time when Lambeth and Addington first flung open their adorable pasturages. It was thrilling to know that Robert Browning was coming to dinner one night, to be grasped by the hearty hand that had written the poems of which a fives competition had procured me a copy. There was but a small party on the night that I remember, and after dinner my father moved up to take the place next him, and beckoned to me to close up on the other side. Somehow a mention came of a volume of Austin Dobson's, and Robert Browning preserved a cheerful silence till some direct question was put to him. Then, drinking off his port, he made a notable phrase.

"Well, some people like carved cherry-stones," he said.

I fancy he always avoided talking of his own works, and that my father knew this, for certainly no allusion was made to them. But, as we rose, he volunteered a question to my father, saying, "What of my work do you like best?" On which my father replied:

"Your lyrics."

Robert Browning gave some great gesticulation; he seems to me now to have rubbed his hands, or jumped or stamped a foot.

"Lyrics?" he said. "I have deskfuls of them."

In consequence, I still faintly hope that some day there may be discovered a great ream of lyrics by Robert Browning, for, as far as I know, "deskfuls" have not yet appeared.

On another occasion Tennyson was there. Of his conversation I have no sort of recollection, the reason for which lapse may be probably accounted for by the fact that he didn't say anything. But I had picked his note of acceptance out of my mother's waste-paper basket and the envelope signed in the bottom left-hand corner, both torn across, so he could not leave me comfortless.

How very odd these dinner-parties, great or small, would have appeared at the present day! There was but one circulation of wine after the ladies had rustled forth, and even when they had gone, there was nothing in the shape of tobacco, which, combined with the indolent progression of the decanter, surely accounted for the austerity of Tennyson. A long sitting of abstemious gentlemen was succeeded by a short sitting in the drawing-room, and then the bell sounded at ten, and the whole company trooped into the chapel for a slightly abbreviated evensong. Sometimes, this service was before dinner; otherwise, at its conclusion, round about half-past ten, the guests departed, for after this long devotional interlude, it was frankly impossible to resume a festive sociability. Already the cigarette-habit had made its footing in most houses, to the extent, anyhow, of a guest, if so decadently inclined, having opportunity of indulging his lust, but neither at Lambeth nor at Addington was there any parleying with the enemy. My father intensely disliked the smell of tobacco, and once only when the present King, as Duke of York, dined at Lambeth, was an after-dinner cigarette allowed. On that occasion I, greatly daring, told my father that he liked a cigarette after dinner (so it was popularly supposed), and for the first time, the gallery of portraits was veiled behind the unusual incense. There were many great stern houses in the eighties, which kept the flag of no surrender flying in the dining-room, but I doubt if any except my father's held out till after the middle of the nineties. He knew of but ignored the existence of a smoking-room at Lambeth and Addington, but neither in drawing-room or dining-room, nor until the hour of bedroom candles (electric lighting being still an exceptional illumination) was there the chance of a cigarette.

A story, *ben trovato*, it may be, was told in this regard, as to how, when a Pan-Anglican conference was in progress at Lambeth and the whole house was buzzing with bishops, my father had occasion late one night to visit the bedroom of one of the prelates, with some paper of *agenda* for next day: He got no answer to his tap on the door, and entered, to find the occupant on his knees before the fire-place. My father, supposing that he was at his private devotions silently withdrew himself, and tiptoed down the corridor again. The devotional tenant, unaware of any entrance, but knowing the rule of the house, continued to inhale his cigar, and puff the aromatic evidence of his crime up the chimney. . . . Though my father knew that his chaplains smoked, he would never acknowledge it, and if a letter, difficultly drafted and brought to him for his approval, bore unmistakable evidences of this aid to inspiration, he would sniff at the original letter and its answer, and say, "He must have written it in a smoking-carriage." And though, again, he knew quite well that all his three sons smoked like chimneys, I have heard him confidently assert that none of us ever did. He would have liked to believe that. In fact he would have liked it so much, that his fervour allowed him to believe it.

But I am sure it never entered his head that my mother smoked. She did: and once after a journey of a day and a night and half a day to the Riffel Alp, my father, absolutely unfatigued, insisted on the whole family getting on to a glacier of some sort without delay. My mother racked with headache, but thinking the air would do her good, came with us, but having gained the glacier, refused to proceed, and sat down on a rock on the moraine to wait for her family's return. She indicated that I should stay with her, and as soon as the family's back was turned she whispered, "Oh, give me a cigarette, Fred." By some strange mischance I hadn't got one, and was only possessed of a small and reeking clay pipe and some tobacco. But I filled and lit it for her, and there she sat smoking her clay pipe like a gipsy-woman, which made me laugh so much that the rest of the family turned round *en bloc* to see what was happening. Nothing appeared to be happening, because she was wise enough to hand the pipe back to me, and on they went. Then she had a little more, and her headache was routed. . . .

That Riffel Alp holiday was one of the most sumptuous. Mountain-climbing with guides and porters is an expensive pursuit, but my father "treated me" straight off to any two first-class peaks I wanted to ascend. My instant first choice was the Matterhorn, and after a few days' gymnastics on less austere summits I set forth, chaperoned by the most zealous of Alpinists, Mr. Toswill, to make this adorable ascent. We slept in the Schwarz-See Hotel, and starting at a moonless midnight to the light of a lantern, stumbled on in that inconvenient illumination till the first hint of dawn made the east dove-coloured and the lantern could be quenched. The excitement of the climb quickened the perceptions, and that opening flower of day was the very glory of the Lord, first shining on the earth. We still climbed in the clear dusk, but high, incredibly high above us the top of the great cliff grew rose-coloured, as the sun, still below our horizon, smote it with day. The sky was clear and the stars grew dim, as the great halls of heaven were slowly flooded with light. Step by step the day descended from peak to shoulder of our mountain till it met us on the rocky stair. Dent Blanche, Rothorn, Gabelhorn, Weisshorn were dazzled with the dawn: looking down into the Zermatt valley was still like gazing into dark clear water.

But that clarity of morning was not for long. On all sides clouds were forming—it is a mistake as a rule to speak of clouds "coming up": they just happen—and before we reached the famous shoulder, it was certain that if we were to make our peak, we must race against the thickening weather. Already the range along the Théodul was blanketed, and mist-wreaths were beginning to form on the east side of our mountain below us. If they stopped there and did not form higher up they would do us no harm, but nobody would choose to be above the shoulder of the Matterhorn in cloud. So at high speed— duly recorded in the Visitors' Book at the hut—we made our peak, opened the bottle of Bouvier (most of which in that low pressure of the air rose like a geyser and intoxicated the snows) and began the descent. The air was notably still: not a breath of wind stirred, but somewhere below us there were boomings of thunder not very remote.

Before we got back to the shoulder a wisp of cloud flicked round the edge of the precipice which plunges a sheer four thousand feet on to the Zmutt glacier, and in a moment we were enveloped by it. The sun was expunged, the cold suddenly grew intense, and snow denser than I thought possible that snow could be, began to fall. In five minutes we wore the thickest white mantles, so too, which was less convenient, did the rocks, which at this point are not only difficult by reason of their steepness, but dangerous because of the downward slope of the strata. The thunder moved up to meet us, in fact we were just beginning to pass into the storm-clouds themselves. The air was highly charged with electricity, for presently the points of our ice-axes fizzled and sang like kettles on the boil. Then below, a light, violet and vivid, leaped suddenly out of the murk of snow, and the thunder reverberated sharp as the crack of a dog-whip. Once our rope got fouled, and we all had to untie ourselves and stand perched on our steps, while the guide wrought to release it. Forty highly exciting minutes enabled us to crawl down through the storm, and reach clear air again, and though I am glad to have dived through a thunderstorm on the Matterhorn, I will willingly dispense with any further experience of the sort. Those forty minutes rattling with ambient thunder were much too tense to allow of conscious alarm, and I never wished I was "safe home" again. But I would never choose to do it a second time.

My second selection was the Dent Blanche, but after starting for it a blizzard made the ascent impossible. So for fear of losing my second big peak altogether—things like the Breithorn, ascents of the Riffelhorn from the glacier, and a subsequent crossing of the eastern face of the Matterhorn were picked up by the way—I chose the Zienal Rothhorn, and with Nellie made an entrancing ascent. There was a huge cowl of snow on the summit, and sheltered by this from the wind we sat for nearly an hour in the blaze of the translucent day. Coming down an ill-fitting boot tore the base of one of her nails, and she was in bed next day with considerable pain. But with what scorn she answered my query as to whether, on her part, the expedition had been worth such a payment. Simultaneously there began a week's bad weather, and we produced a stupendous Swiss *Saturday Magazine*.

My third year at Cambridge, it may be remembered, I had resolved to devote to a strenuous course of the classical tongues, and the autumn of 1889 saw me provided with a shelf of interleaved Latin and Greek authors (in order to make quantities of profound notes on the opposite page); with a firm determination to remember every crabbed phrase in case of finding some approximate English equivalent in passages set for translation from English into Baboo Latin or Greek, and triumphantly dragging it in; with pots of red ink to underline them, and with an optimistic determination of getting a first in my Classical Tripos. Eustace Miles who could work longer and more steadily than anyone I ever came across before or since, became the anchor to keep me moored on the rock of industry, despite the engaging tides and currents that made me long to drift away, and I would take my books to his room and vow that I would remain glued to them as long as he. If I worked alone my infirmity of purpose was something ghastly to contemplate, but the living proximity of a friend who set so shining an example shamed me into industry. He was bound for the same port as I, namely, a first in the Classical Tripos, and was a master in the art of inventing ludicrous phrases which contained the key to dates, and memorized the events of the Peloponnesian War for me in a few unforgettable sentences. We had intervals when we set the table on its side to serve as a back wall for some diminutive game of squash, and then refreshed and dusty we followed the odious symptoms that attended the plague in Athens. I quite lost sight again of the beauty of the classical languages, for just now the learning of them was the mere grinding of the mills that should produce a particular grist. It was no leisurely artistic appreciation, like that which had fitfully inspired me under Beesly and during my last year at school; I but wanted to commit a sort of highway robbery on Sophocles and Virgil, and take from them the purse that should pay my way for a first-class ticket. After two terms of this, for the only time in my life, I was considered to be in danger of growing stale from sheer industry, and for a fortnight of the Easter vacation, in accordance with my father's suggestion, Monty James took two other undergraduates and myself for a bookless tour through Normandy and Brittany. It was nominally a walking-tour, but we went by train, visiting Rouen, Caen, Bayeux, and Lisieux, and finishing up with Amiens and Beauvais. We played quantities of picquet, and the Nixon saga was enriched by a Pindaric Ode in praise of Pnyxon winner in the tricycle race against two Divinity professors. . . .

The last paper in the Tripos, after translations into English from Latin and Greek verse and prose, and translation into Latin and Greek from English, was in classical history, of which I knew nothing whatever, and so I sat up three-quarters of the night and read through the whole of two short history primers. In the few hours that intervened between that degrading process and the history paper, it was impossible to forget crucial dates or events of any magnitude, and by dragging in all collateral information, and dishing it up with a certain culinary skill acquired by years of *Saturday Magazine*, I produced a voluminous vamp of information. And then after some days of waiting came the lists, and the year of Babooism had won its appropriate reward, for, sure enough, I had taken a first. As for the history, I had produced a paper that caused me to be congratulated by the examiner (Dr. Verrall) on my "grasp"—acquired the night before—and was advised by him to take up history for a second Tripos. That, knowing better than he what the tenacity of my grasp really was, I thought better to decline.

Having taken a first (such a first!) my father was more than pleased that, pending the choice of a profession, which I had already secretly registered, I should stop up another year and attempt to perform a similar feat in some other branch of knowledge. Should that also be accomplished, I should be of a status that could see a Fellowship at King's within possible horizons, and he wanted no finer threshold of life for any of his sons than a Fellowship of his college. Here then his scholastic sympathies were completely engaged, but infinitely more potent than they was his desire that we should all of us enter the priesthood of the Church to which, with a unique passion, all his life was dedicated. Arthur at this time, had already been an Eton master for over five years, and had not taken orders, and it was not likely now that he would. I was the next, and when my father more than gladly let me stop up at Cambridge with a view to a second Tripos, for another year, he coupled with his permission the desire that I should attend some Divinity lectures. Never shall I admire tact or delicacy more than his upon this subject. For years while at school he had put before me, never insistently but always potently, his hope that I should be a clergyman, so that now I was quite familiar with it. But at the very moment when a strongly expressed desire on his part might have determined me, he forbore to express such desire at all: if I was to be a clergyman I must have the personal, the individual sense of vocation, and not take orders because he wished it. Already I knew that he wished it, but he would not stir a finger, now that I had come to an age when definite choice opened before me, to influence my decision. He wished me to attend Divinity lectures in order to learn something before I either chose or rejected, but beyond that he never said a word in argument or persuasion, nor even asked me if I had attended these lectures. At the very moment, in fact, when his wish, had he expressed it, that I should take a theological Tripos with a view to ordination, would have had effective weight, seeing that he was allowing me to spend a fourth year at Cambridge, he, with a supreme and perfect delicacy, forbore to put a pennyweight of his own desires into the scale, and welcomed the choice I made of taking up archæology for a second Tripos. He merely wished me to attend a few divinity lectures, and left it at that. Hugh, meantime, triumphantly carrying the banner of early failure which I had so long held against all comers, had unsuccessfully competed, after a year of cramming, in the Indian Civil Service examination, which had been his first choice of a profession. Having failed in that, he was to come up to Trinity in October, unblushing and unhonoured. I passed the banner to him with all good wishes.

There were some weeks of long vacation after the archæological decision was made which I now know to have been loaded with fate so far as my own subsequent life was concerned, though at the time those scribblings I then indulged in seemed to be quite as void of significance as any particular number of the *Saturday Magazine* had been. For one morning, at Cambridge, where I had returned for a few weeks before we went out to Switzerland in August, I desisted from the perusal of Miss Harrison's *Mythology and Monuments of Ancient Athens*, and wrote on the top of a piece of blue foolscap a word that has stuck to me all my life. For a long time there had been wandering about in my head the idea of some fascinating sort of modern girl, who tackled life with uncommon relish and success, and was adored by the world in general, and had all the embellishments that a human being can desire except a heart. Years ago some adumbration of her had occurred in the story that Maggie and I wrote together; that I suppose was the yeast that was now beginning to stir and bubble in my head. She must ride, she must dance, she must have all the nameless attraction that attaches to those who are as prismatic and as hard as crystal, and above all she must talk. It was no use just informing the reader that here was a marvellously fascinating personality, as Maggie and I had done before, or that to see her was to worship her, or that after a due meed of worship she would reveal herself as no more than husk and colouring matter. Explanations and assurances of that sort were

now altogether to be dispensed with. Scarcely even was
the current of her thought, scarcely even were the main
lines of her personality to be drawn: she was to reveal
herself by what she said, and thus, whatever she did,
would need no comment. There is the plain presentment
of the idea that occupied my youthful mind when I wrote
Dodo at the top of a piece of blue foolscap, and put the
numeral "one" on the top right-hand corner; and where
this crude story of mine still puts in a plea for originality,
is in the region of its conscious plan. Bad or good (it
was undoubtedly bad) it introduced a certain novelty
into novel-writing which had "quite a little vogue" for a
time. The main character, that is to say, was made, in
her infinitesimal manner, to draw herself. In staged and
acted drama even, that principle—bad or good—is never
consistently maintained, because other people habitually
discuss the hero and heroine, and the audience's conception of them is based on comment as well as on self-
spoken revelation. Also in drama there is bound to be
some sort of plot, in which action reveals the actor. But
in this story which I scribbled at for a few weeks, there
was no sort of plot: there was merely a clash of minor
personalities breaking themselves to bits against the central gabbling figure. Hideously crude, blatantly inefficient as the execution was, there was just that one new
and feasible idea in the manner of it. What I aimed
at was a type that revealed itself in an individual by
oceans of nonsensical speech.

I wrote with the breathless speed of creation (however
minute such creation was), almost entirely, but not quite,
for my own private amusement. It was not quite for
that internal satisfaction alone, because as I scampered
and scamped, I began to contemplate a book arising out

of these scribblings, a marketable book, that is to say, between covers and for sale. Eventually, for the information of any who happen to remember the total result, I got as far as the lamentable death of Dodo's first husband, and that, as far as I knew then, was the end of the story. Dodo would be thus left a far from disconsolate widow dangling in the air like a blind-string in front of an open window. On the last page of the book, she would remain precisely as she had been on the first; she had not developed, she had not gone upwards or downwards in any moral course; she was a moment, a detail, a flashlight photograph flared on to a plate without the smallest presentment of anything, except what she happened to be at that moment. All this I did not then realize. . . . There it was anyhow, and having finished it, I bundled the whole affair into a drawer, and with that off my mind, concentrated again over the *Mythology and Monuments of Ancient Athens.*

Then followed a few weeks at the Rieder Furca Hotel, above the Aletsch Glacier, opposite the Bel Alp. At that time it was a wooden structure of so light and airy a build that without raising your voice you could talk through the wall to the person next door. Maggie that year was obliged to go to Aix for a course of treatment and my mother went with her, but, even as it was, we nearly filled the little hotel. The weather was bad, an ascent of the Jungfrau which I made in very thick soft snow, after sleeping for two nights at the Concordia hut being the only big (and that an abominable) climb, and there was a great deal of "Cotter's Saturday Night." My father had a larger supply of books than usual, for he was busy with his judgment in the Lincoln trial, to be delivered in the autumn. For a couple of years the case

had been a perpetual anxiety to him. It was doubtful
at first whether he, as Archbishop, possessed the jurisdiction to try it, and while personally (to put the matter
in a nutshell) he was very unwilling to do so, he did
not want the jurisdiction of the See, if it possessed it, to
lapse. The case was one of illegal ritual: and the Church
Association party, at whose instigation it was started, had
obtained their evidence in a manner peculiarly sordid, for
they had sent emissaries to spy on Bishop King's manner
of celebrating the Holy Communion. As their object
was to obtain evidence on that point, it is difficult to
see how else they could have obtained it, but the notion
of evidence thus obtained was revolting to my father.
On the other hand there was Bishop King, a man of the
highest character, of saintly life, an old and beloved
friend of my father's, who was thus accused of illegality
in matters which to the ordinary lay and even clerical
mind were of infinitesimal importance. But the indictment was that he had offended against Ecclesiastical Law,
which my father as head of the Church was bound to up-
hold, so that when, after innumerable arguments and discussion, the Judicial Committee of the Privy Council
found that he had the jurisdiction, he decided to assume
it. That being so, he could dismiss the case as being a
frivolous indictment, but this course undoubtedly would
have caused a split in the English Church, and accordingly he decided to try it. It was heard in February,
1890, and he reserved judgment. It was this pronounce-
ment that occupied him so closely all that summer, and
he finished it in September.

At the beginning of October, Hugh went up to Cambridge, for the assembling of freshmen, and I had still
some ten days which I spent at Addington. Arthur was

already back at Eton, my father and mother and Maggie soon went off on some visit, and thus it happened that Nellie and I for a few days were alone there. We had breakfast very late, with a sense of complete uncontrol, we rode and we played lawn-tennis and talked in the desultory argumentative manner that we both thoroughly enjoyed. In particular we played at "old games," and Beth used to join us. That year the big cedar in the garden was covered with little immature cones, full of a yellow powder like sulphur, and we collected this in glass-topped pill-boxes, part of the ancient apparatus of the moth-collections, shaking the sulphur-laden cones into them, and filling each full to the brim. There was no design as to what we were to do with these: there was just some reversion in our minds to childish "treasures," like the spa and the dead hornet in the aquarium. It was enough to fill these little pill-boxes with the cedar-pollen, and screw the lids on, and know that half a dozen boxes were charged to the brim. We were quite aimless, we saw nobody but Beth, and were wonderfully content. I did a little reading in Overbeck's *Schriftquellen*, and Nellie translated the German part of it to me, to save time. There was nothing more to remember of those days except that delicious sense of leisure and love and liberty: we did nothing except what we wanted to do, and what we seemed to want was to be ridiculous children again. Eventually, after some four or five days, came the afternoon when I had to go back to Cambridge; my father and mother were coming back to Addington that day or the next. Nellie and I parted, greatly regretting that these silly days were done, and made plans for Christmas.

A week or so afterwards, I got a letter from my mother,

saying that Nellie had a diphtheritic sore throat. Anxious news came after that for a few days, but on a certain Sunday I had tidings that she was going on well. Early on Monday morning I got a telegram telling me to come home at once, for she was very much worse. I went round to Trinity to see Hugh, and found he had received a similar telegram. There was a train to London half an hour later, and as I was packing a bag the post came in with reassuring news. But that had been written the day before: the telegram was of later date.

She had died that morning, facing death with the fearless welcome that she had always given to any new experience. During her illness she had not been able to speak at all, but had written little sentences on scraps of paper; after the nature of it was declared she had been completely isolated, but her nurse disinfected these notes and sent them to the others. The first was a joyful little line to my mother, saying that as she had to be in bed, she was going to have a good spell of writing at a story she was engaged on. At the end, the last note but one had been for her nurse; in this she had thanked her and asked, "Is there anything I can do?" Her nurse answered her when she read it, "Let patience do her perfect work." . . . So that was off Nellie's mind. And then last of all she wrote to my mother who was by her bed and she traced out, "I wonder what it will be like. Give them all my love." Then my mother began saying to her, "Jesu, Lover of my soul," and while she was saying it, Nellie died.

That afternoon, we, the rest of us, went out on that still sunny October day and strolled through the woods together, splitting up into twos and threes and rejoining again. My mother seemed to have her hand in Nellie's all the time, telling us, who had come too late, tranquilly and serenely, how the days had gone, and how patient she had been and how cheerful. We recalled all sorts of things about her, with smiles and with laughter, and there was no sense of loss, for my mother brought her amongst us, and never let go of her. Then, back in the house again, there were other arrangements to be made: it was settled that Arthur, Hugh and I should go back to Eton and Cambridge as soon as we could, but after the funeral we must spend a week of quarantine somewhere. How Nellie had got diphtheria was obscure, and it was better that we should not sleep in the house, or run a possible risk of infection. I wanted to see her, but my mother said that what I wanted to see was not Nellie at all, and that I must think of her as I had known her. And as I knew her, so she has always remained for me, collecting the cedar-sulphur, or laughing with open mouth, or grave and eager with sympathy. The glass-lidded pill-boxes were on a ledge of a bookcase, where we had left them a week or two before. My mother had seen them, and thought that there was probably some mystic significance about them, so I told her how Nellie and I had gathered them, and she said, "What treasures: bless her!" Golden October weather it was, with frosts at night and windless days, and the chestnut leaves came peeling off the trees and falling in a heap of tawny yellow below them, each leaf twirling in the air as it fell.

She was buried in Addington churchyard and next her now lies Maggie, and on her other side my mother.

My father, all the time of Nellie's illness, had been hard at work on the final revision of his Lincoln judgment: now the delivery of that was postponed for a little, but not for long. Everyone had to get back normally and naturally to the work and the play and the joy and sorrow of life again, but at the Christmas holidays it was seen how huge a gap had come in the circle which since Martin's death, twelve years before, had grown up together, critical and devoted and wildly alive. No one, when all were so intent on the businesses in hand, had estimated when a play, for instance, must be written and rehearsed and managed, how largely it was Nellie's enthusiastic energy that carried things through. So there was no play that Christmas, and the year after four of us, my father and mother and Maggie and I, were in Algiers, another year they were in Florence, and another Maggie and I were in Egypt, and so that particular blaze of young activity of which Christmas holidays had been the type and flower came to an end. Besides we were all getting older, and there was no Nellie; with her death some unrecapturable magic was lost.

Of the many intimate friendships of my mother's life none was closer than that which had ripened during these years at Lambeth with Lucy Tait, the daughter of the late Archbishop. She had constantly been with us in town and at Addington, and now, after Nellie's death, she made her permanent home with us. Then, when the Lambeth days were over she continued, until my mother's death, twenty-two years later, to devote her life to her.

CHAPTER XII

AN ARCHÆOLOGICAL EXCURSION

AT Cambridge the study of archæology had forcibly taken possession of me by right of love, and at last I was working at that which it was my business to be occupied in, with devotion to my subject. Roman art, so I speedily discovered, was an utterly hideous and debased affair in itself, and the only things of beauty that emerged from Rome were copies of Greek originals, and even then these copies were probably made by Greek workmen. In Roman buildings also all that was worth looking at was stolen from the Greeks, and often marred in the stealing, and the thick mortar between their roughly hewn stones, the facing of them with a dishonest veneer of marble, their abominable tessellated pavements, the odious wall decorations of Pompeii revolted this ardent Hellenist. Now, too, for the first time since I came up to Cambridge, I came under an inspired and inspiring teacher; indeed, there were two such, for it was impossible not to burn when Dr. Waldstein in the Museum of Casts flung himself into Hellenic attitudes, and communicated his volcanic enthusiasm. But more inspiring yet was Professor Middleton: he gave me no formal lectures, but encouraged me to bring my books to his room, and spend the morning there. He used to walk about in a thick dressing-gown and a skull-cap, looking like some Oriental magician, and now he would pull an intaglio ring off his

finger and make me perceive the serene and matchless
sobriety of an early gem as compared with the more
florid design, still matchless in workmanship, of a later
century, or take half a dozen Greek coins out of his waistcoat pocket and bid me decipher the thick decorative letters and tell him where they came from.   He had dozens
of notebooks filled with sketches of Greek mouldings and
cornices: there were sections of the columns of the Parthenon that showed how the drums had been ground round
each on the other, till, without any mess of mortar, they
adhered so closely that the joint was scarcely visible.
There were cedar-wood blocks in the centres of them with
bronze pins round which they revolved; the honesty and
precision of the workmanship could never be discovered
till the column was in ruins.   But there was the very
spirit and ardency of Greece; and as for the great frieze
of horsemen sculptured on the walls of the Parthenon it
was so placed that only a mere glimpse of it could be had
by those who walked in the colonnade.   Yet in honour of
the goddess and in obedience to the imperious craving
for perfection, it, though scarcely to be seen, must be of
a fineness and finish unequalled in all the forums of
Rome.   Then Middleton would take a fragment of Greek
pottery from a drawer, or a white *lekythus* from Eretria,
and show me the mark of the potter's wheel, and how the
white ground was laid on after the baking, and how the
artist with brush delicate and unerring had drawn the
raised arm of the *ephebus* who laid his garland on the
tomb.   There were photographs also from the Street of
Tombs; in one there was standing a young girl with
braided hair.   She it was who was dead, and the mother
stood in front of her lifting the small face upwards with
a hand under her chin, bending to kiss her for the last

time, and such of the inscription as remained ran
XAIPEΠENΘ . . . The rest of the letters was gone,
but that was sufficient, and told how her mother gave
the final greeting of Godspeed and of farewell to
Penthesilea, for in that beautiful tongue "Hail"! and
"Good-bye" are the same word and affectionately wish
prosperity, whether for one who returns to the home, or
goes from the home on the longest journey of all. And
Professor Middleton made me realize the serenity of those
good wishes for Penthesilea: there was a wistfulness on
the part of those who remained, and a wonder and a great
hope, and God knows how that struck home to me. . . .
Or a young man sat languid on a rock, and his hunting
spear was propped behind him, and beside him just one
companion, weary with watching, had fallen asleep.
There was no mother there to send him on his way; his
friend and his hunting-spear were his comrades on earth,
and these he must leave behind him, when to-day he fared
out on his new adventure, further afield than ever his
huntings had taken him. . . . And thus to me, the
supreme race of all who have inhabited this earth became
real. They heard the voice of creation as none other has
heard it, and saw as none other has seen. They realized
in dawn and in nightfall the attainment towards which
all others have fruitlessly striven, showing in marble the
humanity of the divine, and the divinity of man; they
had birthdays for their gods, and for their dead, who
died not, they had the imperishable love that knows not
fear.

Professor Middleton never alluded in any way to this
archæological tripos which I was to challenge after one
year's work. All the morning, three times a week or
more, I used to sit there with my books that I never read,

because he, in his dressing-gown, produced, one after the other, little bits of things which would make me love the Greeks for no other reason than for the artistic joy of their works and days. He knew of course that there was a tripos impending, and this in his view was the best way of preparing for it; while for drier stuff he gave me his notebooks on Vitruvius, which would, with his little exquisite sections and elevations, explain all that I need know about the bones and alphabet of architecture. His whole procedure, as I saw then, and his whole object was to make me want to know, down to their sandals and their salad-bowls and brooches, all that was to be learned of the brains of a god-like race. Once, so I remember, a bitter blizzard white with snow beat against the windows, and from some roof near a slate flew off and crashed in the small court at King's where the mulberry tree grew. "That was Oreithyia," he said, sucking on his pipe. "Boreas loved her, and blew her away. Rude Boreas, you know. You should read up the myths. Most of Greek sculpture illustrates myths."

Since the days when I was fifteen, since Beesly and the *Trojan Queen's Revenge*, there had been no such inspirer. But Beesly dealt only with language, while under Middleton the dry bones which had come together, not only stood up "an exceeding great army," but went about their work, and returned to their homes of an evening, and lived and loved. Beesly had brought me to the portals of the house of the people who made Art, and knocked on the door for me. But Middleton pushed it open, and the gold standard of the Greeks that, theoretically, seven years ago I knew to be the only coinage, was now weighed and was found sufficient, and all else whatever baser stuff might load the opposing balance was found wanting.

It was at some time during that year that J. K. Stephen, the founder of the T.A.F., returned to King's, and instantly for me all the lesser lights of general influence were eclipsed. In presence and personality alike he was one of those who without effort or aim impose themselves on their circle. Had he never said a word, the very fact of his being in the room must have produced more effect that any conversation that might go on round him. He was splendidly handsome, big of head, impressive and regular of feature, and enormously massive in build; slow moving and shambling when he walked, but somehow monumental. He had an immense fund of humour, grim and rather savage at times, at others of such froth and frolic as appeared in the two volumes of verse which he published during the next year, *Lapsus Calami*, and *Quo Musa tendis*. But this bubbling lightness was markedly uncharacteristic of his normal self. That it was there, those two volumes proved, but that particular spring, that light-hearted Puck-like quality, he certainly reserved for his verse, which to those who knew him was in no way the flower of his mind. In the dedication to *Lapsus Calami*, he expresses the desire that the reader should recognize his debt to "C.S.C." (Calverley of *Fly Leaves*), he hopes that some one will think that "of C.S.C. this gentle art he learned," and undoubtedly the reader did think so, for it was certainly C.S.C. whose method inspired some of these poems. But it is just these poems in which he was obviously indebted to Calverley, that are least worthy and characteristic of him. Jim Stephen made, at his worst, amusing neat little rhymes not nearly so good as Calverley's, but, at his best, he made poems, such as "The Old School List," of which Calverley was quite incapable. Both also were brilliant parodists, but here J.K.S. had a far subtler art than the man with whom he hoped his readers would compare him. Calverley's famous parody of Robert Browning, "The Cock and the Bull," does not touch in point of rapier-work J.K.S.'s poem "Sincere Flattery to R.B." The one does no more than seize on ridiculous phrases in Browning, and go a shade further in absurdity: the other ("Birthdays") parodies the very essence of the more obscure lyrics: you cannot read it, however often you have done so, without the hope that you may this time or the next find out what it means. He was the inventor, too, of a peculiarly pleasing artifice with regard to parody, for he put into Wordsworth's mouth, for instance, in pure Wordsworthian phrase, the exact opposite of Wordsworth's teaching, and produced a lament over the want of locomotive power in the Lake district. The effect is inimitable: the poet longs to see in those happy days when Helvellyn's base is tunnelled, and its peak grimy

> The dusky grove of iron rails
> Which leads to Euston Square,

and in lines that almost must have been written by Wordsworth exclaims:

> I want to hear the porters cry,
> "Change here for Ennerdale!"

And I must be forgiven, since so few know the poem, for quoting the postscript to his parody of Browning, sufficient surely to make the poet, for whom Jim Stephen had an immense reverence, turn in his grave in order to laugh more easily. As follows:

P.S.

There's a Me Society down at Cambridge
Where my works, *cum notis variorum*
Are talked about: well, I require the same bridge
As Euclid took toll at as *Asinorum*.

And as they have got through several ditties
I thought were as stiff as a brick-built wall
I've composed the above, and a stiff one it is,
A bridge to stop asses at, once for all.

If the art of parody can go further, I do not know who
has conducted it there. The kindly ghost of Robert
Browning might perhaps shrug his shoulders at "The
Cock and the Bull," and say, "Very amusing": but reading Jim Stephen's R.B. he must surely have winced and
frowned first, and thereafter broken into a roar of his
most genial laughter.

Often (when not indebted to C.S.C.) Jim Stephen's
most apt and biting parodies would be written or spouted
extempore: I remember for instance someone reading a
rather lamentable verse from F. W. Myers in which he
delicately alludes to the godly procreation of children
in the following lines:

Lo! when a man magnanimous and tender,
Lo! when a woman desperate and true,
Make the irrevocable sweet surrender,
Show to each other what the Lord can do.

upon which Jim Stephen without a moment's pause exclaimed:

Lo! when a man obscene and superstitious,
Lo! when a woman brainless and absurd,
Strive to idealize the meretricious,
Love one another like a beast or bird.

This could not be included in *Lapsus Calami*, nor unfortunately would he include one of his most ingenious extravagances, and I cannot find that it has ever been published. The subject matter was that a burglar "desperate and true" awoke in the night and found an angel standing in his room, who asked him whether, being what he was, he would sooner go to heaven or hell, the choice being entirely his. His admirably logical conclusion was as follows:

> The burning at first no doubt would be worst,
> But custom that anguish would soften;
> But those who are bored by praising the Lord,
> Would be more so by praising him often.

He chooses accordingly.

All that year Jim remained in residence at Cambridge; during one vacation he stayed with us at Addington, during another I went over to his Irish home, where, one evening after an argument about Kipling, he took up his bedroom candle saying, "Well, I wish he would stop kipling. Good night." In ten minutes he came back, "I've written a poem about it," he said, and proceeded to read the two immortal stanzas which end,

> When the Rudyards cease from kipling,
> And the Haggards ride no more.

Close friends though we were, I was always conscious of a side of him that was formidable, of the possibility of a sudden blaze of anger flaring up though quickly extinguished again: there was, too, always present the knowledge of that "dark tremendous sea of cloud" in the skirts of which he had been before, and into the heart of

which it was inscrutably decreed that he must go.   There
came a dark December morning; that time the breakdown
was final, and he lived not many weeks.

Once again I made a triumphant tripos in the matter of
archæology, was given an open scholarship at King's, and
immediately afterwards applied for one of those grants
that seemed to hang like ripe plums on the delightful
tree of knowledge.   Hitherto those branches had waved
high above my head, but now they graciously swept downwards and I plucked at the first plum I saw, and applied
for a small grant to excavate in the town-walls at
Chester.   There was reason to suppose that quantities of
the Roman tombstones of the legionaries that had been
stationed there, had been utilized in the building of the
town-wall, and though there were only Roman remains
to be discovered (would that they had been Greek!) the
search for them would be a very pleasant pursuit for the
autumn, and might yield material for a fellowship-dis-
sertation.   To my intense surprise some grant—from the
Würtz Fund, I think—was given me, for the purpose of
discovering, if possible, new facts about the distribution
of Roman legions in Britain.

The family went out to Pontresina that August, and I
with them for a week or two before the work at Chester
began.   There I had a most horrible experience with
Hugh on the Piz Palu, one of the peaks of the Bernina.
Our plan was to make a "col" of it, that is to ascend it
on one side, pass over the top, and descend on another.
We tramped and perspired up southern slopes in deep
snow on the ascent, struck an arête which led to the top,
made the summit, and began to descend by another route.
The way lay over a long ridge swept by the most biting

north wind, from which on the ascent the mountain had screened us, and never have I encountered so wicked a blast. The loose snow whirled up from the rocks was driven against us as if it was torrents of icy rain, piercing and penetrating. Once as we halted, I noticed that Hugh shut his eyes, and seemed sleepy, but he said that he was all right and on we went. He was on the rope just in front of me behind the leading guide, and suddenly, without stumbling, he fell down in a heap. He was just conscious when we picked him up and said, "I'm only rather sleepy; let me go to sleep . . ." and then collapsed again.

He was alive and little more. Raw brandy, of which we had about half a pint, stimulated him for a moment, and soon, after another and another dose, our brandy was gone. There was no question of the inadvisability of giving him spirits, in order to warm him, which is one of the most fatal errors when a climber is suffering from mere cold: there was just the hope of keeping him alive by any stimulant. It was not possible to go back over the summit, and so to get into more sheltered conditions again; the best chance, and that a poor one, was to convey him down somehow along the rest of this bitter ridge, till we could find shelter from the wind. Very soon he became completely unconscious, he could move no more at all, and the guide and the porter whom we had with us simply carried him along the rest of the ridge. The rope was altogether a hindrance, so we took it off, and proceeded in two separate parties. The guides carried Hugh between them, and I followed.

I had no idea after we had made this arrangement if Hugh was alive or not; often I had to wait till they got round some awkward corner, and then make my way after

them. Places that would have been easily traversed by
a roped party, took on a totally different aspect, when two
men unroped were carrying another, and when the fourth
of the party had to traverse them alone. What chiefly
occupied my benumbed mind was the sort of telegram
that would be sent to my father when we got down to the
foot of the glacier below, where there was communication
with Pontresina. Should I be sending a telegram that
Hugh was dead, or should I have slipped, and thus be
incapable of sending a telegram at all, or would nobody
come back? . . . For some hour or so this procession
went on its way: after I had waited for the trio to get
round some rock or obstruction on the ridge, I followed,
and caught sight of them again a dozen yards further
down. Whether they were carrying a corpse or not I
had no idea.

Gradually we came to the end of this ridge. I had
waited for them to scramble over a difficult passage, and
then they disappeared round a corner. One of the guides
had loosened a rock, and when I tried to step on it, it
gave way altogether and rattled down the almost precipi-
tous slope to the side. I had recovered on to my original
standing-ground, but with that rock gone, and being
alone and unroped, it took me some couple of minutes,
I suppose, to find a reliable foothold. When that was
done, a couple of steps more brought me, as it had brought
them, completely out of the wind, and on to a broiling
southern slope. Fifty feet below me there came another
corner, which they had already passed, and I could see
nothing further. I went round that corner, and found the
two guides roaring with laughter and Hugh quite drunk.
He was making some sort of ineffectual attempt to sit
on the point of his ice-axe. He was not dead at all: he

was only drunk. The moment, apparently, that they had got out of that icy blast, his heart-action must have re-asserted itself, and there was a half-pint of raw brandy poured into an empty stomach to render accounts. With thick and stumbling speech, he staggered along, assuring us that he had only been rather sleepy. . . . And so he had, and I emptied the fine snow that had been driven in about my knees through my knickerbockers, and had no need to send any telegrams.

Except for that adventure, which I would gladly have done without, Pontresina was an uneventful place, rather picnicky and wearisome. There was a friend of my sister Maggie there under the sentence of the white death: there was an elderly bishop who attached himself some-what to our party: there was Miss Margot Tennant whom then I met for the first time; and after a rather dull fort-night, I turned back to England to embrace the career, at Chester, of a serious archæologist.

Now there was no particular reason why the Corpo-ration of Chester should allow a young gentleman from Cambridge University to pull the city walls about, in the hope of extracting therefrom Roman tombstones, even though he was quite willing that these monuments, if discovered, should be presented to the local museum. So with a view to securing a warmer welcome, I had got my father to write to the Duke of Westminster at Eaton, and this was a gloriously successful move. I went over to see him, explained the plan, and got his support. He in turn wrote to the Mayor urging the claims of archæ-ology on an enlightened town, and gave me £50 to aug-ment the grant from the Würtz fund. The technical part of the work, the underpinning of the wall, the subsequent

building of it up again in case we extracted Roman tombstones from it was entrusted to the city surveyor: local
subscriptions came in, and tombstones of considerable importance came out, for we found that a legion, *"Legio
Decima Valeria Victrix"* (The victorious Valerian),
whose presence in England was hitherto unknown, had
been stationed at Chester. Professor Mommsen, the his-
torian, must be informed about that, and the copies of
these tombstones must be sent him, and these produced a
letter of congratulation and acknowledgment from the
great man. I skipped with joy over that, for was not
this an apotheosis for the family dunce, that Professor
Mommsen should applaud his work? And again I
skipped when one of the famous post-cards came from
Hawarden, asking me to come over and tell Mr. Gladstone about these finds. The sense of diplomacy spiced
that adventure, for profoundly ignorant though I was
about politics, I had just the prudence to be aware that
Eaton and Hawarden must not be put, so to speak, into
one pocket, since Mr. Gladstone with his policies of
Home Rule for Ireland and the Disestablishment of the
Welsh Church had digged a gulf of liquid fire between
himself and the Duke. There must be nothing said that
could tend to stoke that, and strict was the guard that
I set on my lips.

All are agreed on the sense of the terrific latent energy
with which that quiet country-house was stored: there was
high tension in its tranquillity. You felt that if you
touched anything a great electric spark might flare with
a cracking explosion towards your extended finger. . . .
I got there during the morning and was at once taken to
see Mr. Gladstone. He was in his study, sitting at his

"political" table: that other table was the table where
he worked at Homer, so he presently explained to me, suggesting though not actually stating the image which flew
into my mind, of his boiling over, so to speak, at the
political table, that furnace of fierce contention and
white-hot enthusiasm, and of his putting himself to cool
off from controversy by the Ionian Sea. He instantly
plunged into the subject of Roman legionaries in Britain
as if nothing else really mattered or ever had mattered to
him, and pored over the copies of a few inscriptions I had
brought him. But he wanted more lively evidence than
a mere copy.

"I should like to see the squeezes of these," he said.
"Do you know the only proper way to make squeezes?
You take your sheet of blotting-paper, and after you have
washed the stone, you lay it on, pressing the paper into
the letters of the inscription. Then sprinkle it with
water, but by no means wet your paper before you have
laid it on the stone, because it is apt to tear if you do
that. Then take a clothes brush—not too stiff a one—
and tap the surface over and over again with the bristles.
By degrees you will get the paper to mould itself into all
the letters of the inscription, and where there are letters
apparently quite perished, it will often show you some
faint stroke from which you can conjecture what the
missing letter has been, though it is invisible to the eye.
And let your blotting paper get dry before you remove
it. Otherwise again you may tear it. Yes, we are coming
to lunch: we know," he said to Mrs. Gladstone, who
came in for the second time to say it was ready.

I do not of course pretend to reproduce the precise
wording of this little dissertation on blotting-paper-
squeezes, but there or thereabouts was the substance of it,

E. F. BENSON, ÆT. 22

[Page 269

full of detail, full of fire and gesticulation, as if he himself had invented the science of squeezes, and had done nothing all his life but make them.

After lunch he said he would drive me to St. Deiniol's, the library, chiefly theological and philosophical, that he was arranging, largely with his own hands, from his vast accumulation of books, for the benefit of the district, and in especial, for that of clerical students whose Church he had vainly attempted to disestablish. Soon after lunch it was announced that the carriage was round, and he went to the door. I had supposed that there would be some brougham or whatnot in charge of a coachman; instead there was a pony carriage for two, with a groom holding tight on to the pony's head. Mr. Gladstone, already very dim-sighted, peered at the pony, and said to me, "Wait a minute: that pony's a beast," and hurried back into the house reappearing again with a formidable whip. Then I became aware that he and I were going alone, and that Mr. Gladstone, armed with this whip in case the pony was "beastly," was intending to drive, for he took up the reins, and, as soon as I was in, said to the groom, "Let go, Charles," and whacked the pony over the rump to teach him that there was his master sitting inside. Under this charioteer, blind and aged and completely intrepid, we cantered away to St. Deiniol's, Mr. Gladstone pointing at objects of interest with his whip, and reminding the pony that he would catch it, if he misbehaved. From there, I think he drove me to the station and returned alone. I duly sent him squeezes prepared in the manner he had prescribed, and received a series of post-cards suggesting the probable readings of erased letters, and when next I went to Hawarden that autumn, there were passages he had turned up in the

"Corpus Inscriptionum Latinarum" which bore on this tombstone and on that, discharged at me as if from a volcano. . . .

Six weeks' exploration was enough to exhaust my funds, and I carried my squeezes and my sketches back to Cambridge, there to put the results into shape. . . . And there I found, and re-read with a suddenly re-kindled interest those pages of blue foolscap on the first of which was the heading "Dodo." I had written them chiefly for my own amusement, but now, rightly or wrongly, I had the conviction that they might amuse others as well. But I really had no idea, till I took them out again, what they were like; now it occurred to me that the people in them were something like real people, and that the whole in point of agitating fact was something like a real book, that might be printed and bound. . . . But I instantly wanted another and if possible a story-teller's opinion about it, and sent it off to my mother, asking her to read it first, and if it seemed to her to provide any species of entertainment, to think whether she could not manage to induce Mrs. Harrison (Lucas Malet) or Henry James, to cast a professional eye over it. She managed this with such success, that a few days afterwards she wrote to me to say that Henry James had consented to read it, and give his frank opinion. The packet she had already, on his consent, despatched to him.

Now this MSS. which thus had reached the kindest man in the world, was written in a furious hurry and covered with erasures, that exploded into illegible interpolations, and was indited in such a hand as we employ on a note that has to be dashed off when it is time already to go to the station. This was genially hinted at when late in November the recipient announced to me his judgment in the matter; for he prefaced his criticism with an apology for having kept it so long, and allowed that, in consentng to read and criticize, he had "rather over-estimated the attention I should be able to give to a production in manuscript of such substantial length. We live in such a world of type-copy to-day that I had taken for granted your story would come to me in that form. . . ."

I should like to call the attention of Mr. Max Beer-bohm, our national caricaturist and parodist, to this unique situation. Henry James at that time had lately evolved the style and the method which makes a deeper gulf between his earlier books and his later than exists be-tween different periods of the work of any other artist. Nearest perhaps in this extent and depth of gulf comes the case of the painter Turner, but the most sober and quiet example of his early period is not so far sundered from the most riotous of Venetian sunrises, as is, let us say, "Roderick Hudson" from "The Ivory Tower." Just about now Henry James had realized, as he told my mother, that all his previous work was "subaqueous": now, it seemed to him that he had got his head above water, whereas to those who adored his earlier work he appeared to have taken a header into some bottomless depth, where no plummet could penetrate. At this pre-cise moment when he had vowed himself to psychological analysis so meticulous and intricate that such action as he henceforth permitted himself in his novels had to be sifted and searched for and inferred from the motives that prompted it, he found himself committed to read a long and crabbed MS., roughly and voluptuously squirted on to the paper. With what sense of outrage as he deciphered it sentence by sentence must he have found himself confronted by the high-spirited but hare-brained harangues of my unfortunate heroine and her wordy friends! Page after page he must have turned, only to discover more elementary adventures, more nugatory and nonsensical dialogues. At the stage at which my story then was, I must tell the reader that the heroine was far more extravagant than she subsequently became: She was much pruned and tamed before she made her printed appearance. The greater part of her censored escapades have faded from my mind, but I still remember some occasion soon after her baby's death when she was discovered, I think by Jack, doing a step-dance with her footman. It must all have seemed to Henry James the very flower and felicity of hopeless, irredeemable fiction and still he persevered. . . . Or did he persevere? He wrote me anyhow the most careful and kindly of letters, following it by yet another, delicately and delightfully forbearing to quench the smoking flax.

"I am such a fanatic myself," he writes in the earlier of these, "on the subject of form, style, the evidence of intention and meditation, of chiselling and hammering out in literary things that I am afraid I am rather a cold-blooded judge, rather likely to be offensive to a young story-teller on the question of quality. I'm not sure that yours strikes me as quite so ferociously literary as my ideal. . . . Only remember that a story is, essentially a form, and that if it fails of that, it fails of its mission. . . . For the rest, make yourself a style. It is by style we are saved."

In case the reader has given a glance to *Dodo*, can he imagine a more wisely expressed opinion, that opinion, in fact, being no opinion at all? Never by any possibility could that MS. have seemed to him worth the paper it was written on, or two minutes of his own time. With what a sigh of relief he must have bundled it into its wrapper again!

I suppose I was incorrigible on this question of scribbling, for I was not in the least discouraged. But for the time the further adventures of the book were cut short by its author's Odysseys, for directly after Christmas my father and mother, Maggie, Lucy Tait and I started for Algiers, through which we were to journey together as far as Tunis. After that I was going on to Athens to spend the spring there studying at the British School of Archæology, and it was with a light heart that I clapped Dodo, after this austere outing, back into a drawer again to wait till I could attend to her.

CHAPTER XIII

A CURIOUS incident marked that Algerian tour. Before going, my father told Queen Victoria of his intention, and she had at first been against his travelling so far afield, putting it to him that if his presence in England was urgently and instantly required, there might be some difficulty about his getting back in time. Whether she had in her mind the possibility of her own sudden death she did not explain. But presently she seemed to think that her reluctance that he should be so remote from England was unfounded: she changed her mind and wished him an interesting and delightful journey. So from Algiers we went slowly eastwards visiting Constantine, Tebessa, Timeghad and Fort National on the way, our most remote point from Englar ? –via Tunis on the one side or (retracing our steps) Algiers on the other—being Biskra. We got there late one afternoon, and waiting for my father was a telegram from the Lord Chamberlain, announcing the death of Prince Edward, Duke of Clarence, from influenza, and giving the date for the funeral. My father and I with guides and Bradshaws vainly attempted to find a route by which he could get back to England in time, but such route did not exist. Had this news come that morning he could have got back, so also could he, if the funeral had been arranged for the day after that for which it was fixed:

but just here, at Biskra, and nowhere else throughout the journey was my father unable to return in time. It would perhaps be going too far to say that the Queen had anything in her mind definite enough to call a premonition; but the event happening just then was at least a most curious coincidence. . . . A few hours afterwards a second telegram arrived, from the Prince of Wales who, with great thoughtfulness, begged him not to interrupt his tour.

My father was thus able to realize one of the dearest dreams of his life, namely, to see with his mortal eyes the Carthage which he knew so intimately in connection with his lifelong study of Cyprian. His book on Cyprian which had occupied his leisure for some thirty years was now approaching completion, and long had he yearned to behold the ruined site where Cyprian had worked as bishop, to wander with his own feet over the shores and hills, which, all these years, had been so familiar to him; and that visit to Carthage had for him the sacredness of some pilgrimage for which his heart hungered. His own enthusiasm was so keen that I feel sure that he had no idea that his Mecca could be less to us than to him, and I have the vision of him kneeling on the site of some early Christian church, with his face all aglow with the long-deferred consummation. Just as his appreciation of a picture was mainly due to the nature of its subject, just as his pleasure in music was derived from the words which were sung to it, so now, as his diary records, he saw enchanting loveliness in that bare and featureless hill where Carthage once stood, for Cyprian's sake, and wondered at the want of perception which caused other travellers to find nothing admirable in that bleak place. For once the classical associations of Carthage, the Punic Wars, the subsequent Roman occupation had no lure for him. Cyprian, Bishop of Carthage, was the full moon among the lesser lights of the firmament.

At Tunis I left the rest of them, going on my own special pilgrimage, and via Malta and Brindisi I came to the city already known to me by map and picture, and hallowed by some kind of predestined love. And just as my father was enchanted with that ugly little hill of Carthage because Cyprian had dwelt there, how was I not transported when above mean streets and miry ways I saw the sparkle of that marble crown of temples on the Acropolis? For indeed, from the time that Beesly had read us his *Trojan Queen's Revenge*, some idea, some day-dream of Athens had been distilled, drop by drop, into my blood. Whatever was lovely, whatever must be estimated and esteemed I always laid alongside some Greek standard. Not alone were things directly Greek, like the chorus of the *Œdipus in Colonos*, the chorus in Swinburne's *Atalanta*, the teachings of Middleton, the holy dead in the Street of Tombs tested by the Hellenic touchstone, but whatever moved my heart, the vision of Mary Anderson in the *Winter's Tale*, the joy of athletics, the austere crests of mountains, the forest of Savernake, the Passion-music of Bach, had been instinctively subjected to the same criterion.

The material standard and symbol of that, by this subtle subconscious distillation, had always been the Acropolis, and on this crystalline January afternoon, it was mine to hurry along a tawdry Parisian boulevard, set with pepper trees, to see on one side the columns of the temple of Zeus, and on the other the circular Shrine of the Winds. On the right, as I knew well, I should soon pass the theatre of Dionysus and not turn aside for that

even, and then would come the stoa of Asclepius and a
great Roman colonnade, and for none of these had I a
glance or a thought to spare, for over the sheer southern
wall of the Acropolis there rose the south-west angle of
the Parthenon. And then, with a reverence that was as
sincere as love itself and not less ardent, I mounted the
steps of the Propylæa, with the rebuilt shrine on the
right of that fairy-presence, the Wingless Victory, who
shed her pinions because for all time she was to abide in
Athens; and on the left was the great bastion wall stained
to an inimitable russet by the winds from Salamis, and
between the great Doric columns I passed, and there in
front was a bare scraped hill-top, and glowing in the sunset was the west front of the Parthenon, that serene abiding presence, set for a symbol of what Athens stood for,
and, no less, of the eternal yearning of man for the glorious city of God. Behind rose the violet crown of hills,
Hymettus and Pentelicus and Parnes.

"Holy, holy, holy!" was the first message of it, and
then like the dawn flowing down the cliffs of the Matterhorn, it illuminated all that on earth had the power to
be kindled at its flame. Like the Sphinx it articulated
its unanswerable riddle, and by its light it revealed the
solution, and by its light it hid it again. The architect
who had planned it, the sculptor who had decorated it,
the hands that had builded it and formed the drums of its
columns into monoliths of translucent stone had thrown
themselves into the furnace of the creation that transcended all the wit and the cunning of its creators. They
raised but a fog or a smoke of human endeavour, and
from outside, no less than from the heart of their love,
there dawned for them and for us the light invisible.
Whatever love of beauty was in their souls was tran-

scended and translated into stone; the glory of jubilant
youth and of ridden stallions, of maidens who wove the
mantle of the goddess, of priests and of the hierarchy of
gods was but part of some world-offering to the austere
and loving and perfect presence which they had instinctively worshipped, and, as in some noble trance, had set
in symbol there.   With what wonder must they have beheld the completed work of their hands, and, in their
work, the indwelling of the power that was its consecra-
tion.

A tremendous impression, such as that first sight of the
Parthenon undoubtedly made on me, would be a very
doubtful gain, if it caused the rest of life to seem uninteresting by comparison, for any kind of initiation must
quicken rather than blunt the workaday trivial activities,
and certainly in this case I lost no perception of the actual
in the flash of the absolute.   Athens at that time (to
fuse together the impressions of this and subsequent
years) was the most comic of European capitals; it was
on the scale of some small German principality, and while
aping the manner of Paris in a backwater, claimed descent
from Pericles.   It was *opera-bouffe*, seriously carried out,
imagining itself in fact to be the last word in modern enlightenment no less than in classical romance.   It was
with just that classical seriousness that the Olympic
games were, a little later, reinaugurated here, and with
all the gaiety of *opera-bouffe* that defeated competitors
passionately argued with judges and umpires.   At the
top of the town came "Constitution Square," which com-
prised an orange-garden and a parade-ground, where on
festive occasions the regiments of Guards deployed and
manœuvred, quite, or nearly, occupying the centre of it:
and there have these eyes seen the flower of the Greek

army routed and dispersed by an irritated cab-horse, which, clearly possessed by the devil, galloped and wheeled and galloped again till the Guards had very prudently taken cover among the orange trees, for it was impossible to make any effective military display, when harassed by that enraged quadruped. Sometimes I think that this distressing scene was an adumbration of how, a few years later, that same army bolted through Thessaly on the approach of the Turks. "The host of hares" was the Turkish phrase for them, and Edhem Pasha, then commander-in-chief of the Ottoman army, described to me, when I was at Volo after the Turkish occupation of Thessaly, the battle of Pharsala. "We came over the hill," he said, without enmity and without contempt, "and we said 'Sh-sh-sh' and we clapped our hands, and that was the battle of Pharsala." . . . How complete has been the regeneration of this versatile people may be gathered from their later campaigns against the same adversaries.

On three sides of Constitution Square, were hotels and cafés and the residence of the Crown Prince Constantine subsequently cast by destiny for the ludicrous rôle of "King Tino." On the fourth side the Royal Palace, of a similarly pretentious and ugly style as that which looks over St. James's Park, presented a mean and complicated face to the steam-tramway that puffed through the top of the square on its way to Phaleron. A royal baby, that year or the next, had seen the light, and we foreign but loyal Athenians, what time a bugler stationed in the colonnade of the palace made all kinds of music, craned our necks and focussed our eyes to see the King come forth. But in nine cases out of ten, it was not King George who emerged but a perambulator pushed by an English nursery-maid. But that was the dynastic custom: whenever a royal personage came forth from the palace, the bugler made all kinds of music, so that the inhabitants of Athens might, like good Nebuchadnezzarites, fall down and worship the pink little image. . . . Sometimes, however, their loyalty obtained a more adult reward, for on Sunday afternoon King George would generally go down to Phaleron in the steam-tram, and observe the beauties of nature. On such occasions he was marvellously democratic, and would come trotting across the belt of gravel between the palace and the tram-lines in order not to keep his citizens waiting. There is no doubt that if he had attempted to do so, the tram would have gone without him, leaving him to follow by the next, or study the beauties of nature in his own garden.

He was democratic also towards foreigners. A tourist staying in one of the respectable hotels round Constitution Square, for instance, was quite at liberty to intimate to the Minister of his country that an audience with the King would be agreeable, and in due course some footman from the palace, in gorgeous well-worn livery, would bear a missive with a tremendous crown on the envelope which informed him that King George would give him an audience next day. Or, if you did not express your loyal desire, it would perhaps be intimated that it would be quite in order if you did so, and thereupon, on the appointed morning you would put on your evening dress-clothes (rather green in the sunlight), and a white tie, and a straw hat, and present yourself at the palace door. On seeing this apparition the bugler stationed there has been known to give one throaty blast, thinking that any-one so ridiculously attired must be a royal personage, then, catching the affrighted eye of the visitor, he recognized his mistake, and with an engaging smile, saluted instead. You took off your straw hat (or if it was winter your top-coat and bowler) and were ushered with a series of obeisances into a small bare room, furnished with a carafe of water. Then a door was thrown open, and, as in a dream, you advanced into a small apartment with a purple paper and gold stars upon it, and found the King. He always stood during these amazing interviews, and kept rising on tiptoe with his feet close together, till the instinct of unconscious mimicry made it impossible not to do the same, and he and you seesawed up and down, and talked for ten minutes about his friends in England. He had a long neck, and shoulders like a hock-bottle, and when he dipped them it was a sign that he had sufficiently enjoyed your society. He was very bald, and so also was the Crown Prince, who married the German Emperor's sister. Both father and son (though this will hardly be credited) wrote testimonials in praise of some fluid which, when rubbed on the head, produces or preserves a fine crop of hair. And if the hair-grease did them no good, as it apparently didn't, I hope there was some sort of palm-grease that made their testimonial worth their while.

Queen Olga was Russian, daughter of the Grand Duke Constantine, a wonderfully beautiful woman, whom I had seen first when I came up from Marlborough for the Jubilee of Queen Victoria in 1887. She had an engaging habit when she came round the room at balls or after dinner in order to talk to the guests, of putting her hands on the shoulders of the women she was conversing with, and shoving them back into their seats, so that they should sit down without ceremony. Sometimes she would want to talk to two or three people together, and down they would go like ninepins, while she stood. Behind her came the King still playing seesaw, and behind him the Crown Prince, who did the same to the men he wanted to talk to, and a little while afterwards there was Prince George and Princess Marie, both putting people into their places. It was all very democratic, but also slightly embarrassing, because after large Prince George had pushed you back into a low chair, you had to crane your head up, as if you were talking to somebody on the top of the dome of St. Paul's, the dome inverted being represented by his tremendous and circular waistcoat. After him came Prince Nicholas, but he had always something terribly important and slightly broad, in the shape perhaps of a "Limerick," to communicate. So as these could not be shouted, conversation was held on more reasonable levels.

King George's family, as all the world knows, had made magnificent marriages. He was the brother of Queen Alexandra, and of the Dowager Empress of Russia, and his eldest son had brought as wife to Athens the German Emperor's sister, to whom, I suspect, these bugle-regulations were due. The "in-laws" consequently were often being bugled for, and the tram to Phaleron on a Sunday afternoon would now be a fine target for Bolsheviks. The Crown Princess was constantly engaged during these years on her wifely duties, and the arrival of the Empress Frederick in Athens usually implied that there would soon be fireworks in Constitution Square. But when I write of her, there is no *opera-bouffe* atmosphere that I can attempt or desire to reproduce, for tragic were her past years, bitter her present years, and grim agonies of mortal disease were already making ambush for her. During the three or four ensuing years, when, instead of being at the British School or at a hotel, I spent

some months at the British Legation, where Sir Edwin
Egerton was Minister, I found myself on strangely personal terms with her. She had been a friend of an uncle
of mine, who became a nationalized German after years
of living in Wiesbaden, and starting from that, she
talked with a curious unrestraint. Bitter little stinged
remarks came out, "You are happy in being English";
or "When I come to London I am only a visitor." On
one occasion I was left alone with her on a terrace above
the outlying rooms at the Legation, and to my profound
discomfort, she began pacing up and down with smothered
ejaculations. Then quite suddenly she said to me, "But
Willie is mad!" I suppose I idiotically looked as if this
was some joke, and she shook her outstretched hand at
me, "I mean that he is mad," she repeated. "Willie is
mad." . . . Then quite suddenly, with the arrested
movement of a bird, wounded to death in mid-air, she
ceased from her tragic flight, and came to earth. "If
you are going to bathe again at Phaleron," she said, with
a laugh, alluding to an incident of the day before, "I
must be sure there are no clothes on the beach, before I
sit down to sketch. You came out of the water, and there
was I . . ."

Or the bugle sounded, and there was the unhappiest of
the Czars looking very small beside his cousin Prince
George. Or again, one afternoon, when, by perpetual
permission, I was allowed to seek the shade and coolness
of the palace gardens, I heard the trampling of foot-steps,
and shrill expostulations, from behind a hedge of ole-
ander. Round the corner came the originators of this
disturbance. . . . King George seemed to have taken a
dislike to his sister's hat, and had plucked it from her
head and was kicking it along the garden path, while she

followed remonstrating. "But it's an ugly hat," said
he, delighted to find some kind of umpire, "and therefore I took it and I kicked it, and she cannot wear it
any more. . . ." (Was there ever anything so like the
immortal *Rose and the Ring?*) "My hat!" said the
injured owner tersely, as she recovered her hopelessly
damaged property. . . . "So rude of you, George."

My first spring in Greece was mostly spent out of
Athens, for with another student I was put in charge of
the British excavations at Megalopolis. All the plums
had already been picked out of it, for the theatre had been
completely cleared, and the excavation of the year before
had laid bare the entire plan of the great Council hall,
the Thersilion, built in the time of Epaminondas, so that
this year excavation was equivalent to sitting on a wall
while a lot of workmen removed tons of earth in which
nothing could possibly be discovered. It was not thrilling, but at least one could incessantly talk to them in
what purported to be modern Greek, until it became so.
There had been considerable excitement about Megalopolis the year before, for the British excavators had
thought they had triumphantly refuted the German
theory, announced by Dr. Dörpfeld, that fourth century
Greek theatres had no stage. They had unearthed steps
and columns, which, they considered, proved the existence
of a stage, and, rather prematurely, had announced their
anti-German discovery in the *Hellenic Journal* with
something resembling a crow of satisfaction. On which
this dreadful Dr. Dörpfeld came down from Athens with
a note-book and a tape measure, and in a couple of hours
in the pouring rain had proved quite conclusively, so
that no further argument was possible, that the British,
with a year to think about it, had quite misinterpreted

E. F. BENSON, ÆT. 26

[Page 287

their own evidence, and demonstrated how what they had taken for a stage was merely a back wall. Their researches in fact had merely confirmed his theory. Then he rolled up his measure and went back to Athens. . . . So another and I cleaned up these rather depressing remains, and when that was done we hired mules and went a-wandering through the country and saw the spring "blossom by blossom" (even as Beesly had read) alight on the hills. Blossom by blossom, too, Greece itself, no longer pictured in photographs or bored for in books, opened its myriad lovelinesses, even as the scarlet anemone made flame in the thickets, and the nightingales "turned the heart of the night to fire" in the oleanders by the Eurotas. We visited Homeric Mycenæ, and Epidaurus, the Harrogate of the fourth century B.C., and in archæological intervals I speared mullet by the light of a flaming torch on moonless nights with the fishermen of Nauplia, and ate them for early breakfast, broiled on the sea-shore, before the sun was up. I crossed the Gulf of Corinth and went to Delphi, where the French school were beginning the excavations that were destined to yield more richly than any soil in Greece except the precinct at Olympia. There, too, I went, and if to me the Parthenon had been a revelation of the glory of God, there I took my shoes from off my feet, and worshipped the glory of man, because the Hermes of Praxiteles "caring for the infant Dionysus," embodied, once and for all, the possible, the ultimate beauty of man, even as the Louvre held the ultimate glory of woman. . . . A few weeks more in Athens were busy with the record of the meagre results from Megalopolis, and I left for England, knowing in my very bones that Athens was in some subtle way my spiritual mother, so that on many subsequent journeys, as I went from England there, and from there back to England again, I travelled but from home to home, οἴκοθεν οἴκαδε.

Dodo had been put back in her drawer, after her expedition to Henry James: now for the second time I took her out and tasted her, as if to see whether she seemed to have mellowed like a good wine, or become sour like an inferior one, in which case I would very gladly have poured her on the earth like water, and started again. But I could not, reading her once more, altogether cast her off: she had certain gleams of vitality about her, and with my mother's connivance and help again I submitted her to a professional verdict. This time it was my mother's friend, Mrs. Harrison, known to our admiring family as "Lucas Malet," author of the adorable *Colonel Enderby's Wife*, who was selected to pronounce on my story, and again, I am afraid, it was without the slightest realization of this highway robbery on the time of an author that I despatched the book. Anyhow those two assaults on Henry James and Lucas Malet have produced in me a fellow-feeling for criminals such as I was a quarter of a century ago, so that now, when, as occasionally happens, some light-hearted marauder announces that he or she (it is usually she) is sending me her manuscript, which she hopes I won't mind reading, and telling her as soon as possible exactly what I think of it, and to what publisher she had better send it (perhaps I would write him a line too) and whether the heroine isn't a little overdone (but her mother thinks her excellent), and would I be careful to register it when I return it, and if before next Thursday to this address, and if after next Friday to another, etc. etc., I try to behave as Lucas Malet behaved in similar circumstances.

I do not for a moment say that I succeed, but I can still remember how pleasant it should seem, from the point of view of the aspirant scribbler, that somebody should be permitted to read what has been written with such rapture and how important it all is. . . .

But I can never hope to emulate Lucas Malet's tact and wisdom in her genial, cordial, and honest reply (when she had had the privilege of wading through these sheets), for they still remain to me, who know her answer almost by heart, to be the first and the last word in the true theory of the writing of fiction. Her deft incisions dissected, from lungs and heart and outwards to the delicate fibre of the skin that protects and expresses the life within, the structure of stories, short or long, that are actually alive. First must come the "idea," the life that is to vitalize the complete animal, so that its very hair and nails are fed with blood. . . . And then, since I cannot possibly find words as apt and as sober as hers I will quote from the letters themselves.

"First the idea, then the grouping, which is equivalent to our drama—then a search for models from whom to draw. Most young English writers—the artistic sense being a matter of experience, not of instinct, with most of us—begin just the other way about. Begin with their characters . . . rummage about for a story in which to place them, and too often leave the idea out of the business altogether. . . . One evil consequence of this method—among many others—is that there is a distracting lack of completeness and *ensemble* in so much English work. The idea should be like the thread on which beads are strung. It shouldn't show, except at the two ends; but in point of fact it keeps the beads all together and in their proper relation."

Then, to one already hugely interested in this admirable creed of the art of fiction, Lucas Malet proceeded to a dissection, just and kind and ruthless, of the story as it stood. She hurt in order to heal, she cut in order that healthy tissue (if there was any) might have the chance to grow. She showed me by what process (if I applied it seriously and successfully) I might convert my Dodo-doll into something that did not only squeak when pressed in the stomach, and gave no other sign of vitality than closing its eyes when it was laid flat. In consequence, greatly exhilarated by this douche of cold water, I collected such fragments of an "idea" as existed, revised what I had written, and wrote (in pursuance of the "idea") the second volume, as it subsequently appeared, in those days when novels were originally issued in three or two volumes at the price of a guinea and a half or a guinea. I finished it that autumn, sent it to the publisher recommended by Lucas Malet, who instantly accepted it. It came out in the following spring, that of 1893. I was out in Greece again at the time, and though it was my first public appearance (since *Sketches from Marlborough* may be considered as a local phenomenon) I feel sure that from the time when, with trembling pride, I corrected the long inconvenient galley sheets that kept slipping on to the floor, I gave no further thought to it at all. Bad or good, I had done my best; what happened concerned me no more, for I was quite absorbed in the study of the precinct of Asclepios on the slopes of the Acropolis, in the life at Athens, and in a volume of short stories that I began to write with a pen still wet, so to speak, with the final corrections on the proof sheets of *Dodo*. She was done with, so far as I was concerned, and it was high time, now that I was twenty-five, to get on with something else, before the frosts of senility paralysed all further effort.

For such a person as I happened to be, that, as I then believed and still believe, was the wisest resolution I could make. The habit of immediate activity, physically or mentally violent, had, from the days when butterflies, plants, athletics, friendship, *Saturday Magazines* were all put under contribution to feed the raging energies of life, become an instinct. If there was a kick left in my wholly boyish nature, it had become a habit to kick, and not to save the energy for any future emergency: if there was a minute to spare, somehow to use or enjoy it. To what use that minute and that kick were devoted, so I now see, did not particularly matter: the point was to kick for just that minute. No doubt there are other and admirable uses to which energy may be put; some make reservoirs, into which they pour and store their vital force, and while it increases, screw down their sluice, and let the gathered waters rest and reflect. Such as these probably achieve the most abiding results, for when they choose to raise their sluice, they can, by the judicious use of winch and shutter, continue to irrigate the field which they have determined to make fruitful, for a period that they can certainly estimate. They burn a steady unwavering candle which will always illuminate a fixed area, and from the areas which do not concern them they hide their ray and thus economize their wax and their wick. But how surely are there others who from their very nature are unable to construct their reservoirs or burn this one decorous candle. Whatever head of water there is, it must be instantly dispersed, whatever candle there is, it must be lit at both ends, and if that is not enough, it must be broken in half, and its new ends of wicks kindled and used for the exploration of some trumpery adventure: "trumpery," that is to say, in the vocabulary of the wise and prudent, but how colossal in the sight of the wild-eyed adventurer. And just here, just where a moral lesson should be drawn showing the early decay and the untimely end of these spendthrifts of energy, the whole tendency of Nature lies in precisely the opposite direction to that in which natural and moral economy ought to tend, for it is the careful who grow early old, and the careful investor of energy who declares bankruptcy, and retires in middle life to the club windows, where he shows a bald head to St. James's Street, and a sour visage to the waiters. Somehow so it most inexorably seems, those who spend, have; those who save, lack. Not that the spender could, by the laws and instincts of his nature, have done otherwise than court bankruptcy: not that the investor could have done otherwise than court affluence. But the one careful candle, as a matter of experience, gets blown out, and the irrelevant candle-ends continue to flare. . . .

So, after this second visit to Greece, I came home to find to my incredulous and incurious surprise, that in the interval I had become, just for the focus of a few months, famous or infamous. One of those rare phenomena, less calculable than the path of a comet, which periodically is to destroy the world, had occurred, and there was a "boom" in *Dodo*, and no one was more astonished than the author, when his mother met him arriving by the boat train at Victoria, and hinted at what was happening. All sorts of adventitious circumstances aided it: it was thought extremely piquant that a son of the Archbishop of Canterbury should have written a book so frankly unepiscopal, and quite a lot of ingenious little paragraphists invented stories of how I had read it aloud to my father and described his disconcertedness: the title-rôle

and other characters were assigned to various persons
who happened then to be figuring in the world, but apart
from all these adventitious aids, this energetic and trivial
experiment had—in those ancient days—a certain novelty
of treatment.   There were no explanations; whatever little life its characters were possessed of, they revealed by
their own unstinted speech.   That, as I have already explained, had been the plan of it in my mind, and the
execution, whatever the merits of the plan might be, was
in accordance with it.   It went through edition after
edition, in that two-volume form, price a guinea (against
which shortly afterwards the libraries revolted) and all
the raging and clamour, of course, only made it sell the
more.   It had received very scant notice in the Press
itself; what (as always happens) made it flourish so
furiously was that people talked about it.

But its success apart from the delightful comedy of
such a first act to its author, led on to a truly violent situation when the curtain rose again, for the critics, justly
enraged that this rare phenomenon called a "boom"
should not have been detected and heralded by their
auguries and by them damned or deified, laid aside a
special pen for me, ready for the occasion when I should
be so imprudent as to publish another novel; and they
all procured a large bottle of that hot ink which Dante
dipped for,

> When his left hand i' the hair of the wicked,
> Back he held the brow and pricked its stigma
> Bit unto the live man's flesh for parchment,
> Loosed him, laughed to see the writing rankle,

and since they were proposing to "let the wretch go
festering" through London, they read up Macaulay's re-

view of Mr. Robert Montgomery's poems to see how it was done. If they had not noticed *Dodo*, they would at least notice her successor. Indeed the fairy godmother who presents a young author at his public christening with a boom, brings him a doubtful gift, for when next I challenged attention all these little Macaulays and Dantes uncorked their hot ink, and waited pen in hand till Mr. Methuen sent them their "advance copies." Then, saying "one, two, three—go," they all produced on the birth-morning of the unfortunate book columns and columns of the most blistering abuse that I remember ever beholding in God-fearing journals. This blasted infant was a small work called *The Rubicon*, now so completely forgotten that I must ask the reader to take my word for it that it was quite a poor book. It was not even very, very bad: it was just poor. Critics have hundreds of poor books submitted to their commiserated notice, and they are quite accustomed to that, and tell the public in short paragraphs that the work in question is "decidedly powerful," or "intensely interesting" or "utterly futile," and there is an end of it as far as they are concerned. Had this blasted infant been a first book it would naturally have received no more than a few rude little notices, and perhaps a few polite little notices. But as it was the successor to the abhorred comet it was concertedly singled out for the wrath of the Olympians. The *candidatus exercitus* of the entire Press went forth with howitzers and Maxims (in both senses), with cannons of all calibres, with rifles and spears and arrows and sharp tongues to annihilate this poor little May-fly. That I am not exaggerating the stupendous character of this fusillade can be shown from a few extracts. In those days I used to take in Press-cuttings, and among a heap of more precious relics in a forgotten box I came across the other day a packet of these, which contained such flowers as I could not leave to blush unseen, and I picked and here present a little nosegay of them.

(1) The *Pall Mall Gazette*. (*The Rubicon*, E. F. Benson.)

"MR. BENSON'S NEW PLAY.

Dramatis Personæ.

Exhumée Dodo.   Madonna de Clapham.
Lord Anæmia.   Jelly Fish.
Donjuans (*sic*).   Vulgarities.   Indecencies.
Time, The Middle Classes.   *Place*, Le Pays Inconnu.

Mise en scène, Fluff."

Then follows a short analysis, not so fragrantly precious, and then comes comment.

"All the gutter-elements of *Dodo* are rehashed and warmed up again with no touch of novelty or improvement or chastisement. . . . The Lives of the Bad are interesting assuredly . . . but then they must be living and bad, and these pithless people are only galvanic [galvanized?] and vulgar. *We do not wish to be hard on Mr. Benson.* Let him give three years to investigating the distinctions between good writing and bad writing, between wit and vulgarity . . . and then we should not be surprised if he produced something worth finding serious fault with."

(2) The (late) *Standard*. (A column and a half.)

"Taking the book as a whole, it is an absolute failure. As a rule, the writing is forced and uneasy, the reflections confused or lumbering. The character-drawing is crude and uncertain. It is emphatically one of those books that are sensual, earthly and unwholesome."

(3) *Vanity Fair*.   (One column.)

"Of style he has little : of wit he has no idea . . . of plot there is less in *The Rubicon* than is generally to be found in a penny novelette : of knowledge of Society (if he have any) Mr. Benson shows less here than is usually possessed by the nursery-governess ; and in grammar he seems to be as little expert as he is in natural science : of which his knowledge seems to equal his smattering of the Classics . . . ill-named, full of faults, betraying much ignorance of manners and unknowledge [*sic*] of human nature : a book, indeed, compact of folly and slovenliness : guiltless of any real touch of constructive art ; without form and void : a book of which I fear that I have made too much."

(4) *Daily Chronicle*.   (One column.)

"A PUZZLE FOR POSTERITY.

What will the critical students of, say, two generations ahead, make of the fact that in the spring of 1894 the newspapers of London treated the appearance of a new novel by Mr. E. F. Benson as an event of striking importance in the world of books? The thought that death will rid us of the responsibility for that awkward explanation lends an almost welcome aspect to the grave. . . .

That *The Rubicon* is the worst-written, falsest and emptiest of the decade, it would be, perhaps, too much to say.   In these days of elastic publishing standards and moneyed amateurs, many queer things are done, and Mr. Benson's work is a shade better than the poorest of the stuff which would-be novelists pay for the privilege of seeing in print. . . . A certain interest attaches, no doubt, to the demonstration which it affords that a young gentleman of university training can meet the female amateurs on their own ground, and be every whit as maudlin and absurd as they know how to be.   But the sisterhood have an advantage over him in the fact that they can spell. . . . There are a score of glaring grammatical errors, to say nothing of the clumsiness and incompetency which mark three sentences out of five throughout the book.

Bad workmanship might be put aside as the fault of inexperience, if the young man had an actual story to tell . . . but there is nothing of that sort here. . . . The heroine is from time to time led over to as near [sic] the danger line of decency as the libraries will permit. She is made to utter several suggestive speeches, and once or twice quite skirts the frontier of the salacious. . . ."

(5) *The World.* (Length unknown: I cannot find the second half of it.)

"But, alas! Eva Hayes in *The Rubicon* is quite as vulgar, quite as blatant in the bad taste she is pleased to exhibit on every occasion, as her predecessor *Dodo*, and is dull beyond description into the bargain. From beginning to end of the two volumes there is not one spark or gleam of humour, or sign of true observation and knowledge of humanity."

(6) The (late) *St. James's Budget.* (Six columns.)

"ANOTHER UNBIRCHED HEROINE.

It might have been supposed that the son of an Archbishop was hardly the sort of person to shine in this kind of literature, but Mr. Benson has taught us better than that. Yet our thanks are due to him for one thing: his book consists of only two volumes; it might have been in three. . . .

How they Mate in the 'Hupper Suckles.' . . .
Languour, Cigarettes and Blasphemies. . . .

We conclude this enthusiastic appreciation of Mr. Benson with the bold avowal that we regard *The Rubicon* as almost truly perfect of its kind, and probably unsurpassable. Any one of Shakespeare's most remarkable gifts may be found, perhaps, in equal measure in the writings of some minor author; but none ever had such a union of so many as he. So it is with Mr. Benson. A school-girl's idea of 'plot,' a nursery-governess's knowledge of the world; a gentleman's 'gentleman's' views of high life; an undergraduate's sense of style and store of learning; a society paragraphist's fine feeling and good taste; a man-milliner's notion of creating character: of each of these you may find plenty of evidence in the novels of the day; but nowhere else—unless it be in *Dodo*—will they all be found welded into one harmonious unity as they are here! . . ."

Here is but the most random plucking of these blossoms, but what a nosegay! The flower from *Vanity Fair* grew of course from the same root as that from the *St. James's Budget*, and this is interesting as showing the excellent co-ordination between these different attacks. As a Press-campaign on an infinitesimal scale, I give the foregoing as a classical example. No book, however bad, could possibly have called forth, in itself, so combined an onslaught: every gun in Grub Street was primed and ready and sighted not on *The Rubicon* at all, but on the author of *Dodo*. But herein is shown the inexpediency of using up all your ammunition at once, on so insignificant a target. It was clear that if the respectable journals of London made so vigorous an offensive, that offensive had to be final, and the war to be won. Still more clear was it that, if this was not a preconcerted, malicious and murderous campaign not on a particular book, but on an individual, the entire columns of the London Press must henceforth be completely devoted to crushing inferior novels. *The Rubicon* was but one of this innumerable company: if the Press had determined to crush inferior novels, it was clear that for a considerable time there would be no room in its columns for politics, or sport or foreign news or anything else whatever. Not even for advertisements, unless we regard such attacks as being unpaid advertisements. . . .

So there was no more firing for the present, and it was all rather reminiscent of the tale of how Oscar Wilde went out shooting, and fell down flat on the discharge of his own gun.

The Press, after that, had nothing more to shoot at me, for all their heaviest shells had been launched; so the blighted author walked off, as Mr. Mantalini said, as comfortable as demnition, and proceeded vigorously to write *The Babe, B.A.* and other tranquil works, just as if he had not been blown into a thousand fragments.

The Press-notices, in fact, from which these six extracts are taken, were a huge lark, and one day I found my father (who so far from summoning family councils on the subject never spoke to me about my public scribblings at all) wide-eyed and absorbed in one of these contemporary revilings. Suddenly he threw his head back with a great shout of laughter, and slapped me on the back. "You've got broad enough shoulders to stand that sort of thing," he said. "Come along, are the horses ready?" and out we went riding. But less humorous were certain private kicks which I got (and no doubt deserved) from less ludicrous antagonists. Of these the chief, and the most respected both then and now, must be nameless. He had been so hot in appreciation and so cordial over *Dodo*, politely observing in it a "high moral beauty" that I find him (in this same forgotten box) writing to me, before the appearance of *The Rubicon*, in these words à propos of the growing public taste for realism:

"The public in the next generation will be what you and one or two others like you choose to make it. Good work in any style gives that style vogue. . . . It's ever when you are most serious you are at your best. Work, work and live."

Well, I worked and lived like the devil for strenuousness. Then *The Rubicon* made its appearance, and the same friend took a blistering pen instead:

"If anything could possibly give a more serious blow to your chances of future and legitimate success than the publication of *The Rubicon*, it would be to bring out within three or four years another novel. . . . It does not seem to me that you have formed the slightest conception of the true situation. It is this. Your first book, from accidental and even parasitic causes—things that were not in the book at all—enjoyed an entirely abnormal and baseless success. You have now to begin again, and for several years the public will certainly not listen to you as a novelist."

For the life of me, I cannot now, reading these explosive records over again, determine whether I could have gained anything by paying the smallest attention to them. Logically, it was impossible to do so, for they clearly were directed, as I have said, not against this wretched old *Rubicon*, but against the person who had dared to capture success with *Dodo*. Rightly or wrongly, it seemed to me that vituperation so violent could not be regarded as other than comic. If I was a nursery-governess and a man-milliner, and a gentleman's gentleman it was all very sad, but I was less overwhelmed because I was already terribly interested in the *Babe*, *B.A.* and not at all interested in the *St. James's Budget*, except as a humorous publication, which the *Babe*, *B.A.* tried to be, too. And then there were delightful plans ahead; this autumn Maggie was to come out to Athens with me, and we were to go on to Egypt together, and have a Tremendous Time. . . .

CHAPTER XIV

ATHENS AND EGYPT

SO there was Athens again, with its bugles and its Royal Babies, and its eternal Acropolis, which custom never staled. Maggie jumped into the Hellenic attitude at once, adoring the adorable, filling with the laughter of her serious appreciation the comedy of the life there, enjoying it all enormously, and finding ecstatic human interest in Oriental situations. One day the M.P. for Megalopolis appeared in Athens, and so, of course, I asked him to tea in the Grand Hotel, and Maggie put in some extra lessons in modern Greek with the English vice-consul, in order that a tongue-tied female should not mar the entertainment. The M.P.'s remarks were mostly unintelligible to her, and these I translated back for her benefit, and if she could find a phrase that fitted she slowly enunciated it, and if not she said to him, syllable by syllable, "I should like to see your wife and children, but we are going to Egypt." All the "circles" in Athens embraced at once her cordial and eager humanity. She sketched all morning, and when I came to the rendezvous, there would be a dozen young Greek urchins round her canvas, to whom, as she washed in a lucent sky, she made careful and grammatical remarks. . . . She captivated the heart of the archæologists, and Dr. Dörpfeld who had proved himself so fatal to the theories of the British School at Megalopolis, addressed his most abstruse arguments to her as he announced that "die Enneakrounos, ich habe gewiss gefunden" when he gave his out-of-door lectures. The English Minister, Sir Edwin Egerton, used to wrap her shawl round her, as she left the Legation after dinner, saying, "Now you look like a Tanagra figure," and the Queen asked her in strict confidence, whether the English aristocracy really behaved as her brother said they behaved in that odd book called *Dŏdō*. The answer to that was given in a performance we got up, ostensibly for the amusement of the English governesses in Athens at Christmas, of the *Duchess of Bayswater*. Of course we got it up primarily because we wanted to act, and then it grew to awful proportions. The English Mediterranean Fleet happened to come into the Piræus about then, and Admiral Markham asked if a contingent of two hundred blue-jackets or so might stand at the back of the English governesses. On which, the style of the entertainment had to be recast altogether, and we bargained that, if they came the performance should consist of two parts. The first part should be supplied by sailors, who would dance hornpipes, and sing songs, and the second part should consist of *The Duchess of Bayswater*. That was agreed, and we engaged a large public hall.

Then Regie Lister who was a Secretary of Legation, let slip to the Crown Princess that we were getting up an entertainment for (and with) sailors and English governesses, and she, under promise of discretion as regards her relatives, was allowed to be one of the English governesses. With truly Teutonic perfidiousness, she informed all the Kings and Queens then in Athens what was going on, and just as the curtain was about to go up for *The Duchess of Bayswater* a message came from the palace that the entire host of royalties was then starting to attend it. And so there was a row of Kings and Queens and ten rows of English governesses, and a swarm of English sailors. But we refused to cut out a topical allusion to the Palace bugles.

And at precisely this point, the epoch of those absurd theatricals, the sparkle and comedy of Athenian existence was overshadowed or enlightened for me by the birth of a great friendship. Regie Lister had the greatest genius for friendship of any man I ever met; no one, not even Alfred Lyttelton, had a finer gift or a more irresistible charm for men and women alike. The two, extraordinarily dissimilar in most respects, were identical in this, that they compelled others to love them, because they loved so magnificently themselves. Alfred Lyttelton, for all his exuberant virility, had the feminine quality of giving himself instead of taking, which is what I mean by magnificent love, and Regie's genius in friendship sprang from precisely the same abandonment. There they diverged north and south, for Regie had practically none of the manliness that was so characteristic of the other. But he had superbly the qualities of his defects; in matters of intellect, the direct masculine attack was represented by intuition and diplomacy and extreme quickness, and in matters of affection by a certain robust tenderness, quite devoid of sentimentality. All mankind, whether male or female, is compounded of both sexes: the man without any womanly instincts would be a mere monster; the woman without any grit of manliness in her, a mere jelly-fish, and in Regie's nature the woman had a large share. One quality supposed to be a defect of women rather than men he was quite without: he had no notion whatever of "spite," and was incapable of tak-

ing revenge on anyone who had annoyed or crossed him.
Most shining of all among his delightful gifts was his
instinct of seeing the best in everyone. Wherever he
went in his diplomatic posts, Athens, Constantinople,
Copenhagen, Rome, Paris, or Tangiers, he found, without the least "setting to work" about it, that there never
was so heavenly a place, nor so delightful an entourage.
At heart he was really Parisian; that city, with its keen
kaleidoscopic gaiety, its intellectual and artistic atmosphere, dry and defined as its own air, suited him best,
but this instinct to find everyone with whom he came in
contact delightful, brought out, as was natural, all that
there was delightful in them, and thus his instinct was
justified. He was incapable of being bored for more
than a couple of minutes together, and would have found
something that could be commuted into cheerfulness in
the trials of Job. Whether he liked a person or not, he
always gave his best, not with the idea of making himself
popular, but because that was the natural expression of
his temperament. His amiability made the ripe plums
easily drop for him, but when he had determined to get
something which did not come off its stalk for the wishing,
he had indomitable perseverance, and that rather rare
gift of being able to sit down and think until a method
clarified itself.

With him, then, I struck up a friendship which dispensed with all the preliminaries of acquaintanceship:
there was no gradual drawing together about it, it leaped
into being, and there it remained, poised and effortless.
Often during the ensuing years after he had left Athens
and was at his post in some European capital, we did
not meet for months together, but when the meeting
came, relations were taken up again, owing to some flame-

like quality in him which warmed you as soon as you got near him, without break or sense of there having been a break. Morning by morning he came down to the museum where I was studying sculpture with his paints and sketching-block, and made the most admirable pictures of some Greek head; we took excursions round Athens up Hymettus or Pentelicus, we usually dined together at some house of an evening, where he made cosmopolitan diplomatists act charades or play some childish and uproarious game. Best of all was it to leave Athens, and wander three or four days at a time in the Peloponnese. We cast pennies into the Styx, we lost our way and our mules and their drivers on the slopes of Cyllene, and were rescued by a priest who tucked up his skirts, and hurled huge stones at the savage shepherd-dogs; we slept in indescribable inns, where were all manner of beasts, we bathed in the Eurotas, and lay that night among goats in a shed on the Langarda Pass, and the sorriest surroundings were powerless to abate Regie's enjoyment. And on one unique and memorable day we hunted for the temple at Bassae in a thick fog, and almost despaired of finding it, when out of the heart of the enshrouding mist there came the roar of a great wind that tore the fog into tatters, and lo, not a hundred yards away was the grave grey temple. The flying vapours vanished, chased like frightened sheep along steaming hillsides and through the valleys below, and all the Peloponnese swam into sight, from the Gulf of Corinth to the western sea, and from the west to the bays of the south, and from the south to the waters of Nauplia. . . . Did two more ecstatic pilgrims ever behold the shrine of Apollo?

For the next three winters slices of Egypt were sand-
wiched between visits to Greece. I started with Greece,
went on with Maggie, or on other occasions joined her
at Luxor, and came back to Greece, living, after Regie's
departure for Constantinople, at the Legation with Sir
Edwin Egerton, the most hospitable of mankind. But
the magic of Egypt, potent and compelling as it was, was
a waving of a black wand compared to the joyful spell of
Greece. "All who run may read; only run" was the
Greek injunction: "All who read must run away" seemed
the equivalent in the Nilotic incantation. To get under
the spell of Greece implied a rejuvenation into a world
that was like dawn on dewdrops and gave so sunny an
answer to the "obstinate questionings" that there was no
need even to ask what the riddle had been.

> "All is beauty,
> And knowing this is love, and love is duty,
> What further can be sought for or declared?"

That glittered from the fading shores of Attica, and then
after a few miles of sea, there arose the low and sinister
coast, and as you began to guess at the mystery of the
desert-bounded land you quaked at the conclusion. There
was something old and evil there and as tired as Eccle-
siastes: it preached *Vanitas Vanitatum* instead of singing
the sunny love-spell of Greece, and while its mouth
mumbled the syllables, its relentless hands reared the
pyramids which must stand for ever to the astonishment
of the world as a monument of unimaginative construc-
tion and lost labour. There too it set the Sphinx whose
totally blank and meaningless face, innocent of any riddle
except that of its own soullessness, defies the rising glory

of the sun and the moon of lovers to instil any spark of
animation into its stony countenance. What monsters
to an Attic pilgrim were these gods conceived not in the
kindly image of humanity but as out of some incestuous
menagerie! Here was no deep-bosomed Hera, queen of
gods and men, for the royalty of motherhood; no
helmeted Athene for the royalty of wisdom; no Aphrodite
for the excellence of love sent her herald Eros to an-
nounce her epiphany from the wine-dark sea. The
Egyptian artificers hewed no images of joy and mirth,
they set no Faun nor Satyr dancing in the twilight, no
Hermes held the winds in the flower-like pinions of
his heels, or nursed the god after whom the Bacchantes
revelled, with the smile that so quivered on his mouth
that next moment surely the vitality with which he
tingled, would break through that momentary marble
arrest. Far other were these incongruous composite di-
vinities, all as dead as a hangman's noose, all incapable
of summoning up one quiver of a kindly mirth. As by
some disordered dream of a religious maniac the hawk-
faced god had a cobra for symbol of his divinity; a cow
or a cat or a lion had mated with a man and the offspring
sat there, bleak and appalling, to be worshipped. And
in matter of material, for the glow of the white Pentelic
that holds the sunshine in solution within, even as a
noble vintage is redolent of Provençal summers, these
monstrous forms were presented in dead black basalt, a
frozen opacity of ink.

Into these tight-fisted inexorable hands were given
the jail-keys of death. Egypt was ever the land of graves,
Memento Mori, the sad gospel of its religion. A little
honey, a little pulse, blue-glazed images of slaves who
might still toil for their master in that dim underworld,

images of food in the chambers of the dead, were all
that the pious could provide for the desolate whimpering
soul, feeble as a moth, that went forth on its lonely
journey through dubious twilight.   The crowns and the
sceptres, the gold and precious stones that were buried
with the kings were but a mockery to them of all that
they had quitted; the mightiest monument that Pharaoh
had raised was no more than a flickering beacon behind
him as he trod the dark passage, which cast in front the
shadow of the man that he had been.   The gigantic and
hopeless art, bound hand and foot by the fetters of
hieratic tradition could do no more than multiply monoliths, incredulous of its own greatness and untinged with
the living colour of humanity.   Yet out of this mere
piling up of dead on dead there arose a musty necromantic
magic, awful and old and corrupt, that sat like a vulture
on the sandbanks and was wafted, eternally fecund,
down the waters of the Nile.   All the way up to Luxor,
where we settled down for a time, through the splendour
of noon and the last ray of sunset that turns the stream
into a sheet of patinated bronze, there was present that
underlying sense of woe; and to this day my nightmares
are set on the Nile in the sweet scent of bean fields
beneath the waving of mimosa and of palms, where, by
the terrible river there crouches some abominable granite
god.

I have given a wrong notion of this curious psychic
horror if I have represented it as interfering with enjoyment and interest.   It lay couched and in concealment,
seldom stirring, and belonged I suppose to that subconscious world which, somewhere within us, is absorbed
in its own constructive energies, and only rarely lets news
of itself rise, like a bubble through dark water, into our

controlled and effective consciousness. But cell by cell
was stored with its bitter honey, and my bees must have
been busy, for when a few years later I began to write
a book called *The Image in the Sand* I found the combs
full and ready for my despoiling. How such invention
as is implied in writing a book, exercises itself in others,
I do not know, but I have a very clear idea of my own
case. The material, the stuff out of which the threads
are woven, or, if you will, the stock-pot out of which the
pottage comes, has long been simmering and stewing before the planning, the conscious invention begins. These
two stages, so I take it, are widely severed from each
other; the storing and the stewing have long preceded this
rummage and inspection of what the author wants for his
purpose. But there is, practically always, a second pot
on the fire, subconsciously stewing, the contents of which
concern him not at all, while he is exercising such culinary
art as may be his over the contents of the first. Thus,
while subconsciously I was gathering and shredding into
this second pot, some of these secret and bitter herbs of
Egypt to be used years afterwards, my conscious cooking
powers were altogether absorbed with the stuff I had long
before collected in Greece. In other words, I was busy
with writing *The Vintage* while my subconscious mind
was just as busy on its own office of making ready for
The Image in the Sand. Every morning, and all morning, as we went up the Nile in the post-boat, I used to
carry book and pen and ink to some sequestered corner
where the sun beat full on me, and, while the sandbanks
and the vultures and the wicked old spell of Egypt were
working on my subconscious mind, I exuded on to paper
what I had captured of the sunnier spell of Greece. I
fancy that this must be a mental process common to

most people, and that nobody writes of the interests and experiences which at the moment absorb him. They have to be kept and stored and stewed before they are fit for use; the harvest in fact has long been completed before the grain is ground, or before the baker, later still, is at his oven.

Every winter then, for those three years, and indeed for one year more, tragic and final—I went across to Egypt from Greece, firm in the protection of the sunny gods when I started, and hastening to swing the incense again when I returned. And I must surely have been inoculated with the poison of the darker deities, so that for two years I was immune from their attacks, or perhaps Maggie's excavations in the temple of Mut in Karnak were so thrilling and surprising that "the plague was stayed," or perhaps I made some truce and reconciliation with the hawk-faced gods and the cats and the baboons, or perhaps (as seemed most probable of all) I had imagined a vain thing when for the first time I thought that the iron of these malignant conceptions had entered into my soul, for the early months of the new year in 1895 and 1896 were weeks of incessant exhilaration, the glory of which was this concession, given to Maggie by the Ministry of Antiquities, that she might conduct the excavation of a temple.

Did ever an invalid plan and carry out so sumptuous an activity? She was wintering in Egypt for her health, being threatened with a crippling form of rheumatism; she was suffering also from an internal malady, depressing and deadly: a chill was a serious thing for her, fatigue must be avoided, and yet with the most glorious contempt of bodily ailments which I have ever seen, she continued to employ some amazing mental vitality that brushed dis-

abilities aside, and, while it conformed to medical orders, crammed the minutes with such sowings and reapings as the most robust might envy. When I got to Egypt in the first of these three years she had already obtained permission to excavate the temple of Mut in the horse-shoe lake at Karnak, with the proviso that the museum at Gizeh was to claim anything it desired out of the finds; she had got together sufficient funds to conduct a six weeks' exploration with a moderate staff of workers, and there she was with her fly-whisk and her white donkey, using a dozen words of Arabic to the workers with astonishing effect. She had begun by trenching the site diagonally in order to cut across any walls that were covered by the soil, and another diagonal soon gave the general plan of the unknown temple. All the local English archæologists were, so to speak, at her feet, partly from the entire novelty of an English girl conducting an excavation of her own, but more because of her grateful and enthusiastic personality, and M. Naville, who was engaged at Deir-el-Bahari across the river, came and sat like a benignant eagle on a corner stone, while Mr. Newberry deciphered some freshly exposed inscription. I was given a general supervision, with the object of discovering the most economical method of clearing, of arranging the "throws" of earth (so that those going to the chucking heap should not use the same path as those returning with empty baskets, a plan which entailed collisions and much pleasant conversation between the workmen who were going to and fro) and with making a plan to scale of the temple. A friend of Maggie's kept an eye wide open for possible thefts of small objects, but the genius, the organizer, the chairman of it all was Maggie. After a morning there, she had to get back to Pagnon's Hotel,

lunch quietly and rest afterwards, but presently she would be out again, cantering on her white donkey without fatigue owing to her admirable seat, with a tea-basket on the crupper, and Mohammed the devoted donkey-boy trotting behind with encouraging cries so that the donkey should not lapse into that jog-trot which was so bad for tea-things. At sunset, the work was over, and we made our leisurely way back to the hotel. Maggie rested a tired body before dinner, but exercised an indefatigible mind, working at what was familiarly known as "her philosophy," which eventually took shape in her book, *The Venture of Rational Faith*, or scribbling at one of the charming animal stories, which she published later under the title of *Subject to Vanity*. Then after dinner, the old habits reasserted themselves and we played games with pencil and paper, producing poetical answers to preposterous questions or rooking each other at picquet. Each Saturday, she jingled out with money-bags to the temple of Mut, and paid her workmen, while her native overseer checked the tale of piastres, and waved the whisk to keep the flies off his mistress.

Sometimes there were days off, when one of the three was left in charge, and the two others went far through the fertile land, or ferrying across the Nile, spent the day with M. Naville at Deir-el-Bahari to see what fresh sculptured wall had been reclaimed from the blown sand of the desert, showing the pictured ivory and gold which the expedition of Queen Hatasoo had brought back from the mysterious land of Punt; or we crawled dustily into some newly discovered malodorous tomb in the valley where the kings of Egypt were buried, or visited Professor Petrie at the Ramesseum and exchanged the news of fresh finds. Sometimes I took a holiday from the remote and

swarming past, and with a horse in place of the demurer donkey, went far out into the desert on the other side of the Nile. Pebbles and soft sand, hard sand and rocks succeeded each other in slope and level, and the horse whinnied as he sniffed the utter emptiness of the un-breathed air. One kite hung, a remote speck in the brazen sky, and the silence and the solitude wove the unutterable spell of the desert. There, out of sight of all that makes the planet habitable, your horse alone made the link with the ephemeral living world; all else was as it had been through uncounted centuries, and as it would remain for centuries to come, until the spinning earth grew still. In the desert the past and the future are one, and the present, dwindled to a microscopical point, is but a shadow of time in the timeless circle of eternity. Old wicked Egypt was no more than that; the dynasties were whisked away like an unquiet fly, that persists for a little, but not for long.

Luxor would be full of southerly-going dahabeahs and English tourists during this month of January, and I can see Maggie waving her long fine-fingered hands in impotent despair, as I brought her an invitation from some friend that she and I would dine on one of these dahabeahs to-night or next night or the night after. "How am I to get on with my work," exclaimed this out-raged invalid, "with all these interruptions? Won't it do, if we ask them to tea at the temple?" That certainly usually "did" quite well, for while Maggie was making tea, the cry of "Antica!" would arise from the diggers, and she popped the lid on the teapot, and we turned to see what had been unearthed. Once it was the statue of the Rameses of the Exodus, which would tremendously excite the visitor, but left us cold, for he was already

plentifully represented. Or it might be a scribe of the
eighteenth dynasty whom to-day you may see in the
museum at Gizeh, and better even than that was a superb
Saite head, such as I may behold at this moment if I
raise my eyes from the page, or best of all it was the
image of Sen-mut himself, to see which, again, you must
go to Gizeh. That was the crown and culmination of
the digging and worthy of an archæological digression.

Sen-mut, we knew, was the architect of our temple, and
of the temple of Deir-el-Bahari across the river, and the
mysterious thing in connection with him was that wherever his name and his deeds appeared in hieroglyphic
inscriptions they had always been defaced, and an inscription about King Thothmes III, nephew and successor
of Queen Hatasoo, to whose reign the activities of Sen-
mut belonged had been superimposed. Sometimes the
deletion was not quite thorough and you could read Sen-
mut's name below some dull chronicle of King Thothmes.
What the reason for these erasures had been was hitherto
only conjecture: now, on the close of this bright January
afternoon the riddle was solved, and we found ourselves
the accidental recoverers of a scandal nearly four thousand years old. For Sen-mut was but a common man,
"not mentioned in writing" (i.e. with no ancestral records), and he speaking from the inscription on the back
of this statue of himself which he had dedicated told us
that, "I filled the heart of the Queen (Hatasoo) in very
truth gaining the heart of my mistress daily . . . and the
mistress of the two lands (Upper and Lower Egypt) was
pleased with that which came forth from my mouth, the
Priest of Truth, Sen-mut. I knew her comings in the
Royal house, *and was beloved of the ruler.*"

Here then was the reason for all these erasures: there

had been a scandal about the intimacy between this "common man" and the Queen; so, when she died, and her nephew succeeded, he caused all mention of Sen-mut to be erased, and covered up the blank spaces with majestic records of his own achievements. It was his design to destroy all evidence of this disreputable or at least undignified affair, and hammer and chisel, at his order, were busy to delete all hint of Aunt Hatasoo's indiscretions. Pious King Thothmes was all but successful in this piece of family pride: only just one record escaped his erasing hand. But now, four thousand years later, Maggie dug up that solitary omission.

I know that there must have been clouds on these halcyon days of winter, but they passed and prevailing sunlight was dominant again. Once Maggie got a chill as she lingered by the horse-shoe lake, and developed a congestion of the lungs, but when she was allowed to leave her bed again and go out, she was carried in a sort of litter, by her own express decree, to the beloved excavation again, and made a delighted progress round the fresh clearing, ordering that some mason must be at once employed in piecing together the huge lion-headed statues which had been discovered in the fore-court of the temple, and in setting them in place again. She was more dubious about certain abominable baboons that crouched in a small chamber within the temple, whose awful ugliness seemed better left alone. . . . Then over us both passed the cloud of slightly disquieting letters from my mother. My father was overtired, and *Would* go on working: he had attacks of breathlessness if he rode, a sense of oppression on his chest that was not mitigated by his remedy of thumping it. But no one, least of all the sufferer, took these things at all seriously, Maggie got better, my

father received no alarming report from his doctor, and
my mother, as these clouds seemed to melt, added them
to her general list of the workings of "unreasonable fear,"
that ghostly enemy of hers, whom she was for ever com-
bating and holding at arm's length, but never quite
slaying.

Arthur, during these Græco-Egyptian years, had slid
into the groove of a career; he was a house-master at
Eton, prosperous and popular, though from time to time
his own cloud beset him, and out of it he would an-
nounce that the burden of his work was quite intolerable,
and that he could not possibly stand it for another term.
But this was a fruitful Jeremiad, for it relieved his mind,
and he buckled to with renewed energy and that amazing
gift of getting through a task more quickly than anybody
else could have done it, without the slightest loss of thor-
oughness, and he added to the work that was incident to
his profession an immense literary activity of his own,
producing several volumes of verse, and experimentaliz-
ing in those meditative essays in which before long he
found his own particular *métier*.   Hugh, in the same way,
after studying at Llandaff under Dean Vaughan, had
taken orders in the English Church and was attached to
the Eton Mission at Hackney Wick, so that of the three
sons I was the only one who had not settled down to any
career.   By this time archæology, as a scholastic profession, was already closed to me, for Cambridge could not
go on giving me grants indefinitely, and in order to crown
my days of classical learning with a final failure, King's
had not decorated with a fellowship either the work I
sent in on the Roman occupation of Chester, or on certain
aspects of the cult of Asclepios.   So, in deference to my
father's wishes, I took the first step towards getting a

post in the Education Office, collected and sent in testimonials, and craved employment there as an inspector or examiner, I forget which. This regularized matters: that was a respectable employment, and by sending in those testimonials I was doing my best to be respectably employed, and pending appointment I could go on writing, thus treading the path that by now I fully meant to pursue. At no time was it definitely agreed that I should become anything so irregular as a writer of novels, and I suppose that if I had been appointed to a post in the Education Office, I should have taken it up. But those in whose hands the appointment rested thought that the author of *Dodo* would be a very indifferent educator, in spite of these brilliant panegyrics from his tutors, and for aught I know those testimonials are dustily filed there still.

But neither Arthur nor Hugh thought of their present vocations in their present form as their lives' work; Arthur, at any rate, had not the slightest intention, as events proved, of plucking the rewards which his profession as schoolmaster was soon to offer him, and when headmasterships came within his reach he did not put his hand out to them. Hugh's case was only a little different; the direct service of God was now his choice and his passion, but as evolution of that progressed in him, it took him out of the English Church altogether. No one ever questioned that his joining the Roman communion and taking orders there was anything but a matter of irresistible conviction with him, but what would have happened had that conviction taken hold on him before my father's death it is impossible to say. I cannot imagine any human relation, any *pietas* restraining Hugh when he had the firm belief that it was by divine guidance that he so acted: on the other hand I cannot imagine what the effect on my father would have been; whether he could have beaten down his own will in the matter, as my mother did, and have accepted this without reserve at all, or whether it would have been to him, as the death of Martin had been, an event unadjustable, unbridgable, unintelligible, a blow without reason, to be submitted to in a silence which, had it been broken, must have been resolved into bewildered protest.

Apart from their present professions both Arthur and Hugh were moving towards the pursuit, that of authorship, which was soon to take at least equal rank with their other work. Within ten years it was as an essayist, a writer of delicate meditative prose that Arthur was most widely known, and to this he devoted the flower of his energy, while Hugh served his Church not as a parish priest, but as preacher and as writer of propagandist novels, novels with the purpose of showing the dealings of God through His Church. As works of art his sermons far transcended his books, an opinion which no one I think who ever listened to that tumultuous eloquence could doubt. They carried his untrammelled message; while he preached, he could say with supreme instinctive art all that in novel-writing he had more indirectly to convey: his sermons had an overwhelming sincerity which made the delivery of them flawless and flame-like. When he wrote he was never quite so inspired: the message was the same, but it had to be wrapt about with the allegory of ordinary life, he had to convey it in terms of country houses or historical episode, and the sermon which was the underlying intention was often a handicap to the art of story-telling. But it was towards his books that his inclination tended; his joy of achievement lay in the written, not in the spoken word.

Then came the closing summer of this period, after which the whole stage and manner of life was altered altogether. That year I had stayed late in the south, going on from Athens to Capri, and laying the foundation then of that Italian castle of dreams, which was afterwards to take a more solid form. Maggie had supplemented Egypt with a cure at Aix-les-Bains, but in August we were all together again at Addington, and once more, as before Nellie's death, and never since then, there were hundreds of small cones on the cedar that scattered the sulphur-like powder. Arthur came there before he went to Scotland, Hugh had a holiday release from the Eton mission, Maggie was established there deep in the collation of the results from the digging at Luxor. Soon my father and mother were to start on a tour through Ireland, and when September saw their departure, Maggie and I stayed on for a little and then drifted off on different visits. We were all free to stop at home if we liked, and ask friends there; Addington was just an ark for any wandering family doves, picnicky as my mother said, but there it was. . . Maggie and I saw my father and mother off, and as from my first remembered days and ever afterwards when he wished "good night" or "good bye," he kissed me, and said, "God bless you, and make you a good boy always." Then, after he got into the carriage, he waved his hands with some affectionate and despairing gesture, saying, "I can't bear leaving you nice people here," and the carriage turned, and went up the slope in front of the house. A very few days afterwards, Maggie and I went off on our ways, leaving Beth at the front door, saying, "Eh, pray-a-do come back soon."

I had trysted with a friend to spend a few days at Addington early in October, and arrived there to find a letter from him that he was prevented, and I was in two minds as to whether to stop here alone, or go off on some other visit for the Sunday. That scarcely seemed worth while, for I had learned that my father and mother were leaving Ireland that day, and would spend the Sunday with Mr. Gladstone at Hawarden. The Irish tour therefore was over, and they would be back on Monday. Beth and I talked about it, and she said, "Nay, don't you go away to-day, you be here for when your Papa and Mamma get back. Have a quiet Sunday, you and me."

It was arranged so: and after lunch on Sunday I went out for a long walk through the myriad paths of the Park, where the beeches were russeting and the squirrels gathering the nuts, and came home in time to have tea with Beth. There was a telegram for me on the hall-table, and glancing at the sender's name first I saw it was from Mrs. Gladstone.

"Your father passed over quite peacefully this morning," it said. "Can you come with Maggie?"

I did not comprehend at first what it meant. My father was a very bad sailor, and it was quite possible that Mrs. Gladstone had merely telegraphed the little news that he was comfortably back in England. For one or two or three long seconds which seemed like hours, I tried to think that this was what she meant. But then my father had crossed not "this morning" but on Friday: and why should I "come with Maggie"? I suppose that the comprehension of the real meaning of this message was only a matter of a moment, and I think the envelope of the telegram was scarcely crumpled up in my hand before I knew. Just then, Beth, having seen my entry from the window of her room, came down to tell me that she had got tea ready. And she saw that something had happened, for her hands made a quivering motion, and then were clasped.

"Is there any trouble?" she asked.

I could get up to London that night, but not to Chester. I slept in the Euston Hotel and went on by an early train next morning.

My father and mother had arrived at Hawarden on Saturday: he was very well and in tremendously good spirits, and sat up late that night talking with Mr. Gladstone. They had all gone to early communion on Sunday morning, returned for breakfast, and walked again to church for the eleven o'clock service. Mrs. Gladstone and they were in a pew together, and during the Confession, my father sank back from his upright kneeling, and did no more than sigh. . . . He bowed himself before his Lord, as he met Him face to face. . . .

INDEX